A History of Free Verse

A History of Free Verse

CHRIS BEYERS

THE UNIVERSITY OF ARKANSAS PRESS
FAYETTEVILLE 2001

Manufactured in the United States of America

05 04 03 02 01 5 4 3 2 1

Designed by Ellen Beeler

♾ The paper used in this publication meets the minimum requirements of the American National Standard for Permanence of Paper for Printed Library Materials Z39.48-1984.

Library of Congress Cataloging-in-Publication Data

Beyers, Chris, 1962–
A history of free verse / Chris Beyers.
p. cm.
Includes bibliograhical references (p.) and index.
ISBN 1-55728-701-5 (alk. paper) — ISBN 1-55728-702-3 (pbk.)
1. English poetry—History and criticism. 2. Free verse—History and criticism. 3. American poetry—History and criticism. 4. English language—Versification. I. Title.
PR509.F7 B49 2001
821.009—dc21 00-011419

To Michelle and Willie

Contents

Acknowledgments ix

Introduction *1*

Chapter One: The Problem of Free Verse *13*

Chapter Two: The Loose Tradition in Verse from Cowley to Eliot *61*

Chapter Three: The Haunting of Wallace Stevens *101*

Chapter Four: Straight Talk, Straight as the Greeks *135*

Chapter Five: The Parsing Meter and Beyond *179*

Conclusion: Avoiding Prosody? *223*

Notes *237*

Works Cited *255*

Index *273*

Acknowledgments

"1(a". Copyright © 1958, 1986, 1991 by the Trustees for the E. E. Cummings Trust, from *Complete Poems: 1904–1962* by E. E. Cummings, edited by George J. Firmage. Used by permission of Liveright Publishing Corporation.

"Mid-day" [excerpt] by H. D. Doolittle, from *Collected Poems, 1912–1944,* copyright © 1982 by The Estate of Hilda Doolittle. Reprinted by permission of New Directions Publishing Corp.

"Flash Cards," from *Grace Notes* by Rita Dove. Copyright © 1989 by Rita Dove. Used by permission of the author and W. W. Norton & Company, Inc.

"Measure," from *Field Guide* by Robert Hass. Copyright © 1973 by Robert Hass. Used by permission of Yale University Press.

"The Man Whose Pharnyx Was Bad," "The Load of Sugar-Cane," "Earthy Anecdote," and "To the Roaring Wind, " from *Collected Poems* by Wallace Stevens. Copyright 1923 and renewed 1951 by Wallace Stevens. Reprinted by permission of Alfred A Knopf, a Division of Random House, Inc.

"Fine Work with Pitch and Copper" [excerpt], "The Descent of Winter" [excerpt], "The Winds" [excerpt], "The Term" [excerpt], "To a Poor Old Woman" [excerpts], and "10/14" [excerpt] by Willam Carlos Williams, from *Collected Poems 1939–1962, Volume II,* copyright © 1944, 1948 by William Carlos Williams. Reprinted by permission of New Directions Publishing Corp.

"THE," by Louis Zukofsky. *Complete Short Poetry.* p. 232. ©1991 Copyright 1966 Louis Zukovsky. Reprinted with permission of The Johns Hopkins University Press.

Introduction

In 1918 C. E. Andrews, seeking to deal judiciously with what he considered to be the new phenomenon of free verse, remarked,

> Unless the modern school develops some principle of length and flow of rhythms, and some sense of grouping, of climax, of form, they will have only the temporary vogue of startling novelty. ("The Rhythms" 194)

As sensible as Andrews's statement may sound, he turned out to be dead wrong. Free verse became the ascendant form for twentieth-century American poetry, yet there still is no generally recognized principle of form or rhythm. This book, then, addresses what is perhaps the most pressing problem of twentieth-century poetics: how to define and understand the form that dominated the century.

The difficulty of my task is compounded by the fact that there is little apparent agreement over the definition of the term *free verse*. Nevertheless, the lack of consensus regarding the nature of free verse has not prevented critics from having strong feelings about it. When the free verse of the New Poets first started appearing in British and American magazines, many were convinced that the new movement was antithetical to everything that made poetry poetry. In 1913, Wallace Rice complained that free verse denied "poetry, alone among all the arts, a technic" (371). That same year, an unsigned commentary in the *Dial* characterized free verse as "bedlamite ravings" ("The Muse" 245); a year later, another commentator in the *Dial* described it as a kind of rant "that is not even doggerel, for doggerel at least admits the claims of rhythm" ("New Lamps" 232). H. Houston Peckham's definition of free verse, written in 1917, was "poetry without metre or rhyme or reason" (145).

Nowadays it is easy to read these kinds of statements as salvos in a larger cultural war. The same can be said for the statements in favor of free verse. In 1913, the poet that John Reed would a month later call in the pages of *Poetry* "Mr. Aggressively Contemporary Pound" (112) wrote,

> I said in the first article in this series ["America: Chances and Remedies"] that the two things requisite in the renaissance were enthusiasm and propaganda. For America, I would say that the one thing lacking is simply the propaganda. (*Ezra* I.140)

Pound's activities at this time, as well as those of Harriet Monroe and others, surely had a promotional edge to them. Indeed, by 1920 Llewellyn Jones was remarking that the salient thing about free verse was not "its actual achievement" but instead "the intense propaganda promoted by its writers" (384). The sense of taking sides is evident even in the letters of Wallace Stevens, a poet who could be as aloof from the cultural wars as Pound was confrontational. "Why do you scorn free verse?" he wrote Ferdinand Reyher. "Isn't it the only kind of verse written with any kind of aesthetic impulse in back of it? . . . I am not exclusively for free verse. But I am for it" ("Letters" 390). The bibliography of Eddie Gay Cone's dissertation, "The Free-Verse Controversy in American Magazines, 1912–1922," demonstrates the intensity of the debate: it begins with a twenty-one-page list of articles commenting on free verse—articles that appeared just in American magazines, just in the decade noted in the title.

Timothy Steele remarks that this tradition of propaganda "has discouraged attempts to place the free-verse movement in some kind of historical perspective" (292). The dearth of historical studies of free verse has led Donald Wesling and Enikö Bollobás to comment that

> a theory of free verse . . . has to be formulated in such a way that it would bring free verse out of its mysterious black hole. It has to prove that free verse is not a specimen of antipoetry, a breed of literary counterculture, but a natural child of prosodic pluralism. ("Verse Form" 540)

The second sentence describes a major task of this study, and I will attempt to revise the first assertion by recovering, not formulating, the various theor*ies* of free verse as promulgated by the Moderns.

"We have lived long enough with free verse and metrical verse to see them on even terms," Charles O. Hartman wrote in 1980. However, his claim that the "vitriol has evaporated" (8) has not proven to be the case, as he did not anticipate the new surge of vitriol arising from friction between New Formalist (or expansive) and Language poetics. Steele, for example, not only seeks to historicize free verse, but also to "assess it" (292). His New Formalist analysis of free verse, *Missing Measures* (1990), concludes with the argument that free verse has "no positive principles" except an outdated "novelty." The form, Steele argues, actually promotes political dictatorship; more traditional poetry invites the kind of skeptical inquiry salutary for a democratic society. On the other side of the fence is Joseph M. Conte, who ends his study of postmodern form, *Unending Design* (1991), with a "Polemical Conclusion" that pits the "cultural neoconservatives" writing traditionally metered poetry against "leftist" free-verse poets (275). He concludes that a "retrogressive revival" of traditional form "will inevitably create a stagnant and derivative poetry"; those following "exclusively postmodern" notions "will sustain the creative energy" of "poetry's unending design" (282).

Determining whether traditional or free verse better fosters liberal democracy and creative energy is beyond the scope of this book. In order to make their pronouncements, Conte and Steele must posit then proceed from a notion of what constitutes the true essence of poetry; in doing so, they replicate the common approach to free verse in the twentieth century. Why this approach so often produces polemics is perhaps made most clear by H. T. Kirby-Smith's *The Origins of Free Verse* (1996). In his treatment of the theory of organicism, Kirby-Smith refuses to "allow" the concept "as a basis for discussion of free verse." Emerson's statement (in "The Poet") that form is dependent on soul, Kirby-Smith explains, is insufficient because Emerson, Coleridge, and all the other organicists misunderstood the nature of the human soul. Kirby-Smith then outlines the soul's actual nature (it turns out the soul has a material basis).

Such an argument is, to say the least, startling in a book of literary criticism. Kirby-Smith justifies the critique by stating that "the grandiose claims of organicists require a far-reaching refutation" (36), but what is more strikingly demonstrated is that those who attack organicism because it is not true or logical are actually engaging in what amounts to sectarian debate. Kirby-Smith might just as well argue that Christianity is not logical. Generally, those testing organicism (or other such poetic myths) against "reality" or "truth" underestimate the complexity of the theory while overstating the degree to which poets take the theory literally. There is no recorded instance, for example, of Samuel Taylor Coleridge or Charles Olson trying to create poems by watering sheets of paper and then setting them out in the sun.

A History of Free Verse examines the enabling myths, including organicism, that Modern writers used without judging these ideas according to whether or not they are true. I will also focus on Modernist free-verse practice. Unlike previous studies such as Kirby-Smith's, there is no attempt here to define ultimately or delimit what the term *free verse* means; rather, I am exploring what the term was *thought* to mean and the complex relationship between these theories and the poems they were meant to describe. In this approach, I differ markedly from such studies as Hartman's *Free Verse* (1980) and Wesling's *The New Poetries* (1985)[1] Both books are, in my estimation, *sine qua non* for anyone serious about free-verse theory, but both pursue an accurate and inclusive definition of a slippery term and sift through the various theories trying to find out which one is closest to the truth.

In treating free verse without trying to assess it or to measure it "truly," my procedure is only unusual in that it examines free verse in the same way that other verse forms are treated. Take, for instance, the sonnet. Most of my readers, I suspect, are aware that the term *sonnet* originally meant a short song, but for English poetry came to designate a fourteen-line rhyming lyric poem in iambic pentameter, often, but by no means exclusively, addressing the topic of love. There are many specific sorts of sonnets: Italian, Spenserian, Shakespearean, Miltonic, and so forth. However, the practitioners of the sonnet have often been as keen to innovate as they have been to follow rules. A number of poems in the seminal sequence, *Astrophil and Stella,* for example, are not sonnets by the above definition, and there are arguments about whether, for example, George Meredith's *Modern Love* sequence—sixteen-line poems responding to the conventions of love poetry and sonnet sequences such as *Astrophil and Stella*—are actually sonnets. There are those who find sonnets embedded in other poems, and a fair number of critics willing to consider the notion of a free-verse sonnet.[2]

The question of whether these poems are "really" sonnets seems senseless to me. While at the *New Trends in Poetry* conference a while back, I presented a paper at the same session as the poet Alfred Dorn, who read a paper on the New Formalist sonnet. During the question-and-answer period, Dorn was asked to define the sonnet, with the underlying question as to whether or not a fourteen-line loosely metrical poem with off-rhyme instead of true rhyme is "really" a sonnet. Dorn declined to make such a judgment, and nobody else wished to either. What we all cared about is whether looking at a poem in the context of the sonnet tradition helps readers experience and understand both the poem and the tradition to which the poem responds.

Likewise, the notion that we should "assess" free verse seems nonsensical. It is there; some people like it and some do not. Free verse seems rather singled out for judgment, though the only thing the verdicts ever indicate is the predilection of the jury. This book addresses free verse as poetic form is generally addressed, by searching for its roots and paying close attention to the poets' statements about their chosen form. Rather than naively treating these statements as fact, I will treat them as aesthetic choice, as a kind of myth. Further, I will argue way that these myths often appear in the poetry as a kind of formal allegory.

While the use of the word *allegory* in this context sometimes indicates an allegiance to deconstruction, it is not meant so here. My study is more in the line of *Fictions of Form in American Poetry,* in which Stephen Cushman points out that poets' assumptions about the nature of poetry and the significance of form constitute an important fiction. He is quick to add that calling these assumptions "'fictions' is not to judge their truth value, not to call them wrong or false" (5). The fact that these fictions have generated so much fine poetry attests to their power. The poets' assumptions constitute a "figurative discourse," that, "although not strictly a part" of a poem, "often develop or extend" it. In addition, like John Hollander, I often find these sorts of fictions within the poems themselves. Hollander argues that poetic forms often function not only as a "special linguistic framework," but also "are themselves momentarily made fictional, or allegorized" (*Melodious* 164) in the poem. That is to say, poets will often assign a kind of meaning or value to a particular poetic structure, and then use that structure consistently within a poem (or within the poet's whole corpus) to accompany certain ideas, emotions, or attitudes. Like Hollander, I use the word *allegory* to stress the somewhat arbitrary nature of these fictions. In my view, the meanings poets think into poetic form are by no means inevitable or natural. Further, the term *allegory* helps indicate the coherence and dynamism of much free-verse form. The allegorical hero of John Bunyan's *Pilgrim's Progress* does not just stand there, symbolizing the Christian Man; he goes on his various travails, managing to push aside Mr. Doubter, slog through the Slough of Despond, and arrive at the Celestial City. His interaction with other allegorical figures helps delineate his full character. Likewise, free-verse form often exhibits a kind of metafictional coherence organized by its poet's beliefs, and the poems make meaning in the process of their unfolding.

My argument is that, in order to understand free-verse theory, free verse's history and its relation to the past must also be understood. I endorse Dorothy Z. Baker's view that whenever a poet "works within a given poetic form—the sonnet, blank verse, rhymed couplet—he or she is calling up his literary past, and, in some manner, reflecting on the legacy of the past" (1). Clearly, a poet writing a sonnet must have some knowledge of the sonnet's rules, as well as making a conscious effort to follow them. However, for free verse the issue is greatly clouded, since the rules for free verse are not well known or agreed upon. Still, the poets' theories about free verse's relationship to the past is one of the most fruitful sites of what Cushman calls its "figurative discourse."

The historical parts of this study mean to address two audiences. The first consists of those who consider free verse, for better or worse, formless and completely new. I intend to show them that the forms often assumed to be an author's unique and organic response to the world and language are actually that author's participation in an established tradition. The second is that group of readers who have noticed connections between free and more traditional verse, but never really put them together. The criticism of T. S. Eliot and Wallace Stevens, for example, is replete with offhand remarks about the similarities between the practice of these authors and that of previous generations. In their entries on free verse, poetry handbooks often mention many of the authors discussed here as possible precursors to twentieth-century free verse. *A History of Free Verse* traces the specific philosophical and technical lines of development.

I have necessarily created a narrative, one that is somewhat different from that offered by most literary histories. I bring together canonical works in what may be called noncanonical ways, and introduce a fair number of noncanonical, or less canonical, works. In addition, the history I am offering is what Marianne Moore would call a "congenial" one—that is to say, one that takes into account the theories that poets and critics have created to explain poetic form. Poets have written, "this is how to hear my poems," and I have tried to read them in this way. Nevertheless, I have not taken the next step and *believed* the poets. I have taken care to remark frequently on other ways to read and hear poetry. In addition, by stressing the fictive nature of these theories, this history rather opens the way for a more cultural study of poetic form, though I have not made it my task to trace any particular ideology as that term is generally understood today.

My reluctance to uncover ideologies stems from my historicist and aesthetic approach. If, as is often asserted, ideology is inescapable, then at least polemics are avoidable. What I mean by this is evident in my differences with Annie Finch, whose book *The Ghost of Meter* examines many of the same formal allegories that I do here. While Finch shares my historicist concerns, we differ widely on how we apply our historical understanding. Finch's chapter on Emily Dickinson is a case in point. Finch argues that Dickinson perceived iambic pentameter as a vehicle for patriarchal authority because, by the middle of the nineteenth century, the meter *was* actually the instrument of authoritative patriarchy. To prove this, she cites the opinions of a number of well-respected critics: Roland Barthes, W. H. Auden, Sandra Gilbert and Susan Gubar, John Hollander, and others. Noticeably absent from the mix is Dickinson herself[3] or any other nineteenth-century poet.

Was iambic pentameter the instrument of patriarchy in the nineteenth century? The poet and novelist Charlotte Perkins Gilman did not seem to think so. Her poem "One Girl of Many" (1880) describes a woman who, due to social conditions, turns to prostitution. "These disgraceful creatures" are prostitutes:

> Only one girl of many, 'Tis a need
> Of man's existence to repeat the deed.
> Social necessity. Men cannot live
> Without what these disgraceful creatures give.
> Black shame. Dishonor. Misery & Sin.
> And men find needed health & life therein. (116)

It is hard to see where in these bitter lines, which state that men find their "health" in destroying women, Gilman has been "inevitably involve[d] in duplicity or bad faith" (19), as Finch would have it. Most do not consider the author of "The Yellow Wallpaper" to be an advocate of patriarchy. A more historical view is that, as I will show in chapter 2, in the nineteenth century iambic pentameter was often used as a site for meditation and statement. Since most poets were conventional politically and philosophically, and since many nowadays call the conventional opinions of these years "patriarchal," it is indeed true that many poems in iambic pentameter did express patriarchal ideas. However, that does not mean that individual poets could not use this meter for their own purposes and, as in Gilman's poem, use the tradition of iambic pentameter to voice ideologies counter to the prevailing one. Finch may be correct in her argument that Dickinson perceived the iambic pentameter as patriarchal (though, again, she does not cite anything by Dickinson indicating this), but to argue that there is one set of associations around a meter imposes an unnecessarily monolithic ideological reading upon a broad spectrum of poetry. If it is the case, as the Language poets would have us believe, that all assertion bolsters phallocentricism, then the problem is the assertions, and not the marshalling of ten syllables per line.[4] I hope to show that Finch's assessment amounts to a kind of prosodic essentialism that, for all its historicist trappings, is actually ahistorical.

Thus, while in essential agreement with Marjorie Perloff's argument, that "there is no prosodic form that isn't, at least to some degree, historically bound and culture-specific" ("Return" 136), I seek to complicate the ways in which we conceive of the history and culture that are in part determining poetic form. Too often, the very critic looking to connect culture to versification posits general agreement where there was actually much debate. Consider these words from Marina Tarlinskaja:

> Every poem written in Spenserian stanza brings to mind *The Faerie Queene,* together with its images and style. Every tragedy written in unrhymed iambic pentameter is perceived against the background of Shakespearean tragedies, with their character types, plots, and stylistic couplings. Each verse form has accumulated many layers of associations during the long period of its use by generations of poets. (494)

Throughout she implies a relatively stable communal interpretation of traditions for which there is little evidence. Certainly, the undergraduates I have taught in survey courses can read excerpts from *Childe Harold* quite untouched by the shadow of Spenser; indeed, they are generally surprised to find that a work in iambic pentameter has ten syllables per line, even if they have read the work before in other classes. Thus, Tarlinskaja's "associations" are only available to a reader familiar with a certain body of knowledge. Trying to construct this reader leads to serious theoretical difficulties, especially for free verse, a point I will address in the conclusion of this book. But even granting the arguable notion that *all* blank-verse plays bring to mind Shakespeare, a cursory glance at the ever-burgeoning amount of Shakespearean criticism demonstrates that the composition of "the background of Shakespearean tragedies" varies from reader to reader. In short, a meter or form has no inevitable meaning. Individual poets think certain meanings *into* certain forms, and which poets we choose to read, and how we choose to read them, comprises our traditional associations. If the Modern period has taught us nothing, it is that "tradition" is a term that seems solid but is actually quite fluid.

As I have said, my main focus is historical and aesthetic, and there is little here that most readers will find obviously political. However, this study does make one important contribution to the debate on the politics of poetic form. I have just argued that it makes no sense to say that alternating ten stressed and slack syllables is political; instead, the more accurate formulation is that certain poets associate certain ideas with certain forms. Far from arguing that prosodic theory is inherently apolitical, what I mean to show is that it is a battleground for competing ideologies, a constant struggle to re-allegorize the "meaning" of form to serve successive sociocultural agendas. Delving into those agendas is not my task, but I will show that it is untenable to say, like a graduate student in a qualifying examination, "in the nineteenth century, they felt . . ." without acknowledging that there were others at the same time feeling something quite different. One theoretical problem with finding ideologies in works not overtly political is that too often critics find surprisingly coherent ideologies, sometimes if not generally by employing methodologies that are speculative and premised on certain procedures of reading (such as identifying the poem with the poet). It makes more sense that the theory of poetic form would be as contradictory and inconsistent as most people's ideas are.

Moreover, the finding of consistent ideologies, even in an era where those ideologies are stated and relatively easy to find, often underestimates the cultural processes that produce ideology in the first place. For example, Jorie Graham told Mark Wunderlich that one trend in today's poetry is a "synthesis" of apparently contradictory "aesthetic devices." She continues,

> I'll have students simultaneously influenced by Susan Howe and Sharon Olds—or by elements of their styles—students for whom these two poets, for example, don't seem to embody any prohibitive polarity of purpose or belief. When they learn (or "lift") stylistic devices from these recent forbears, they don't seem to lift the ideological or political assumptions that gave rise to those styles—what made them "hard-earned" in other words. And these are by no means people who are in any way naive, or unaware of the implications of what they are choosing to ignore. It fascinates me, worries me, and in many ways delights m . . . to see them sample and synthesize and invent without feeling the need to be accountable to the beliefs that gave birth to those voices and styles they imitate.

What Graham has identified as a characteristic of contemporary poetry is in fact the general pattern of history. Her students, as she stresses, are not politically uninvolved or naive; rather they are re-allegorizing their forms in ways that address what they believe to be the pressing issues of their day, and will one day live to see their allegories and ideologies retheorized by their students.

I hope that all this talk about ideology does not discourage those who I suspect will comprise most of my audience, the "poetry people" who simply love poetry for its own sake. For them, a main interest in this book should be its exploration of the chief pleasure of verse: its music. Like Wesling and Hartman before me, I find that trying to understand free verse leads to a prolonged inquiry into what poetry sounds like (or, more accurately, is supposed to sound like), and that means a long investigation of prosody. Prosody is devalued in some circles, and prosodic criticism in general is notorious for sponsoring cranks. Yet the "science of verse," as Sidney Lanier called it, has made a real comeback in recent years. There have been books advocating new prosodic systems (by Alan Holder, Richard Cureton, and Donald Wesling); *Meter in English,* a multi-critic debate on meter; and book-length prosodic studies of single authors, including Herbert, Wordsworth, and Hardy, and so forth. Subjectively, I can say that everywhere I go I meet somebody intensely interested in it. It seems to me that there is, and always has been, a sizable underground of poetry aficionados who really care about poetic rhythm.

It is worth noting that many of the critics most interested in poetic rhythm are poets themselves. I examine not only what I consider to be an essential feature of what is generally called poetry, but also one that is one of the poet's day-in and day-out concerns. The approach to prosody I offer here, like my approach to free-verse theory, aims at description rather than prescription. I am seeking a congenial prosody as well; rather than trying to shoehorn every poem into the same system, I proceed from the notion that differing prosodies are better gauges of different poems—that is, that there are different free-verse prosodies.

This book begins with a survey of definitions of the term *free verse.* I show that while most definitions lack descriptive power, they do display important beliefs about the nature of poetry, the way that poems are composed, and how readers apprehend poetic rhythm. After explaining the prosodic problem that free verse foregrounds (and which makes the term difficult to define), I then outline four categories of free verse: long-line verse, short-line verse, "haunted" poetry, and poetry that avoids tradition. These genres exhibit differing conventions governing the line, proceed from differing notions of organic form, and hold differing assumptions as to what part of the human consciousness poetry addresses. Since long-line free verse is relatively well understood, I summarize and discuss it in chapter 1, while devoting the rest of the book to the less understood genres.

Chapters 2 and 3 consider poetry written under the "ghost-of-meter" paradigm. Chapter 2 contextualizes the poetics of Eliot's "The Love Song of J. Alfred Prufrock," with special attention to sublime theory and the way that the poem reacts to the conventions of late-century magazine verse. I then turn to the way that Eliot's other major poems are similarly "haunted." Chapter 3 uses the paradigms developed in chapter 2 to examine how Wallace Stevens's poems use prosody to build meaning.

Chapters 4 and 5 explore short-line poetry. Chapter 4 surveys the history of the short line and shows its connection to classical literature and translation theory. I then show how the poet Louis Untermeyer called "the perfect imagist," H.D., created her line as an outgrowth of these influences, and spend some time defining the procedures of short-line poetry. Chapter 5, like chapter 3, uses the paradigms of its preceding chapter to read the career of William Carlos Williams. The chapter concludes with a comprehensive examination of the theoretical claims and practical difficulties of Williams's "variable foot."

The final chapter examines poetry whose fiction of composition insists that it avoids prosody. The chapter also looks at the influence of Modern free-verse theory on contemporary poetry by examining a few poems by Phil Levine, Robert Hass, and Rita Dove. In the end, I propose that the study of prosody can be historicized and made relevant to the types of cultural issues such aesthetic concerns are often thought to ignore. While prosody may never completely fulfill its promise of being the science of verse, it can help reveal a poet's most deeply held beliefs regarding culture, language, human desire, and the order—or disorder—of the world.

CHAPTER ONE

The Problem of Free Verse

In his standard bibliography of versification, T. V. F. Brogan comments that the term *free verse* is "useful" just "so long as one does not inquire further into what it means" (*English* 402). The sense of exasperation in Brogan's remark stems from the fact that, while defining free verse was a persistent theoretical occupation of the twentieth century, free-verse practice remains poorly understood. My argument is that most have been so stimulated by free-verse theory (and the accompanying polemics) that they have underappreciated the essential fact that free verse is a *lineal* form—in fact, a group of differing lineal forms. Still, the theory of free verse is "useful" because it helps show how Modern free-verse poets developed their forms into full-fledged genres. Further, later poets have generally followed the contours of the debate as articulated in the teens and twenties, so that the arguments of the Moderns are still potent today. In all, this chapter begins by discussing the definitions of free verse and ends by detailing the genres of free verse and some of the main tenets of free-verse theory as developed in the Modern period.

The definitional problem of free verse has been exacerbated by the unusual attitude many of the Moderns took toward the form. Poets, when they innovate, are typically keen to justify their innovation. For example, John Milton explains to the readers of the preface to *Paradise Lost* that his "neglect" of rhyme is not "to be taken for a defect, though it may seem so perhaps to vulgar readers"; in fact, the blank-verse line used in the epic "recoverd" an "ancient liberty" enjoyed by Homer, freeing the poem "from the troublesome and modern bondage of rhyming," that, in longer poems, produces an unmusical "jingling" (6). Blank verse, Milton argues, is not just different; it is markedly better because it is more pliant, avoids the unnatural and ornamental technique of his contemporaries, and provides a sophisticated and beautiful music for the refined reader. Thomas Campion (for his quantitative verse), Coleridge (for his accentual verse), and Hopkins (for his sprung rhythm) offer comparable justifications.

In this respect, the free verse of the Moderns poses a special problem. Compare Milton's preface to the comments of two Modern free-verse poets, T. S. Eliot and William Carlos Williams. The former was probably the most influential poet during the Modern period, and the latter has emerged as one of the more influential since. In 1917, Eliot told his readers that "*Vers libre* does not exist" (*To Criticize* 183). Twenty-five years later, he continued to argue that "no verse is free for the man who wants to do a good job" (*On Poets* 31).[1] Williams, who wrote the entry on free verse for *The Princeton Encyclopedia of Poetry and Poetics* (1974), said in 1913, "I do not believe in vers libre, this contradiction in terms." He continued,

> Vers libre is prose. In the hands of Whitman it was a good tool, a kind of synthetic chisel—the best he had. In his bag of chunks even lie some of the pieces of rhythm life of which we must build. This is honor enough. Vers libre is finished—Whitman did all that was necessary with it. Verse has nothing to gain here and all to lose. . . . (orig. ellipsis; *Interviews* 66–67)

It is not that Williams maintained some sort of personal distinction between the terms *vers libre* and *free verse* or that he went on to change his mind. In 1961, he told Walter Sutton,

> there is no such thing as free verse. It's a contradiction in terms. The verse is measured. No measure can be free. We may say Whitman's verse is a typical example of what is spoken of as free verse. Now Whitman never called it free verse. (*Interviews* 38)

The only thing that seems to have changed in the forty-eight years between the statements is that Williams decided that even Whitman never wrote free verse.

I can think of no other formal movement for which two of its most important practitioners disclaim their chosen form's very existence. The two poets seem to be saying that, even if free verse does exist, it is not the kind of poetry that anyone should want to read. In the context of the contemporary debate on free verse, however, it becomes clear that the two are responding to a specific strain of polemics about free verse, trying to clear themselves and other like-minded poets from the charge that the freedom of "free verse" means a total lack of poetic control and form. In the Modern period as today, the "problem" of free verse has been caused largely by the divisive debate about the form, a controversy that has prevented much substantive work on what the form *is.* Even handbooks disagree radically, but these disagreements disclose crucial elements of free-verse theory.

As Graham Hough remarks, "One quite appropriate reason for caution in approaching the term," free verse, "is that we are not at all clear about what, in English, it means" (158). Roger Fowler likewise finds the term vague and "dated," but adds, "some word is needed" (79) to describe nontraditional poetry. In fact, William Pratt has said that the lack of consensus about free verse's definition has meant that the term needs "redefinition each time it is mentioned" (25). *The Guide to Modern World Literature* (1972) provides the spectrum for which the phrase is employed: free verse "embraces anything from prose to a verse that is only fairly irregular in a strictly metrical sense" (426). A large number of readers regard free verse in the same way that many people regard pornography: they do not know how to define it, but they recognize it when they see it.

Many find the term one that merely designates what a poem is not. This was Eliot's main objection to *vers libre:* "I can define it only in negatives," he wrote, "(1) absence of pattern, (2) absence of rhyme, (3) absence of metre" (*To Criticize* 229). In 1930, George Stewart likewise proffered only a negative definition, as did Clement Wood twelve years later, and A. F. Scott's *Current Literary Terms* in 1965.[2] More recent books likewise avoid making positive statements. *The Writer's Encyclopedia* (1983), for example, tells its readers that free verse is poetry "in which the length of lines is not measured by a specific number of units," adding,

> Thus any piece
> of writing that is broken in-
> to lines of irregular length, may be
> called free verse, whether
> it advertises nylons, records Sam-
> son's celebration of light,
> or explains prosody as drily
> as this (421)

Less witty but similar definitions appear in *Literary Terms and Criticism* (1985), *The Poet's Dictionary* (1989), and the fourth edition of *Benet's Reader's Encyclopedia of American Literature* (1991).[3] "This manner of describing free verse," remarks

Harry Warfel, "merely indicates that it is not poetry according to the rules of syllabic, accentual, or quantitative prosodies" (232). Again, these descriptions do not state what free verse *is*.

While such "negative" definitions only assert that free verse is not traditional, definitions seeking to specify the form's actual characteristics are usually more interested in taking sides than in describing. Writers such as Stewart and Wood take the negative definition of free verse as evidence that free verse has no form at all.[4] In the Modern period, hostile or puzzled commentators often echoed Raymond Alden's assertion of 1913 that free verse "abandoned all standards of form" and suppressed "all evidence that a particular composition is animated by any directing intelligence" (386–87). This point was asserted many times during the teens and twenties. It is one reason that Eliot and Williams dismissed the term.

However, advocates of free verse often do little to convince skeptical readers that free verse really does have form. In lieu of presenting principles, free verse's defenders often assert that there are rules yet do not specify what those rules might be. *The Reader's Encyclopedia of American Literature* (1962), for example, tells its readers that "the really noteworthy writers of 'free' verse have set up for themselves disciplines of sound and rhythm as severe as any under which Chaucer, Pope, or Tennyson worked" (356). Period. End of entry. Hough asserts that free-verse poems have "a planned and intricate organization" that is nonetheless "indescribable" (173). Clearly these writers are responding to the propaganda that free verse is formless, and perhaps to the assertion, prominently forwarded by Max Eastman in 1916, that free verse is "Lazy Verse" (139). In short, the response to the unprovable claim that poets write free verse because they are too lazy to learn traditional techniques has often been the unsupported claim of rigor.

One difficulty in specifying these rules is the general perception that free verse is extremely variable. Because of this, Paul Ramsey argues, to be "true," any definition must be "untidy and unexciting" (99). Some have taken such untidiness as a sign of inexpressible profundity—that is to say, the difficulty in describing the form is often translated to mean that the form surpasses all description. For instance, Walter Sutton concludes a study on Walt Whitman's form by asserting,

> Whitman's free verse poems demonstrate that poetic form is an open rather than a closed system, susceptible always to redefinition and further development in

> the shifting perspective of the reader. The form of the work is a potential of its verbal structure. Although it may be discussed from various viewpoints, no analysis or interpretation can be commensurate with its complexity, however simple it may appear at first reading. Any analysis which presents itself as systematic and definitive is false to the nature of the poem, perhaps to the temporary advantage of the critic. (23)

Sutton's comments can be neatly separated into two categories. The first two sentences regard organic form, an important concept that I will return to later. The second two sentences, however, constitute a significant statement of belief. Why shouldn't some superintelligent, hyperaesthetic genius be able to fashion an explanation more complex than the thing?[5]

My point is not that critics write more sublimely than poets do. However, Sutton's remarks contain a curious assertion of unutterable transcendence in poetry characteristic of a significant branch of free-verse theory. In discussions of traditional verse, such aspects as theme, characterization, and the effect on the reader are sometimes thought to be beyond precise definition. But the poem's form is usually considered relatively knowable. The "thoughts too deep for tears" in Wordsworth's Immortality Ode may be something for which there are no exact words, but that the idea is expressed in iambs and that "tears" rhymes with "fears" is classifiable. In addition, Wordsworth's participation in the nineteenth-century English ode tradition has been identified and well analyzed by Stuart Curran,[6] among others. However, many who appraise free-verse form attempt to place what used to be the most discernible part of poems into the category of things impossible to discuss.

Sutton is not the only one who finds something ineffable about the form of free verse. *The Teacher's and Writer's Handbook of Poetic Forms* (1987) informs its readers that

> The point of free verse is not that it has thrown the traditional rules of poetry out of the window; it means that every poet who writes in this form must create his or her own set of rules. These rules are based on our personal thought patterns, our sense of how the poem should look on the page, our deepest feelings about life itself. (85)

Here again, rigorous, unspecified rules are asserted, with the additional implication that free-verse form is so intimately connected with being human that to describe it would be tantamount to understanding the essence of humanity.

Similarly, Wayne Dodd finds that, for him, free verse ("at its best") feels like "an ur-language, original and personal and accurate" ("And the Look" 36). For Dodd, poetry is born free but is everywhere in chains; only free verse returns poetry to its origins in human utterance. Dodd's assertion about accuracy must be taken, like Sutton's on complexity and *The Teacher's and Writer's Handbook*'s on feelings, on faith.

Eliot's negative definition of free verse does have one positive aspect: by stressing how the line of free verse differs from that of traditional verse, it helps indicate free verse can be understood as a lineal form, like iambic pentameter. Since the definition of traditional verse's lineal form centers on rhythm (an iambic line, e.g., has a certain disposition of stressed syllables), those seeking to define free verse positively have sought to describe free verse's rhythm. While later critics such as Sutton and Dodd often insist on the inexpressible profundity of free verse's rhythm, the Moderns themselves tended to tell their readers that their poetry was measurable using the most up-to-date equipment. In 1913, for example, Alice Corbin Henderson argued that free verse was rhythmic by insisting that free verse, like all poetry, exhibited the "inherent, scientific divisions of rhythmic wave lengths" that are regulated by "the law of balance," and appear in a "poetic interval" ("Poetic" 71). Henderson did not specify further,[7] so how these rhythms are measured remains a mystery; instead, she implies that what she describes is so clearly manifest that any researcher could detect it.

A year later, also in *Poetry,* Amy Lowell picked up Henderson's argument, renaming her "wavelengths" as "simply curves," and reiterating that the "length and shape of the curve" distinguishes poetry from prose. She added that perhaps the "characteristic of poetry" is "return," which she defines as various sorts of cohesive patterning, such as rhyme and anaphora. She continues, "Sometimes the return is indicated more in idea than in absolute words, but in poetry it is always present in some form, to give the balance that produces the effect of music on the ear" ("Vers Libre" 213). Though the notion that the sound of a poem should echo its sense is by no means peculiar to free verse—it is of course one of Alexander Pope's tenets—saying that free-verse lines mimic the *idea* being represented begs the question, what do ideas *sound* like? What rhythm do they convey?

The strategy of using the language of science to validate poetic technique is a familiar one in Modern criticism. Ezra Pound constantly referred to science—in *The Spirit of Romance,* for example, he remarks that "Poetry is a sort of inspired mathematics" (5); Eliot, in "Tradition and the Individual Talent," invites his readers "to consider, as a suggestive analogy, the action which takes place when a bit of finely filiated platinum is introduced into a chamber containing oxygen and sulphur dioxide" (*Sacred* 53); in *Prepositions,* Louis Zukofsky several times explains why science is poetry and *vice versa;* Williams claimed that his "variable foot" put Einstein's theory of relativity into metrical practice. As Timothy Steele argues, by aligning themselves with scientific progress, Moderns not only implied that their poetry was precise and accurate, but also that traditional poetry was "intellectually backwards or instrumentally inferior to newer methods of composition" (14). Such assertions were often made more to invest aesthetic opinions with the authority of objective verifiability than to suggest a way to verify objectively. Responding to the notion that free verse is lazy verse, Lowell and Henderson use the language of science to signal that free verse is at least as controlled and rigorous as traditional verse. In addition, both imply that free verse is closer to the essential nature of poetry than traditional verse—that free verse is the naked exercise of the very law of poetry. This idea implies a critique of traditional versification and an ontology of poetry that constitute one of the most persistent aesthetic ideas in the twentieth century.

This critique and ontology can be seen more clearly in Pound's significantly titled essay, "The Tradition," which appeared a few months before Lowell's article. In the essay, Pound asserted that "cadence" was the organizing principle of free verse. Cadence is his version of Henderson's "poetic interval," and, like Henderson's interval, it is not defined. Nonetheless, Pound's comments and the source that sparked them are worth considering at some length, since they are central to free-verse theory.

"As to the tradition of *vers libre*" Pound informed readers of *Poetry,* "Jannaris in his study of the Melic poets comes to the conclusion that they composed according to the feel of the thing, to the cadence, as have all good poets since. He is not much inclined to believe that they were much influenced by discussions held in Alexandria centuries after their deaths" (*Ezra* I.211).[8] Pound's insistence that the practice of free verse stretches back to antiquity means to answer criticism in the *Dial* that free verse dismisses all tradition. More important for this discussion, he wishes to bifurcate what we mean when we say poetic tradition. On the one hand is the mistaken tradition of mainstream nineteenth-century poetics; on the other is the tradition of poetry itself. What is called the tradition, he argues here and elsewhere, is too often a derivative technique practiced by second-rate poets and extolled by second-rate critics, neither of whom knows what poetry *really* is. When Pound goes on to tell his readers that if they want to find good free verse, they should "turn at random to the works of Euripides . . . or to almost any notable Greek chorus," he is not only trying to establish his credentials as a critic who knows these texts, but also asserting that twentieth-century free verse has, potentially at least, the musicality of ancient literature. By returning to Euripides and Homer, Pound returns to what he considers to be the source of Western poetry, a kind of poetry not corrupted by the simplifications of later criticism. Euripides and Homer were not trying to be Tennyson or Keats; they were writing poetry, *real* poetry.

So much for the polemics; a closer look at the prosodic theory of Antonius N. Jannaris brings us closer to Pound's own theory.[9] In *An Historical Greek Grammar Chiefly of the Attic Dialect,* Jannaris remarks that the Attic dialect of Greek is a "merely historical *abstraction,* that is an *artistic* language which nobody spoke but still everybody understood" (4). In his first two appendices, he expands upon this idea. He takes issue with the notion that the accent marks in ancient texts reflect the manner that the ancients pronounced their language, claiming that the system "was far too subtle and complicated for practical purposes." By the third century these accent marks were used "with the object of facilitating the rhythmical reading and understanding of 'ancient' texts" whose "language had by this time become obsolete and incomprehensible" (508). Thus, the received prosodic system was based on an appraisal of a language no longer current. Jannaris argues that "the theoretical and often irreconcilable precepts of the Alexandrian grammarians, or rather of their Byzantine excerptors and commentators" only provide "incidental and second, often even third, hand and mostly speculative information" of questionable value. When Pound comments that Jannaris did not think the Melic poets were influenced by later discussions in Alexandria, he is apparently referring to this passage.[10]

As a result of this historical process, later Greek poets "laboured under the double disadvantage of painfully copying both the metre and diction of their classical predecessors, two elements surely extinct from the living language of their time" (523). Thus, the fully developed system of quantitative prosody is an "artificial method founded upon precedent practice" (524–25). That is, later prosodists surveyed Attic poetry, described what they read, and then turned their descriptions into prescriptions for future poetry. Geoffrey Horrocks points out that, although more recent linguists have complicated this interpretation of Greece's linguistic history, Jannaris's view "reflects the sympathies of most linguists . . . of the nineteenth and twentieth century" (6).

If the Attic poets did not write according to rules formulated long after they were dead,[11] what rules or principles did they use? Jannaris's answer is that, since ancient verse was "never meant to be *read*" (517) but instead meant to be sung, "metre and music were inseparable from each other" (518). Considering this, the "indisputable fact" is that the ancients only "knew what constitutes the soul of poetry among all nations: they knew rhythm, that is the regular recurrence of thesis and arsis" (526–27). This is what Pound calls "the cadence, the feel of the thing." It is also what Henderson termed "the poetic interval" and Lowell called "return." It is the musical rhythm that appears in poetry.

The theory that poetry's basis is musical is also apparent in Pound's subsequent remark that, since a composer writing music in 4/4 time does not have to use four quarter notes per measure, poets should have an analogous freedom. He thus implies that writing in, say, strict iambic pentameter is like writing a symphony using only quarter notes (this early statement anticipates Pound's third principle of Imagism: "compose in the sequence of the musical phrase and not in the sequence of a metronome" [*Ezra* I.119]). Free verse, then, has a rhythmic standard that it reaches via a greater variety than traditional verse reaches its metrical standard.

But what is the standard? Pound's musical analogy may suggest that free-verse poets use quantitative, not accentual, rules. Musical notation measures duration as well as accent, and Melic poetry helped create a quantitative tradition. Lowell soon jumped on the quantitative bandwagon; later that year, she told Joyce Kilmer that "to a certain extent, 'cadence'" is "dependent on quantity" (Kilmer 8). Likewise, Harriet Monroe argued in 1913 that "English verse is as quantitative as Greek verse, because its primary values depend quite as essentially upon the time-values of its syllables, upon its marshaling of long and short syllables in feet of a given length" (*Poets* 290). Of course, unlike the well-established outlines of Latin verse, the rules for an English quantitative verse have never been recognized by a significant number of people,[12] so these writers are asserting the influence of an alternative prosodic system that does not exist in English in any generally accepted way. The musical analogy does not help clear up the issue, since composers of music have strict rules for duration that they could easily find by consulting a handbook, whereas Pound concludes his comments on free verse by telling his readers that "treatises" are "useless" for a poet, who can only learn from examining with an unprejudiced mind the "finest examples" (*Ezra* I.212). Again, we are left with a definition of free verse and its rhythm that leaves crucial points unexplained.

Despite the vagueness of the formulation of free-verse rhythm, Pound's comments imply a potentially devastating critique of traditional versification.

Jannaris argues that Attic versification is artificial; the "soul of poetry for all nations" is simply "rhythm," what Pound calls "the feel of the thing." Traditional English versification is quite a remove from such a natural feel for rhythm. Derek Attridge points out that Latin prosody "was the result of an attempt to impose upon one language [Latin] a metrical system natural to another, Greek" (*Well-Weigh'd* 17). Since English prosody was modeled on Latin prosody, it might be fairly said that English prosody is an artificial abstraction based upon the artificial abstraction of Latin prosody, which itself was based upon the artificial abstraction of Greek prosody. Further, as was the case for Greek prosody, the accepted rules of English verse were hotly debated long after there was a significant body of English poetry. All this goes to prove the justice in Wesling's remark that the "lack of an adequate metrical theory has never prevented the writing of poems" (*Grammetrics* 10), a fact much in evidence today where there is abundance of free-verse poems but no consistently cited prosody of free verse.

More important, Jannaris provided the Moderns with a theoretical justification for the idea that poetic rhythm is created solely from the poet's sense of rhythm, as well as for the corollary that the traditional rules of versification are arbitrary strictures under which poets mistakenly believed they had to "labour." Jannaris's argument also appeals to Modern internationalism, for he tells his readers that he is outlining the rules for "all nations." Applying such conclusions to Modern poetry, it would seem (as Henderson and Lowell imply) that free verse follows no law but the very law of poetry. Traditional versification, on the other hand, is based upon abstractions that are archaic if not wholly false, and upheld by blind adherence to received authority.

However, Jannaris's argument also contains the seeds of a counter-critique of free verse. If poetry is *not* speech, but music—an art—then the notion that decorums of poetry should be "natural" is mistaken. Most, I suspect, do not believe themselves living in perpetual opera; music is something composers and musicians make intentionally, and differs from naturally occurring ambient noise. Artificiality, then, is no argument against rules for versification, since poetry is in this sense artificial. Moreover, if poetry takes its essence from music, then the fact that the received rules of versification do not accurately reflect the poet's living language is inconsequential. Looked at this way, it can be said that traditional versification is an attempt to imbue poetry with music, which, Jannaris argued, was the basis of Homer's notions of poetry, and thus the basis of poetry itself.

Other writers fared no better than Pound in speaking precisely about free-verse cadence. In 1916, Edward Storer said that the length of free-verse lines are determined "according to some almost unconscious combined action of the eye and ear, pressed into service by the dominant impulse of the poem" (154); in the same year, Henry B. Fuller argued that free-verse poets must "sense" their themes, "perhaps best subconsciously—as a matter of flow cadence" (517). Assuming Storer's "dominant impulse" is the same as cadence, both writers interpreted Pound's "feel of it" psychologically.[13] But assuming cadence stems from the unconscious only begs the question, what does the unconscious sound like? If we don't know, then it seems unwarranted to assert that poems mimic it.

In 1919, John Gould Fletcher offered a definition centering on cadence, couched in language that promises a more quantifiable definition. Yet his article only introduced an essential prosodic problem without giving a real solution. "A vers libre poem depends upon uniformity and equality of rhythm," he wrote, not "an even metronomic succession of beats"—Fletcher's debt to Pound is clear here—"but in contrasted juxtapositions of lines of equal beat value, but of different metrical origin." To illustrate, he quoted his own poem marked for scansion:

/ / /
I have fled away into deserts
/ / /
I have hidden myself from you,
/ / / /
Lo, you always at my side!
/ / /
I cannot shake myself free.
/ / /
In the frosty evening
/ / /
With your cold eyes you sit watching,
/ / /
Laughing, hungering still for me,
/ / /
I will open my heart and give you
/ / /
All of my blood, at last.

"The first thing to be noticed about this," Fletcher comments, "is that there are exactly the same number of beats in every line" ("Rational" 12)—a strange thing to say, since he scans the third line as having four beats. Even overlooking this blunder,[14] his formulation would make free verse nothing more than accentual verse. The scansion makes it clear that his phrase, "different metrical origin," means mixing iambs, trochees, anapests, and dactyls.

However, a reader without Fletcher's scansion might read the poem quite differently. For example, the stress on "In" on the fifth line seems forced. I hear the line as having only two stresses. Fletcher argues that though his scansion of the sixth line "may be unpleasant to some people," it is a "*suspended* line"; the influence of the previous and succeeding lines determines its rhythm. But of course, in order to detect such contextual prosody, the reader must somehow have divined the accentual regularity. A reader without this knowledge may read the line as balancing successive stressed syllables:

```
                /   /      /  /
With your cold eyes you sit watching
```

Line seven could easily also have four stressed syllables:

```
/         /         /     /
Laughing, hungering still for me,
```

No doubt other readers can find other readings of these lines. In short, although the lines can be read in the way that Fletcher proposes, readers not told *a priori* of the scheme may not detect it. To my ear, Fletcher's scansion seems at times odd, even arbitrary.

The problem of defining cadence has lasted well beyond the Modern period. Symptomatic of the problem are the entries on "cadence" in *Crowell's Handbook for Readers and Writers* (1925), *The Reader's Companion to World Literature* (1956), and *Benet's Reader's Encyclopedia* (3d ed., 1987), which all identify cadence as the rhythmic principle to free verse, and then do not define cadence either in the entry on free verse or in a separate entry. Handbooks that do define cadence often do not clear up the issue. Louis Untermeyer's *Forms of Poetry* (1926) says that poetic cadence is the "fall of the voice in reading and speaking, as at the end of the sentence" (6), which cannot explain cadence as a rhythmic principle for free verse. More recently, *A Dictionary of Literary Terms*

(1972) defines cadence as "The rhythmic flow, or sequence, of sounds in writing and speaking" or "the beat of any rhythmic activity" (62); cadence in Babette Deutsch's *Poetry Handbook* (1974) is "a rhythmical unit, similar to the musical phrase, when recurring, gives symmetry to verse when a strict metrical pattern is wanting" (24); Holman and Harmon's *A Handbook to Literature* (1986) explains that cadence is a "rhythmical movement" which "sounds the 'inner tune' of a sentence or verse" (69). *A Reader's Guide to Literary Terms* (1960) is perhaps most revealing. Cadence is "the natural rhythm of language determined by its inherent alternation of stressed and unstressed syllables." Since competent English speakers stress some syllables and not others, the sequence of stresses automatically qualifies as a rhythm. This would suppose that poets have nothing to do at all, since language (by this definition) is inherently rhythmic. However, *A Reader's Guide* quickly qualifies its definition: "When more precisely used in verse, the term cadence refers to the arrangement of the rhythms of speech into highly organized patterns" (22). Readers of this book will not be surprised to hear that these "highly organized patterns" are not specified.

These explanations presuppose a rhythm—the poems are "symmetrical," "highly organized," and have an "'inner tune'"—yet none specify the pattern. Barbara Herrnstein Smith argues that cadence is "inherently nonquantifiable" (87), but has no doubt that it exists. Like negative definitions of free verse, "cadence" is useful in its own way, designating the presence of a hard to demonstrate rhythm; ultimately, though, it is an anti-term designating a rhythm that does not conform to any established model.

As with other aspects of free-verse form, the inability to define rhythm is often taken to mean that the term designates something supersophisticated and hyperaesthetic. John Cunliffe remarked in 1916 that free verse "demands greater subtlety of rhythmic perception both on the part of the reader and on part of the hearer" (104). In much the same manner, Lowell told her readers that the distinction between free verse and prose sometimes "requires a delicate ear to detect it" ("Vers" 217).

This point is still often asserted. Free verse's defenders frequently have the air of someone pulling rank. For instance, Alan Golding says that readers of free verse always must be tense—they cannot "relax" into a meter as readers of, say, Longfellow can (69). "Some readers dislike" free verse, Louis Simpson told the *Ohio Review,* because it "demands that they pay attention to every syllable" (57). Implicitly, traditional verse encourages laziness and inattention. This argument is an offshoot of the argument that free verse follows extremely complex rules peculiar to itself. Indeed, proponents of free verse sometimes justify their claim that free verse is musical by simply quoting a poem and saying, "Doesn't that sound beautiful?" while implying or stating outright that anyone who does not hear it is dull or intransigent. Thus, Dodd, seeking to explain that "there is a difference between meter and rhythm," writes, "Listen to this poem by Robert Bly," quotes the poem, and then "And this one by James Wright," quotes another poem, and then concludes, "This is a poetry that sounds like us" ("Art" 8). In an earlier article, Dodd stated that "those who don't hear the music" of free verse "are, I believe, either tone deaf or not listening" ("And the Look" 36). Dodd offers no further direction for those who cannot (or will not) hear. Time and again, readers are told they must simply believe that the rhythm is there—and that they must work very hard to hear it.

In the teens, many felt that free-verse poets were asking readers to construct music that simply did not exist. In 1916, for instance, H. E. Warner dismissed the notion of free-verse cadence:

> As a matter of fact, the vers librist does not divide his lines on cadence or any regular principle. They consist of a single syllable or a handful of words according to individual whim. It is free but not verse except in some perverted meaning of the term. (572)

Warner disparages psychological interpretations such as later forwarded by Storer, asserting that cadence is based on a "whim," instead of a deep welling from the human consciousness. More recently, Brad Leithauser assailed free verse as an impoverished genre "whose prosody is limited to enjambment" (7). Clearly, he hears no subtle cadence. Dodd and Simpson may well contend that readers such as Leithauser and Warner are too closed-minded to hear free verse. However, by advocating a kind of readerly connoisseurship, they posit another ontology of poetry, one that involves the reader. And the hostile reader's response to such rhetoric is often to challenge free verse's status as poetry by stating, "I don't hear anything."

The indeterminateness of cadence (and the resultant disagreement between Dodd and Leithauser) is a central problem of free-verse rhythm, which is itself a particularly knotty part of the larger problem regarding the rhythm of poetry. I have been quoting Modern poets on this issue, but there is a field designed to study the rhythm of poetry, that of prosody. Like Wesling and Hartman (who subtitled his book on free verse, *An Essay on Prosody*), in this examination of the lineal form of free verse, I find it useful to turn to the problems of prosodic theory that free verse brings to the forefront.

Those who posit "cadence" as something the attuned can hear are insisting that readers have to interpret texts. While poststructural theory continues to explore the implications of this, Walter Prichard Eaton argued the basic notion in 1919 when he noted that "it is the reader, not the writer who sets the tune" ("Influence" 495) for free verse. Eaton made this comment about free verse instead of about poetry in general because he assumed that most readers know how to read poetry in traditional measure.

Why? Although it is often (and truly) remarked that prosodists disagree on just about everything, there is one principle upon which most agree. This principle is sometimes ascribed to I. A. Richards, though Richards himself never claims it as his own, and indeed refers the reader to Coleridge. He could have as easily referred the reader to Poe, Wordsworth, or any of a number of others. Richards summarizes the thinking of prosodists in this way: "Instead of a strict conformity to a pattern, an arrangement of departures and returns to the pattern has come to be regarded as the secret to poetic rhythm" (215–16). Similarly, Hartman makes the distinction between "meter" (the strict pattern) and "rhythm" (the conformity, departures, and returns to the pattern). Thus, the meter is actually an "abstraction" (22). Though not all prosodists use these terms in this way, I will adopt this nomenclature for this book. "Meter" is the overall governing prosody—for example, iambic pentameter—and "rhythm" is the way that lines of poetry conform and do not conform to the meter's pattern.

Jannaris, as I have shown, argued that Greek meter was an abstraction because his investigation in comparative linguistics indicated Alexandrian prosodists did not adequately describe the rhythm of the poetry they studied. He maintained that the peculiar history of the Greek language and its transmission led to the artificiality of Greek prosody. The phenomena he discovered are prevalent in many, if not most, languages. Recognizing both meter and rhythm is important, Richards argues:

> The pattern [i.e., the meter] is only a convenience, though an invaluable one; it indicates a general movement of the rhythm; it gives a model, a central line, from which variations in the movement take their direction and gain an added significance; it gives a firm support, a fixed point of orientation in the indefinitely vast world of possible rhythms. (219)

John Hollander styles the meter a "metrical contract" (*Vision* 558)[15] between the poet and reader, whereby both the poet and the reader share assumptions about poetic rhythm. This is the reason that Eaton said readers must make the rhythm for free verse. He thought there was a defined contract for traditional poetry but not for free verse.

The names of Richards and Coleridge may make the concept of a metrical contract suspiciously New Critical, and it is true that the New Critical work *Understanding Poetry* uses traditional scansion extensively. However, the general assumption can be found in prosodic theory from the classical period to the present day. Longinus, for example, warns against being "overly-rhythmical" lest an audience feel "the effect not of words but of rhythm" and "foresee the due ending themselves" (293). In *Orator,* Cicero takes up the issue of prose rhythm, which he likens to poetical rhythm, just without the "definite and fixed law" (473) of verse. Still, he argues, the ear perceives prose as rhythmical, and thus the ends of sentences should be rhythmic "since the ear is always awaiting the end and takes pleasure in it" (475).[16] Cicero clearly refers to a shared set of expectations between readers and writers, as does Samuel Johnson in his life of Abraham Cowley: "The great pleasure of verse," Johnson wrote, "arises from the known measure of the lines and the uniform structure of the stanzas, by which the voice is regularized and the memory relieved" (I.47). In the middle of the nineteenth century, Harriet Martineau took Matthew Arnold's verse to task in a way that clearly refers to a shared set of rhythmic expectations: she takes issue with "the promise of meter which so many of [Arnold's poems] make to the eye but which break to the ear" (136). In the twentieth century, the idea has been extended by writers like Hollander (in "The Metrical Frame") and Finch, who in *The Ghost of Meter* uses it to incorporate social and political conditions in her theory of "metrical code." Even Alan Holder, who professes great disdain for conventional metrical theory, uses the notion of a shared set of expectations for his "phrasal" prosody.[17]

The metrical contract helps narrow the gap between poet and reader. Like a judge considering cases according to precedent, a reader familiar with a fair amount of poetry can have a fairly good idea as to how a poem is to be read; also like a judge, he or she may decide to disregard a precedent if special circumstances warrant. The contract pledges that the writer will not diverge from meter without a reason, and that the reader should be able to detect "an added significance" in departures from the pattern—under the terms of the agreement, divergences receive special prominence. Even Pope, regarded by many as a touchstone of metrical smoothness, emphasizes the added significance of metrical variation in *An Essay on Criticism:*

> Some Beauties yet, no Precepts can declare,
> For there's *Happiness* as well as *Care.*
> *Musick* resembles *Poetry,* in each
> Are *nameless Graces* which no Methods teach, }
> And which a *Master-Hand* alone can reach.
> If, where the *Rules* not far enough extend,
> (Since Rules were made but to promote their End)
> Some lucky LICENCE answer to the full
> Th'intent propos'd, *that Licence* is a *Rule.*
> Thus *Pegasus,* a nearer way to take,
> May boldly deviate from the common Track;
> Great Wits may *gloriously offend*
> And *rise* to *Faults* true Criticks *dare not mend;*
> From *vulgar Bounds* with *brave Disorder* part,
> And *snatch* a *Grace* beyond the Reach of Art,
> Which, without passing thro' the Judgment, gains
> The *Heart,* and all its End *at once* attains. (ll. 141–57)

Wittily, Pope's own rhythm mirrors the point he makes—the lines that propose deviating from the meter ("Musick resembles . . ." and "May boldly . . .") themselves deviate from meter, and a line discussing license itself takes license with two elisions. The passage argues that (when penned by a Master-Hand), lines departing from meter contain beauties greater than ("beyond the Reach" of) those that conform strictly.

Apart from this general principle, prosodists do not agree on very much. They disagree about the import of a particular meter, the meter of specific poems, and the rhythm of particular lines. Most recognize that the conventional notation of stressed and unstressed (or slack) syllables does not begin to measure the gradation between sorts of stresses. Poe (in "The Rationale of Verse") and Otto Jespersen use a 1 to 4 system for just this reason, and there are other more complex systems.[18] However, anything beyond the stress/unstress system starts getting into an increasingly subjective area, the very place where the reader most makes the rhythm. Jespersen remarked in 1933 that "we have no means of measuring stress objectively by instruments; we must have nothing to go by except our ears" (110). Since then, we have much more complicated instruments, but we are no closer to identifying rhythm conclusively. Jespersen implies a uniformity of ear simply not manifest in prosodic criticism.

"The mysterious glory which seems to inhere in the sound of certain lines," Richards points out, "is a projection of the thought and emotion they invoke" (216). In other words, because English speakers use stress (and duration, and so forth) to make meaning, how you perceive the rhythm depends on how you understand the passage—and the way you interpret a text is in turn influenced by all sorts of extrarhythmic considerations. Moreover, two readers agreeing on the precise interpretation of a text may still create different rhythms, if one feels regularity is important to the idea, while the other believes a conversational rhythm more fitting.

Although the meter of traditional poetry can usually be detected with some assurance, the rhythm can only be determined by considering meaning and context. This is why free-verse rhythm is especially difficult to ascertain. As Hartman pointed out, "prosody, if it is to function as a prosody, must be shared" between writer and reader (13). Even if free verse fashions a brand-new, superorganized prosodic system, (Hartman again) it "is not prosody as far as the reader is concerned, because he does not share the secret" (21). If, as it is frequently asserted, free verse lacks prosody, then the reader has in Richards's terms no way to navigate the possibilities of reading. It is not just that free verse lacks the comfort of a consistent meter; it lacks a stable framework allowing the reader to detect with confidence what departs from the pattern and thus receives special prominence. The generally articulated principle of "cadence," as I have shown, merely indicates that the poem departs from traditional rhythm, and offers no contract for the reader. This difficulty is evident in Alan Helms's frustration over some of A. R. Ammons's poems. Helms writes, "[T]he ghost of prosody hovers in these lines but it never asserts itself: we are halfway through the poem, yet it is still not clear how Ammons expects us to hear his words" (251). He continues, "[I]f a poet can satisfy us that there is some sort of rationale for the disposition of line in a nonmetrical poem, we become willing to commit ourselves to the harder job of reading" (260). Helms's "harder job of reading" suggests, perhaps, the frequently asserted notion that free verse demands more from the reader. However, it seems to me that the difference in readerly attention between free and traditional verse does not amount to more or less attention, but different *kinds* of attention. Which demands more alertness: attending to two patterns (meter and rhythm), or attending to one more unpredictable pattern?

The need for some sort of shared set of expectations is especially great for new movements in lineal form. As I have noted, Milton, Coleridge, and Hopkins all wrote prefaces to help alert their readers to the terms of their new contracts. When free-verse poets eschewed traditional rhyme and meter, they discarded a contract that readers and writers had traditionally shared. Since "cadence" offered no clear terms of agreement, it stands to reason that many early free-verse writers should have felt some anxiety over how to ensure a correct reading of their poems. The many early explanations of free verse, almost all of them by practicing poets, can be understood as efforts to allay this anxiety over rhythm. Though many explanations came from poets not generally highly regarded today, they were influential in the Modern period, and their attempts often mirror those made by poets who do frequently appear in today's anthologies. Fletcher's scansion of his own poem, for example, obviously attempts to alert readers to the way the poetry was supposed to sound; likewise, Lowell published a scansion of H.D.'s "Oread" around the same time.

Rhythmic anxiety is evident in the poetic practice as well. Vachel Lindsay's early verse often included marginal glosses instructing the reader how to read the poem. For example, the note to the first verse paragraph of Lindsay's "The Firemen's Ball" explained the passage was *"To be read or sung in a heavy, buzzing bass, as of a fire-engine pumping"* (123)—which gives both rhythmic and intonational directions.

Lindsay, of course, was an extreme case. Monroe commented that the free-verse movement "has called typography to its aid" (*Poets* 322) to help indicate rhythm. Often the effect was far from subtle. I am not the first to point out that when Pound's "In the Station at the Metro" first appeared, it looked like this:

> The apparition   of these faces   in the crowd :
> Petals   on a wet, black   bough . (*Ezra* I.137)

The gaps seem meant to help readers group the words into free-verse equivalents of metrical feet. But Pound was not alone in this procedure. Robert Alden Sanborn's "Lento" in *Others* of 1915 does the same thing:

> The hours   wait them   at the gate,
> Sighing   As the little feet   tick by (48)

Space also could be used mimetically, as in Henderson's poem, "Humoresque": "not t o o m u c h money / nor q u i t e e n o u g h love!" (100). Something similar occurs in the early poetry of E. E. Cummings. The first of his "Chansons Innocents" in *Tulips and Chimneys* (1923), with its goat-footed lame balloonman whistling "far and wee," is well known for being imitative, but it also suggests a way the poem should be read aloud. The second poem in the series begins,

hist   whist
little ghostthings
tip-toe
twinkle-toe

If anything is being imitated, it is a nursery rhyme. Cummings is fairly obviously playing with pauses between words. Similarly, the end of the poem is set to emphasize rhythm:

for she know the devil   ooch
the devil   ouch
the devil
ach   the great
green
dancing
devil
devil

devil
devil
          wheEEE (25)

Thus Cummings's visual poetic conjoins his aural one. This expressive use of space to emphasize rhythm can be seen as the aesthetic (and perhaps decadent) offspring of such poems as James Whitcomb Riley's "Little Orphant Annie," which uses this impressive refrain:

An' the Gobble-uns 'll git you
          EF you
                    Don't
                              Watch
                                        Out! (370)

Again, space emphasizes rhythm.[19] But Cummings soon moved away from such obvious uses of space. Consider, for example, this poem from 1935:

sh estiffl
ystrut sal
lifs an
dbut sth
epoutin(gWh.ono:w
s li psh ergo
wnd ow n (444)

The typography obfuscates the rhythm. Had he written this fifteen years earlier, he might have arranged it this way:

he stiffly	struts
all ifs and	buts
the pouting	
who	now
slips her	gown
	down

Though my lineation is conjectural, clearly by 1935 Cummings had moved beyond Rileyan effects and was less concerned that readers would misconstrue his rhythm.

A more common way to indicate cadence was to use ellipses. Poets in the first few decades of the twentieth century used ellipses more often than do most contemporary poets, usually at the end of the line to suggest a kind of profound trailing off into the ineffable. It was a favorite technique of bad poets attempting to invest their poems with sublimity not otherwise evident. Free-verse poets, not averse to this sort of thing themselves, often used ellipses for rhythmic purposes. In part V of Skipwith Cannell's "Poems in Prose and Verse," for example, readers of 1913 found regularly positioned ellipses:

At night . . . I will descend . . .
Wearied . . . into the valley . . . (172)

The periods do not indicate lacunae or profound silence—the grammar demands that the reader, so to speak, connect the dots—but the slow cadence appropriate to a tired speaker, much like Eliot's spiritually exhausted J. Alfred Prufrock's locution, "Asleep . . . tired . . . or it malingers" (*Complete* 5). John Rodker's "London Nights" (1914) uses ellipses to indicate rhythm:

> Stress of the crowd . . . and the whole of it mute . . .
> Tunics that thrill in the light till you look at his face
> With a rush of hate . . . and hate for the grace
> Of the slavey wooing the brute.
> Stress of the crowd! (122)

The grammar encourages the reader to take the lines as a semantic whole, so that the ellipses serve to indicate the slower rhythms of lines one and three, as opposed to the quicker ones of two and four, in a very elementary kind of counterpoint.[20] A similar rough counterpoint can be found in F. S. Flint's "Four Poems in Unrhymed Cadence" (1913), the title of which announces a concern for rhythm:

> They fall . . . they fall . . .
> I am overwhelmed,
> and afraid. (138)

The lines also model something free-verse poets discovered in the teens—that, in poems with short lines, poets could control readers' readings to a great extent by using punctuation. The above passage, for example, uses nine words and four punctuation marks.

Alfred Kreymborg's *Mushrooms* (1916) (a volume of verse with a subtitle—*A Book of Free Forms*—announcing allegiance to the free-verse movement) often uses a good deal of punctuation to help readers make out rhythms. The commas of the last lines of "Vista," for instance, are placed to indicate two lines of iambic tetrameter with a caesura (and a trochaic substitution on the final line):

> Love
> ah yes, ah yes, ah yes indeed
> verily yes, ah yes indeed. (5)

"Children" is more accentual:

They live; we exist.
They feel; we think.
They come; we go.
They play; we fumble.
They dream, awake; we dream, asleep.
They sleep; we toss.
We cannot be.
But let us try. (57)

Thirty-three words, sixteen marks of punctuation: the systematic punctuation (and hypermetric line) is reminiscent of most editions of *Beowulf,* which also has been heavily punctuated by editors to give the reader a clear idea of the rhythm. With its unvarying syntax, Kreymborg's poem gives readers a great deal of direction as to how to hear the poem's rhythm.

Constance Lindsay Skinner's "Songs of the Coast-Dwellers" (1914), adaptations of Native American songs, similarly uses a good deal of punctuation:

"Lega-a-a-to'q—co-omes!"
See Me!
Grinding, flashing, my long, white, many, fierce, little, teeth,
I run, I run, I run—Ki-ki-ki-y!—
To eat my big little supper. (10)

It seems unlikely to me that Skinner has Englished the song very effectively, but readers of free verse in the teens often encountered noise like "Legato'q" and "Ki-ki-ki-y" (these turn out to be proper names) serving rhythmic purposes. As usual, an extreme example can be found in Lindsay. Again from "The Firemen's Ball," a passage glossed "*Bass—much slower*":

CLANGARANGA, CLANGARANGA,
CLANG . . . CLANG . . . CLANG.
CLANG, CLANG, CLANG!
CLANG . . . A . . . RANGA
CLANG . . . A . . . RANGA
CLANG . . . CLANG . . . CLANG . . .
LISTEN . . . TO . . . THE . . . MUSIC . . .
OF . . . THE . . . FIREMEN'S . . . BALL . . . (16)

The imitative link to the rhythmic could hardly be more overt. Lowell's prose poem (she called it "polyphonic prose") "The Bombardment" (1914) employs onomatopoeic sounds to underscore rhythms:

> Where are the people, and why does the fretted steeple weep about in the sky? Boom! The sound swings against the rain. Boom, again! After it, only the water rushing in the gutters, and the turmoil from the spout of the gargoyle. Silence. Ripples and mutters. Boom! (60)

The use of echoic words here is about as subtle as Lindsay's "boomlay, boomlay, boomlay, BOOM" refrain in *The Congo*—a poem Lowell admired—and readers of "The Bombardment" would have little trouble finding where the strongest stresses were to be put.

Lowell's many articles on free verse demonstrated that she thought of herself as an expert. Since she was a proponent of "cadence," her verse often self-consciously strives for rhythmic effect. Before the following poem, she asks her readers, "Could I reproduce the effect of music in another medium? Could I? The reader must determine":

> Thin-voiced, nasal pipe
> Drawing sound out and out
> Until it is a screeching thread,
> Sharp and cutting, sharp and cutting,
> It hurts
> Whee-e-e!
> Bump! Bump! Tong-ti-bump!
> There are drums here,
> Banging ("Music" 150)

If you hear Stravinsky's "Grotesques" in these lines, Lowell has succeeded. If you do not, the poem has very little to offer, since it is really only about sound. In this context, Wallace Stevens's early nonsense seems rather conventional. Take "Ploughing on a Sunday," for example:

> Tum-ti-tum,
> Ti-tum-tum-tum!
> The turkey-cock's tail
> Spreads to the sun (20)

While echoing a horn, the onomatopoeic words also announce a kind of rhythm.

A few principles emerge from these examples. First, since traditional contracts no longer held, early free-verse poets often provided their readers with fairly unmistakable contracts in order to make their rhythms clear, often using punctuation and typography to make the rhythm so obvious that a reader would truly have to be dull to miss it. These poems also seem to be written so as to give them a clear sense of "return," and thus effects tend to happen in groups of two or more. Indeed, if early critics of free verse had attended more carefully to the poetry they criticized, they likely would have complained about the over-obviousness of rhythm, rather than the reverse.[21] Moreover, many of the passages quoted above, such as Rodker's, are arguably metrical.[22] Some of the new rhythms, then, were actually replays of the old ones.

However, by the thirties, both Cummings and Eliot had abandoned such overt devices, and poets in general became less intent on announcing their rhythms. This suggests that something changed in the general approach to poetry. Certainly, much of today's free verse is lightly punctuated, and sometimes not at all. Because most Moderns were by no means populist, less explicit contracts make sense, as do the explicit contracts of an avowedly populist writer like Lindsay. Historically, what happened was that free-verse poetry started evincing less concern about guiding the reader because new contracts between free-verse poets and readers familiar with Modern poetry began to emerge. This study elucidates those contracts.

Although the notion of a shared set of expectations between writer and reader is hardly a Modern idea, the lack of explicit terms for these emerging contracts has often led to differing views of what they are. Of course, the precise expectations for *any* literary form or genre are always subject to debate and interpretation, and thus it is not an indication of either readerly philistinism or writerly laziness that the term *free verse* has proven difficult to define.

The central reason why the definitions reported in the previous pages have not succeeded is that they approach free verse as if it were one indissoluble lump. All-inclusive definitions of free verse, if they are not "negative," must be vague because the works generally categorized under the label were actually composed under differing prosodies. A parallel situation might be that of someone trying to define the rhythmic principle underlying *Piers Plowman, The Rape of the Lock,* and Campion's "Rose-Cheeked Laura." Such a person might conclude, as Smith does of free verse, that the rhythm of traditional poetry is "nonquantifiable." But if these poems are separated and considered within the differing traditions, their rhythmic principles are more easily categorized. I call the various lineal forms of free verse "genres" because attending the formal categories are other shared assumptions about rhythmic contracts, typical themes, philosophical ideas, and so forth. Since there is considerable evidence that Modern poets read and learned from one another, lines of influence are comparatively simple to draw.

My argument for types of free verse is not that these categories exist as some sort of linguistic or transcendental fact; they exist because poets believe that they do. The genres are nowadays sufficiently well established that, for example, Carolyn Kizer's poem, "Amusing Our Daughters," praises Robert Creeley for being "Good at reciting long-line or short-line poems" without explaining what she means by the two terms. Clearly, she finds a difference between the two kinds of verse (and if it is Creeley, it is free verse).

While it is not quite true, as Reg Saner suggests, that nobody has attempted to "separate wavelengths in the free verse spectrum" (6), most of the attempts to do so are dogged by the same problems which have ever dogged free-verse theory. As I have shown, a promotional or antipromotional bent has historically accompanied free-verse theorizing. Often, free verse is valued or denigrated simply because it is not traditional. Further, simply ascribing profundity to a form (and sensitivity to the reader who can appreciate it) does little to elucidate that profundity. Still, I do not claim that I am the first to propose genres of free verse. In fact, a growing consensus acknowledges that there are categories. The entry on "free verse" in *The New Princeton Encyclopedia of Poetry and Poetics* (not the entry written by Williams in *The Princeton Encyclopedia of Poetry and Poetics*) makes this point without firmly defining the categories. Those who have been willing to specify have often done so, as it were, from above, without much attention to lines of development. For example, William Patterson and Ramsey posit categories of free verse based on their own formal analysis. Paul Fussell's chapter on free verse in *Poetic Meter and Poetic Form* identifies a number of common techniques, but the only genre he distinguishes is the "lyric-epic" (85). Though Hartman and Wesling attend to the continuity of greater aesthetics, their descriptions of free verse are largely acute comments on a few poems and, like Fussell, they do not offer more general categories. Christoph Küper has suggested categories that have some similarity to mine,[23] though he does not go into much detail nor does he provide examples and aesthetic context.

Classifying free verse into genres runs counter to much free-verse theory, especially the idea that a poem's form is intimately connected to its author's personality or historical circumstances (e.g., it is often said that the fragments of *The Waste Land* reflect the fragmentation of the postwar world). However, locating a free-verse poem in a genre need not force the conclusion that history and personality do not influence a poem. In fact, identifying which aspects of a poem participate in a particular tradition should make it easier to isolate the distinctly personal, political, and so on. The point of establishing categories of free verse is not to deny differences among poems, or, like the third-century grammarians, to establish a set of regulations, but rather to understand how the Modern poets modified traditions in their emerging forms. I am only treating the term *free verse* in the way that other formal terms, such as *ode* or *sonnet,* have generally been considered. My categories follow the historical traditions free verse adapted and have the additional virtue of being relatively easy to identify, so that two critics who agree on little else can agree on these basic formal categories.

To begin: the most identifiable type is poems using the long line. I hesitate to call them Whitmanian—though his influence on later long-line poets such as Sandburg, Edward Carpenter (in *Towards Democracy*), and Allen Ginsberg, is great—because Whitman did not invent the form. Whitman's scholars are quick to point out parallels in translations of the Bible (particularly the poetical books such as Job and Psalms), Smart's *Jubilate Agno,* Ossian, and Blake. Whitman is not even the first long-line poet from America. Twelve years before *Leaves of Grass* was published, the transcendentalist poet Christopher Pearse Cranch wrote "Correspondences," with long lines such as these:

> Man consciously uses figures of speech every moment,
> Little dreaming the cause why to such terms he is prone,
> Little dreaming that every thing here has its correspondence,
> Folded within its form, as in the body the soul. (609–10)

Further, if *Leaves of Grass* gives a reader reason to credit Whitman with audacity, poetic vision, and a commitment to innovation, *Proverbial Philosophy,* a collection of long-line poems written five years before the first edition of *Leaves,* provides no such sanction for Martin Tupper, who was seeking to be derivative: he wanted to add to the store of biblical proverbs using the manner of the King James Bible. Long-line verse, then, was by no means the invention of Whitman. It was well established enough for an otherwise conventional poet such as Tupper to use the form. Whitman was merely long-line poetry's greatest writer.

The most salient feature of long-line poetry is the length of its lines. "Long," of course, is a comparative and not absolute judgment. It so happens to be the case that, in English, poetic lines tend to be the length of iambic pentameter or tetrameter, so lines longer than that seem to be long; in Whitman's case, the lines are often much longer. Yet more than line length determines long-line poetry. As Hollander points out, in such poems, "the sense of line terminus is crucial: each line has become a larger unit of utterance" (*Vision* 231), so that "the integrity of the line as a unit" is always maintained. He adds, perhaps a little too positively, "There can be no enjambment in oracular poetry" (232).

Long-line poems tend to be long in terms of the number of lines as well. A favorite technique is the catalogue, often signaled by anaphora, such as the "Moloch" section of *Howl,* or section three of "Starting from Paumanok." Listing is a part of the assumed vatic expansiveness of the genre. Long-line poetics encourage, it would seem, enthusiastic and often syncretic religious philosophies. Ideally, each element of a long-line catalogue is elevated by its incorporation into the body of the poem, categorized and thus provided with a unifying significance. Fussell (in *Poetic Meter*) notes that the catalogues juxtapose as much as they unite. Fussell quotes from part of this passage of *Song of Myself:*

> The bride unrumples her whiter dress, the minute-hand of the clock moves slowly,
> The opium-eater reclines with rigid head and just-open'd lips,
> The prostitute draggles her shawl, her bonnet bobs on her tipsy and pimpled neck,
> The crowd laugh at her blackguard oaths, the men jeer and wink to each other
> (Miserable! I do not laugh at your oaths nor jeer you;)
> The President holding a cabinet council is surrounded by the great Secretaries,
> On the piazza walk three matrons stately and friendly with twined arms (36)

Fussell calls the comparison between the prostitute and the President "one of Whitman's happiest near-juxtapositions" (79). It would seem to be a kind of political statement. The poem's parenthetical statement makes it clear that the speaker does not wish to degrade the prostitute, though the President and his aides lose something of his pretensions to uniqueness (signaled by capital letters) due to the juxtaposition with the prostitute and the matrons. However, all are subsumed within a larger vision, a greater inclusiveness whose breadth critiques and incorporates the smaller circles of President and Secretaries as well as matrons and friends.

A common assumption about Whitman's verse is that it was written, in

Langston Hughes's words, "without the frills, furbelows, and decorations of conventional poetry, usually without rhyme or measured prettiness" (359). However, apart from breaking the pentameter, Whitman's language could be rather conventional. Consider this passage from *Song of Myself,* section 5:

> Loafe with me on the grass, loose the stop from your throat,
> Not words, not music or rhyme I want, not custom or lecture, not even the best,
> Only the lull I like, the hymn of your valvèd voice. (27)

The lines employ many conventions of metrical verse, including syntactical inversion and a grave accent to indicate the pronunciation of a syllable generally elided in normal speech—two liberties that came about, paradoxically enough, to help writers keep the meter. It thus may be said that (as Ezra Pound tended to argue about Whitman), in freeing himself from meter, Whitman accepted the chains of the other conventions of traditional verse. However, it might be more accurate to say that Whitman both liberated himself from meter and accepted the liberties that traditional poets granted themselves, "encompassing" both, W. D. Snodgrass notes, in a system Whitman felt was more "democratic" (592).

Long-line poetics, then, do not discard traditional poetics so much as they incorporate them. Snodgrass points out that while Whitman often uses "slang and/or coinages," there is also a "surprising amount" of "highly literary" language (587). Though using a mixed diction is by no means peculiar to long-line poetry, it is a persistent characteristic. Section 6 of *Song of Myself* begins, "A child said *What is grass?*" then offers some answers:

> I guess it is a uniform hieroglyphic,
> And it means, Sprouting alike in broad zones and narrow zones,
> Growing among black folk as among white,
> Kanuck, Tuckahoe, Congressman, Cuff, I give the same, I receive the same. (28)

The definitions rove from a child's words to the educated, poetic diction of "uniform hieroglyphic" and to points in between. This aesthetic pluralism recurs in the 1855 preface to *Leaves of Grass,* when Whitman argues that "the finest poems or music or orations or recitations" all come from the same source and are essentially similar (454). Long-line poetry, then, incorporates prose, so long as it is impassioned and translated by the speaker's consciousness.

Long-line poets clearly understood this part of the tradition. Sandburg, likewise, was fond of mixing registers, usually juxtaposing slang with more high-flown language. This is evident in "Who Am I?":

> Down in the sounding foam of primal things, I reach my hands and play with
> pebbles of destiny.
> I have been to hell and back many times.
> I know all about heaven, for I have talked with God.
> I dabble in the blood and guts of the terrible.
> I know the passionate seizure of beauty
> And the marvelous rebellion of man at all signs reading "Keep Off." (110)

Though a reader of today may find these lines clichéd, readers habituated to genteel traditions in the early part of the twentieth century often found Sandburg's use of slang, such as "blood and guts" and "to hell and back," as an earthy and perhaps "manly" antidote to a tradition grown effete.[24]

Ginsberg combines the taboo and earthly with angelic orders in *Howl:*

> who let themselves be fucked in the ass by saintly motorcyclists and screamed
> with joy,
> who blew and were blown by those human seraphim, the sailors, caresses of
> Atlantic and Caribbean love (128)

The operative mode of long-line poetry is a heightening inclusion. The point of long-line poetics is that it is *all* poetry.

Another genre of free verse, short-line poetry of the sort exemplified by Williams and H.D., stems from quite different poetics. Much different from long-line integrity, the shortness of the lines ensures that, unless the poem is to be made up of extremely short sentences, the poem must be enjambed, often strongly so.[25] Short-line poems do not often mix registers in the way the long-line poetry does, and, unlike long-line poems, do not mix in a line of a different length (as Whitman at times did). In general, long-line poems incorporate; short-line poems exclude. A fuller discussion of short-line aesthetics will appear in chapters 4 and 5 of this book.

If these two types of free verse are easily identifiable, the next two may not be so clear-cut. These categories stem from a notion often ascribed to Eliot that free verse is haunted by meter. The metaphor is not original to Eliot. It appears in Stephane Mallarmé's essay, *"Crise de Vers"* (1886),[26] which seeks to explain what Mallarmé calls the *"exquise"* and *"fondamentale"* crisis in literature (159). The poetry of Jules Laforgue, Mallarmé explains, offers the reader the *"charme certain du vers faux."* Laforgue's line is false because of its *"infractions volontaires"* of the received rules of verse and its *"savantes dissonances"*—all of which appeal to our *"delicatesse"*(163–64). Of course, such a formulation assumes the reader must have delicacy in the first place, and thus Mallarmé is another theorist implying that it takes a sophisticated, perhaps supersubtle, reader to appreciate free verse. This reader must be familiar with the poetry's traditions, because *"la réminscence du vers strict hante ces jeux à côté"*(164)—that is, a reader can perceive the falseness and the dissonance only if that reader "remembers" the pattern that is not actually present but haunting off to the side somewhere. Thus, the reader apperceives not only the actual rhythm, but also the meter the rhythm avoids, and feels, exquisitely, the difference between the two.

Eliot picks up many of these ideas, naturalizing them by relating them to *Hamlet:*

> The ghost of some simple metre should lurk behind the arras of even the "freest" verse; to advance menacingly as we doze and withdraw as we rouse. Our freedom is only truly freedom when it appears against the background of artificial limitation. (*To Criticize* 187)

Such a poetic is much more than Pound's characterization, "the skilful evasion of the better known English metres" (*Ezra* II.249). That meter hides behind an "arras" indicates that Eliot's figure puts meter playing the role of Polonius, and its complexity is based on Eliot's notions on Polonius. Oddly enough, the way that Eliot talks about *Hamlet*'s textual history in "*Hamlet* and His Problems" mirrors how he talks about poetic form in "Reflections on *Vers Libre*." In the former essay, Eliot argued that *Hamlet* had a serious structural flaw, in that it did not harmonize the "revenge-motive" (97) of its source material with "Shakespeare's play" about "the effect of a mother's guilt on her son" (98). He finds "little excuse" for "the Polonius/Laertes and the Polonius/Reynaldo scenes" (97–98). Eliot thought Polonius was a part of Shakespeare's source material that the playwright did not integrate into *Hamlet,* arguing that the character was not sufficiently transmuted by Shakespeare's genius. Connected with the "intractable" older material, Polonius is part of the tradition Shakespeare was writing in, but not the matter Shakespeare intended to convey.

Prosodically, Eliot puts Polonius in the role of meter. Thus, poems in this genre often set up some sort of implied categories of language, moving from Polonius to Hamlet and back again, relying on old Polonius when Hamlet "naps" or otherwise cannot organize his excitement. Such a poetic differs from long-line aesthetics because Polonius is not incorporated into *Hamlet;* instead, through juxtaposition, differing sorts of poetic faith and language are tested against prosaic fact—sometimes older, more traditional poetic language against a new sensibility. That is to say, in these poems readers hear either different voices (instead of the bardic voice of, say, Whitman) or the modulations and registers of a single speaker. This is, on a linear level, the type of reinterpretation typical of the eighteenth-century mock epic, when a speaker often sets up, then deliberately deflates, an epic voice. Like Polonius in *Hamlet,* meter may be a nuisance, may even be nefarious, but expunging it is a mistake. I will discuss this more fully in the next two chapters of this book.

A fourth kind of free verse is the sort that, as Graham Hough puts it, "avoids tradition" (173). While ghosts of iambs and anapests abound in Eliot, other poets seem unaffected by such specters or indeed actively avoid them. Roy Fuller writes that such free-verse poets "must watch it" (45) lest they inadvertently lapse into meter, a comment that echoes one made decades earlier: so various are the meters available to a poet, Pound wrote, that "fanatical vers librists will escape them with difficulty" (*Ezra* II.250). In the Modern period, especially the early period, the most often cited test case for whether or not free verse was poetry on formal grounds was not Pound or Eliot (though Pound and Sandburg were often the case studies for testing the subject of poetry), but Edgar Lee Masters's *Spoon River Anthology,* a collection which often does not seem to refer to iambic pentameter.

Uzi Shavit, while discussing Hebrew free verse in relation to American free verse under the assumption that all free verse is basically the same, argues, "The main difference between meter-base rhythm and free verse is that the reiterated unit in metrical rhythm is identical, whereas the recurring unit in free verse is merely similar" (66). However, assigning a "reiterated unit" in these lines from "Lydia Puckett" by Masters seems difficult:

Knowlt Hoheimer ran away to the war
The day before Carl Trenary
Swore out a warrant through Justice Arnett
For stealing hogs.
But that's not the reason he turned a soldier. (50)

Of course, if "recurring unit" is defined loosely enough, *any* prose can be found to have some sort of reiteration, yet in this poem the matter-of-fact speaking voice seems to interfere with a more traditional rhythmic reading. Something similar occurs in D. H. Lawrence's "How Beastly the Bourgeois Is":

> Isn't he handsome? Isn't he healthy? Isn't he a fine specimen?
> Doesn't he look the fresh clean Englishman, outside?
> Isn't he God's own image? tramping his thirty miles a day
> after partridges, or a little rubber ball?
> wouldn't you like to be like that, well off, and quite the thing?
> Oh, but wait!
> Let him meet a new emotion, let him be faced with another man's need, let him
> come home to a bit of moral difficulty, let life face with a new demand on his
> understanding,
> and then watch him go soggy, like a wet meringue.
> Watch him turn into a mess, either a fool or a bully.
> Just watch the display of him, confronted with a new demand on his intelligence,
> a new life-demand. (2127–28)

If you try to rouse up a metrical ghost in such a poem, it seems to me that you will miss the entire tone. As Pound argued, such is the variety of metrical feet in English and classical prosody that feet can be assigned, but meter as it is traditionally understood does not appear.[27] Neither does the poem qualify as long-line poetry generically, though certainly its lines are long. The poem does not use the bardic voice, mix high and low diction, nor enfold its elements in an exalting whole. It seems more profitable to simply note that this poem is either unactivated by the metrical tradition or actively avoiding it.

Lawrence's account of free verse underscores this. Free verse is, or should be,

> direct utterance from the instant, whole man. It is the soul and the mind and the body surging at once, nothing left out. They speak all together. There is some confusion, some discord. . . . It is no use inventing fancy laws for free verse, no use drawing a melodic line which all the feet must toe . . . We can get rid of the stereotyped movements and the old hackneyed associations of sound and sense. (*Selected Literary Criticism* 87)

Lawrence goes on to argue that any rules lead to "unfree verse" and not at all the "new substance" of *vers libre.* Far from establishing a "reiterating unit," for

Lawrence free verse has no "finish":

> It has no satisfying stability, satisfying to those who like the immutable. None of this. It is the instance; the quick; the very jutting source of all will-be and has-been. The utterance is like a spasm, naked contact with all influences at once. It does not want to get anywhere. (88)

Lawrence contends that free verse's intense and direct "contact" with the world precludes it from being formally balanced. By implication, poetry achieving any sort of balance is at a remove from the subject, and thus less lively and probably insincere. This sort of writing caused Pound to speak of "vers-libre fanatics" (*Pound/The Little* 73), and Eliot and Williams to discount free verse altogether. Unstable freedom might have been Lawrence's goal, but many poets were after something quite different. Pound, for example, thought such a poetry avoiding all known meter tantamount to "verse with absolutely no rhythmical basis" (*Ezra* II.250).

My categories of free verse have the virtue of grouping poems together in terms of their most noticeable formal aspects; attached to these forms are comparable relations to the traditions of verse and approaches to rhythm. In the Modern period, these formal decorums often indicated differing attitudes as to what constitutes poetic language. This chapter concludes with two issues—organicism and the poetry/prose debate—that help illustrate the stances taken by differing genres of free verse. I delineate below the main currents of thought as they appeared in traditional poetics and as the Moderns adapted them. Further discussion of these issues, concentrating on how these concerns helped direct the decorums of different free-verse genres, will appear in succeeding chapters. I offer here an overview.

The idea of organicism, Holman and Harmon assert, "has been pervasive for the past 150 years" (351). Nonetheless, as Paul Douglas points out, though many have connected Modernism and Romanticism, "one river left unnavigated" is organicism (253). I will begin this discussion with a presentation of eighteenth-century ideas, because the traditions the nineteenth-century poets reacted against—which in turn the Modern poets adapted—were stated clearly in the eighteenth century. Although succeeding chapters will show that, like prosodic theory, organic theory was by no means uniform, it is useful to review the nuances of the received theory.

In *An Essay on Criticism,* Pope appeals to nature, but finds the rules of poetry "*Nature Methodiz'd*" (1. 89). Hence, meter was first discovered in its raw state, say in the pulsating rhythms of the sea, and then made more orderly and regular. Pope argued that "Expression is the *Dress* of *Thought*" (1. 318)—that is, a poet has a thought, then dresses it up to make the best impression in company. Augustan writers tended to consider "natural" writing to be the style and genre their audience recognized as appropriate. Hence, they found it "natural" to be, or to want to be, well dressed. As Fussell points out, the "more general contemporary aesthetic theory" of the eighteenth century was "the principle of gratification of the sense of expectation, rather than the experience of surprise" (*Theory* 49).

To a large extent because of I. A. Richards, Coleridge's views were particularly important for Modern poetics. While Pope used organic metaphors to adorn his thought appropriately, Coleridge put the notion at the center of his conception of the world. Hans Eichner points out that it is well recognized that Coleridge sought to replace Pope's Deist, clockmaker God with a more active divine principle. Coleridge applied his active divine principle to aesthetics. Like Pope, he thought poems should follow rules ultimately found in nature, but since the universe was so tractable, and since in nature general rules are constantly tempered and even suspended, each poem should operate under rules intrinsic to itself.[28] Thus, when trying to clear Shakespeare of the charge that because his plays did not always follow classical rules they were therefore malformed, Coleridge distinguishes between "mechanic" and "organic" form:[29]

> The form is mechanic when on any given material we impress a pre-determined form, not necessarily arising out of the properties of the material, as when to a mass of wet clay we give whatever shape we wish it to retain when hardened. The organic form, on the other hand, is innate; it shapes as it develops itself from within, and the fullness of its development is one and the same with the perfection of its outward form. Such is the life, such the form. (*Shakespearean* I. 198)

Since poetry is one of the "living powers" (*Shakespearean* I. 197) it should operate under organic rules. This should not be taken to mean that the poem is therefore without form and "lawless," but that the laws should be "of its own origination" (*Shakespearean* I. 198). Coleridge cautioned the poet not to "misinterpret" the precedents of poetry as "a positive causation" and "become a slave of things of which he was formed to be the conqueror and sovereign" (*Collected*

4.I.518). Metrically, this suggests that the poet should not, as Pope presumably did, regard the traditions of English verse as the dictates of nature. Instead, the poem ought to follow more natural rules of its own devising, rules that develop from "within" itself.[30] Coleridge, however, does not specify these rules.

At this moment, readers of this book may be experiencing a sense of *déjà vu.* Coleridge's assertion of unspecified self-generating rules and his assumption of balance is precisely the model proposed time and again for free verse. Coleridge also states outright what many free-verse theorists imply: these organic principles work when they are used by a "true genius" (*Shakespearean* I.197). Further, Coleridge does not present explicit rules so much as suggestive metaphors. M. H. Abrams characterizes Coleridge's criticism as "a very jungle of vegetation . . . growing in tropical profusion. Authors, characters, poetic genres, poetic passages, words, meter, logic become seeds, trees, flowers, blossoms, fruit, bark, and sap." Abrams also calls attention to Coleridge's notion that poetry assimilates something other than itself into itself as "an organism converts food into its own substance" (169).

This "'coadunating faculty'" explains why Coleridge so frequently wrote in meter. It is sometimes maintained that the Romantics thought meter itself organic or were just confused on the entire issue. For example, Steele claims, "For poets like Coleridge and Goethe (and Wordsworth), metrical organization and organic expression do not conflict. Rather they are part of the same natural law" (196). Others assert the Romantics were simply befuddled. George Saintsbury has little patience for any Romantic theorizing,[31] and Wesling suggests that the Romantics thought "poetic meter . . . should at best originate in immediate experience" (*New Poetries* 54), but that logical difficulties caused much "equivocation" (*New Poetries* 64). Though surely Coleridge's voluminous writings contain some equivocations, the fact is that the Romantics by and large did not consider meter itself organic. Chapter XVIII of *Biographia Literaria* explains that meter originated in "the balance of the mind effected by the spontaneous effort which strives to hold in check the workings of the passion" (*Collected* 7.II.64)—that is, passionate words are balanced and checked by the need to put them into meter. Words must be "formed into metre *artificially,* by a *voluntary* act," and thus meter is at a remove from the original, spontaneous utterance; however, in the resulting poem they will appear as a "union" (*Collected* 7.II.65) which will "increase the vivacity and susceptibility both of the general feelings and of the attention" of the reader (*Collected* 7.II.66). Meter is thus an alien element assimilated into the poem, creating a greater whole. Percy

Shelley, in his "Defence," makes a comparable point, arguing that the imagination produces images and language that have relations "to thoughts alone" (VII.113). Meter frees the mind from mere self-referentiality and allowed the poem to "unveil the permanent analogy of things" (VII.115).[32]

Whitman extends this strain of organicism. Like Coleridge's readers, readers of Whitman encounter a profusion of natural metaphors, and Whitman at different times compares a poem to blood, a body, a tree, a river, a country, a planet, a planetary system, and the whole "kosmos." Like Coleridge, Whitman did not believe he was mixing metaphors, but describing different aspects of a greater whole. This is made clear in a note to "Democratic Vistas":

> we have peremptorily to dismiss every pretensive production, however fine its esthetic or intellectual points, which violates or ignores, or even does not celebrate, the central divine idea of All, suffusing universe, of eternal trains of purpose, in the development, by however slow degrees, of the physical, moral, and spiritual kosmos. (516)

It makes sense, then, that even Whitman's prosodic comments should celebrate the All. The other principles of organicism Coleridge promulgated—that poems are growing unities, assimilating outside elements, and evolving from internal sources of energy—are easily found in Whitman's explanations of poetry.[33] Regarding meter, however, Whitman departs from Coleridge. Whereas Coleridge found meter a useful contrivance to help give form to poems, Whitman argues more radically in the 1855 preface to *Leaves of Grass:*

> The poetic quality is not marshaled in rhyme or uniformity . . . The rhyme and uniformity of perfect poems show the free growth of metrical laws and bud from them as unerringly and loosely as lilacs or roses on a bush, and take shapes as compact as the shapes of chestnuts and oranges and melons and pears, and shed the perfume impalpable to form. (454)

Unlike Coleridge, Whitman extends organicism to meter itself. "The spirit and the form are one" (510–11), Whitman says, and "smooth walks, trimm'd hedges, poseys and nightingales" may be appropriate for British poets nurtured by a culture rooted in feudalism, but an American dedicated to the "true idea of Nature" is satisfied only with a poetic that embraces the entire "kosmos" (515). By associating English meter with the ornamental artificiality of English topiary, Whitman claims a greater organicism for his poetic, which does not need the regularizing superaddition of the inorganic to harmonize it. Whitman did acknowledge that perhaps the expansive and thus potentially self-indulgent spirit of the poet's "pride" needed checking. Instead of positing the need for an inorganic formal analogy-making device, as Shelley did, Whitman proposed an organic counter-spirit: the poet's "sympathy" which is "as measureless as its pride and the one balances the other" (456).

This notion of metrical laws growing freely sanctions Whitman's poetic practice. His language and prosody could be quite conventional on occasion, because Whitman was seeking to incorporate and grow from traditional practice. Even Whitman's line has "grown" beyond the traditional limit of ten or twelve syllables. Whitman's organicism differs from Coleridge's in one more important aspect. He conceived his grand conjoining unity as one requiring a reader to bring it to fruition. In "Poetry To-day," he quotes Charles-Augustin Sainte-Beuve approvingly that "'To-day,'" the greatest poet is one exciting the reader's "'imagination and reflection,'" one "'who leaves you much to desire, to explain, to study, much to complete in your turn'" (545). Similarly, in "Democratic Vistas," he proposes a "new theory of literary composition for imaginative works of the very first class." It is a poetry that places special demands on the reader:

> Books are to be call'd for, and supplied, on the assumption that the process of reading is not a half-sleep, but, in the highest sense, an exercise, a gymnast's struggle; that the reader is to do something for himself, must be on the alert, must himself or herself construct indeed the poem, argument, history, metaphysical essay—the text furnishing the hints, the clue, the start or frame-work. Not the book needs so much to be the complete thing, but the reader of the book does. (523)

Here, of course, is a precursor to the persistent argument that free verse needs an especially subtle reader.[34] These comments suggest one reason Whitman's poems often try to incorporate the reader. To take two familiar examples: "Poets to Come" concludes that its speaker is "Leaving it to you to prove and define it / Expecting the main things from you" (12); the last three words of *Song of Myself* are "waiting for you" (75). The celebrator of America needs, finally, a reader—presumably an American—to complete his song. This has a large impact on Whitman's cataloguing. Readers must recognize or invent specific relations between items in a catalogue—that is, a reader must provide the greater coherence, and how much meaning is found in the juxtapositions marks the degree to which that reader is willing to share, at least provisionally, the writer's organic faith.

Whitman's departures from English traditions should not obscure his important relations to them. At the core of both Coleridge and Whitman's poetic is the belief in an active, organic, divine principle. This had a profound impact on the way the writers thought and wrote. Neither poet shied away from asserting God—be it Whitman's "All" or Coleridge's assertion that artistic creation is "a repetition in the finite mind of the act of creation in the infinite I AM" (*Collected* 7.I.304)—as a final guarantor of organic rhythm.

Since the basic idea of nineteenth-century organicism was that poetry ought to express and partake of the divine creative principle that shapes the world, a considerable problem faced Modern writers endorsing the myth: they did not believe in, or were reluctant to assert the existence of, God. The force that ensured relatedness and unity was unavailable to many Modern writers. Douglas argues,

> although Modernist aesthetics remain profoundly Coleridgean, and therefore essentially organicist, modernist writers deny this heritage by breaking vehemently with Romantic pride, with the Romantic faith in the innocence of expression. They have also taken on the burden of another world to be "organized": the linguistic and psychological realm of James, Saussure, Bergson, Whitehead, Freud, Royce, and Heidegger. (254)

It seems to me, though, that instead of incorporating another world, the Moderns often looked to replace an all-encompassing organicism with a less extensive one in which they could believe. To take a familiar example, when Eliot cited Sir James Frazer and Jessie Weston in the "mythic method" of *The Waste Land,* he was trying to create the kind of multireferentiality Coleridge and Whitman assumed came with tapping into the divine.

Douglas focuses his discussion on Eliot and points out that despite his reluctance to endorse the term *organicism,* Eliot used many organic metaphors. Douglas shows that Eliot shared Coleridge's view that (in Eliot's words) a poem is an "entelechy" of organically related parts and that the received rules of art are not necessarily natural. Eliot said poets must "scrupulously guard against measuring living art and mind by dead ideas of order" (qtd. in Douglas 262). Yet Douglas does not discuss the many instances in which Eliot posits decidedly inorganic metaphors for poetry. In "Ezra Pound: His Metric and Poetry," Eliot quotes Pound approvingly that when "one has the proper material for a sonnet, one should use the sonnet form; but . . . it happens very rarely to any poet to find himself in possession of just the block of stuff which can be perfectly modeled into a sonnet" (*To Criticize* 167). Though the artist is controlled to some degree by his material, the work of art is not growing out of some inner source of energy; instead, it is shaped by the conscious activity of the artist. Significantly, Coleridge used a similar artist-as-sculptor metaphor to describe mechanic form.[35] Eliot returns to his inorganicism later in the essay when he says, "Words are perhaps the hardest materials for art" (171). Again, the metaphor implies rigidity instead of vital adaptability.

In "Reflections on *Vers Libre,*" Eliot also asserts the inorganic nature of art. "Not to have perceived the simple truth that some artificial limitation is necessary," he claims, "except in moments of the first intensity is, I believe, the capital error of Mr. E. L. Masters" (*To Criticize* 187). This is not organic assimilation, but a recipe for a kind of heterogeneous poem: moments of intensity surrounded by artifice. The model for free verse Eliot picked up from Mallarmé, the "ghost" of meter haunting less regular lines, is similarly heterogeneous:

> the most interesting verse which has yet been written in our language has been done by taking a simple form, like the iambic pentameter, and constantly withdrawing from it, or taking no form at all, and constantly approximating a very simple one. It is this contrast between fixity and flux, this unperceived evasion of monotony, which is the very life of verse. (185)

Fixity and flux, or stones and trees: this is a mixture of the inorganic and the organic.[36] In a sense, such a mixed aesthetic exemplifies a kind of organic crisis, in which poems seek but rarely accomplish resolution. Instead of combining, the differing modalities maintain their boundaries and critique each other as vehicles of truth or value.

Though Eliot's explanation does not explain all of free verse, it does a good job with his own. Consider these lines from "J. Alfred Prufrock":

> Let us go, through certain half-deserted streets,
> The muttering retreats
> Of restless nights in one-night cheap hotels
> Of sawdust restaurants with oyster shells:
> With streets that follow like a tedious argument
> Of insidious intent (*Complete* 3)

The third and fourth lines are in regular iambic pentameter. Mathurin M. Dondo, in his study of French *vers libre,* points out that in some poems by French *vers librists,* "the measure is kept with regularity despite unequal lines" (75), and notes that, for example, a poem by André Spire could be printed in traditional form simply by relineation. Something similar is evident in "Prufrock."

"There is a great deal, in the writing of poetry, which must be conscious and deliberate," Eliot says in "Tradition and the Individual Talent," and the unity achieved by such works as Cyril Tourneur's *The Revenger's Tragedy* is a "balance of contrasted emotions," a "structural emotion," a "new art emotion." It is a unity specific to art, and not, as Coleridge would argue, an entrance into transcendent truth nor even an expression of the writer's feelings. Indeed, art is "an escape from personality" (*Sacred* 58).[37] Eliot then, posits a local organicism, where inorganic elements stand between more inspired, organic ones.

In the same vein, Hart Crane, writing after Eliot, said he tried to "give the poem as a whole an orbit or predetermined direction of its own. It would establish it as free from my personality." Hence, Crane shares with Eliot the idea that art is a system enclosed within its own "orbit," apart from the poet's "personality," not coextensive with it. As if to demonstrate his endorsement of organicism, he quotes from Coleridge to authorize his opinions. Similarly, in 1925, Edith Sitwell argued that "Poetry is primarily an art, not a dumping-ground for emotions" (26), likewise citing the authority of Coleridge (and Goethe).

Harriet Monroe's organicism provides an instructive contrast. Far from creating its own orbit apart from the poet's personality, Monroe argued that the "free-verse movement has been essentially a plea for personal rhythm, for the poet's independence in working out his most expressive form and using it without prejudice" (*Poets* 322–23). Given his remarks on impersonality, Eliot could have hardly enjoyed her appraisal of *The Waste Land* as the "unstudied spontaneity" of "the changing torture of" Eliot's "soul" (105)—a far cry from careful chiseling.

Monroe and others often asserted the decisive influence of the poet's personality in the forms of poetry. I have already cited the "unconscious" source of cadence as posited by Fuller and Storer. Monroe wrote of Sandburg, "Mr. Sandburg's free-verse rhythms are as personal as his slow speech or his massive gait" ("Carl" 90), and in the same year Harry Hansen endorsed Theodore Maynard's view that Sandburg was a "free verse poet" by "fate" and "natural bent" (40); Hansen went on to claim that Sandburg's poetry was simply "an example of a man writing himself down, and not attempting to pour himself into a standardized mold" (90). Such a view extends the principle of organicism to the point of strongly suggesting Sandburg's poetry is the inevitable result of his intrinsic personal qualities.

In another essay, Monroe's elevation of the personal and experiential causes her to praise the rhythms of Pound's early poems, which, she says, "recapture the primitive simplicities and disregard efficient regularities. They play with rhyme or not, but always follow their own wilful way and ride the changing moods as lightly as a sparrow" (*Poets* 14). In these comments, Monroe endorses an organicism that seems almost arbitrary; she posits nothing to check the poem's freedom. She finds fault with *A Draft of XXX Cantos* because it sinks "too deeply in the mental easy-chairs of the library" and so detached Pound "from currents and growths essential to his full development," leaving him unable "to strike root richly into cultures unresponsive to certain secret needs of his soul" (19). Eliot found an organic unity within the confines of art; Monroe believed literariness prevented organic growth. Instead, she called for poems that "flash their lights into the subconscious and make us thrill with a sense of discovery" (*Poets* 76). I find nowhere in her critical writing a concern for unity. The very sort of uncontrollable inwardness the best poems express in their form, it would seem, resists the sort of harmonizing necessary for unity. Instead, Monroe praises "fecundity and energy" (*Poets* 85) and implies throughout her writing an organicism that resists what today is called closure.

In this respect, her thought is very much like that of Kreymborg's. The poems of *Mushrooms,* the preface says,

> spring up over night in my heart—the reason let philosophers guess. This much I know, this I can tell: myriads and myriad have I found down there, but only a handful have I plucked . . . One was a mood of pain, frail form, another a whimsical spirit, one was some black-browed child of Lear—I carry them up to my hothouse attic, up to my gardener for cultivation. (1)

Kreymborg's "cultivation," denoting both farming and learning, adds a conscious element to organicism—as does the notion that he had to seek out his poems—but the mushrooms-in-the-basement metaphor strongly suggests the unconscious, "secret soul" Monroe found lacking in Pound.

If Eliot's organicism can be said to reinterpret Coleridge skeptically, Monroe and a "free-verse fanatic" like Lawrence are clearly in the tradition of Whitman's undiluted organicism. However, by adhering to the principle that nothing inorganic should enter the poem, and then defining the traditions of verse as inorganic, Lawrence uprooted the traditions Whitman (ostensibly at least) wanted to grow out of. Symptomatic of the difference between the Good Gray Poet and some of his twentieth-century extrapolators, the earlier poet's frequent word for the articulation of his poems is "chant," which suggests some artistic control as well as hierophancy. Lawrence described a poem as a "spasm" which is involuntary. Most poets preferred, as Kreymborg did, to shape their spasms somewhat, but an organicism that precludes "unity" has remained a prevalent poetic in the twentieth century. In all, twentieth-century poetry is not characterized by Organicism so much as by differing organicisms.

In the introduction to her study on poetic and prosaic rhythm, Winifred Crombie argues that "to understand 'free verse,' we are obliged to engage the distinction between verse and prose" (1). In the same way that organicism is an important concept of Modern free-verse form—not because it necessarily describes the nature of poetry or language, but instead because it constitutes a belief that helps generate and direct free-verse form—so does the poetry/prose debate also merit serious consideration.

That Modern poets concerned themselves with the difference between poetry and prose is plain. Reflecting on the Modern revolution, William Butler Yeats remarked that the general feeling was that "Poetry must resemble prose, and both must accept the vocabulary of their time" (95). Eliot likewise looking back, commented, "It was one of our tenets that verse should have the virtues of prose" (*On Poets* 160). In the teens and twenties, Pound, Eliot, Ford, Lowell, Fletcher, Aiken, Williams, Flint, Arthur Davison Ficke, and many others wrote articles outlining or blurring the distinction between poetry and prose.[38]

In addition, the new forms of twentieth-century literature provide clear evidence that writers were thinking and rethinking the demarcation between prose and verse. Williams's *Spring and All* and *Kora in Hell* blended prose and poetry, as does Jean Toomer's *Cane*. Some critics consider chapters of Dos Passos's trilogy of novels, *USA*, poetry, and some nowadays consider Gertrude Stein's more abstract books (like *Tender Buttons* and *Useful Knowledge*) poetry, usually erotic love poetry, though the books look like collections of aphorisms, or, perhaps, table talk. Likewise, some parts of James Joyce's *Ulysses* and large parts of *Finnegan's Wake* are often thought of as poems, and *Portrait of the Artist* contains both poetry and highly poetic prose. Further, while some prose approached the condition of poetry, some poetry moved in the other direction.

The Norton Anthology wonders if David Jones's *In Parenthesis* ought to be considered a poem even though it is set as one, and, I have already pointed out that Masters's *Spoon River Anthology* seemed to many to be more like prose than poetry.

In addition, the outstanding and perhaps most controversial characteristic of Modern poetry is the inclusion of prose into the body of a longer poem. While it is not difficult at all to find pre-Modern prose works quoting poetry, few poems contain prose passages, and those that do make clear demarcations.[39] Many earlier writers allude to prose, but this is very different, formally, from including prose passages as part of the poem's texture.

Such a pervasive trend in Modernism has attracted critical attention, though generally discussion centers on the Moderns' complex relationship with source materials. Studies that come within the scope of this book have generally taken one of two tacks: some, such as Hartman and Steele, have attempted to settle the debate by positing an accurate relationship between prose and poetry,[40] while others have sought to generalize Modern opinion about prose and poetry, usually citing only Pound, Eliot, and those in close orbit to the Pound circle. Glenn Hughes's study of Imagism (rather old now but still often cited) reports a wider range of opinion, but does not suggest that the debate affected the production of poetry.

One faction maintained that there is an insuperable wall between prose and verse. Traditionalists like W. D. Howells felt that poetry without meter was not poetry at all, but "shredded prose" (634). For poets such as Lowell, Henderson, and Fletcher, the difference between free verse and prose is that free verse had a cadence peculiar to poetry that sensitive readers could hear. This cadence differed from prose rhythm in that it created for the reader a greater sense of repetition and patterning. In this vein, in "The Borderline of Prose," Eliot asserted that "there is prose rhythm and verse rhythm" (159); he found a prose poem by Richard Aldington uneven and therefore flawed because it mixed the two. Robert Bridges in a similar vein argued that "free verse is good and theoretically defensible" if it "can create expectancy without the old metrical devices" (654)—that is, meter and rhyme. Thus Bridges's principle excludes many of Masters's epitaphs and much of Lawrence's poetry. I have shown that some argued that free verse does have a built-in "expectancy" (by "law").

Others took the more palpable fact that poetry is printed in lines to argue that lineation marks the difference between poetry and prose. Eaton argued this several times. However, for various reasons, this view was not very prevalent.

Those proposing cadence as the distinguishing feature of poetry dismissed lineation. Lowell told Kilmer, "Typography is not relevant to the discussion [of whether free verse is poetry]. Whether a thing is written as verse or prose is immaterial" (8). John Livingstone Lowes agreed, and to prove his point he printed some of Lowell's polyphonic prose as poetry and some of her poetry as prose, concluding that both were equally poetic. More generally, the typographical definition did not satisfy many writers because they believed poetry operated on a different plane of consciousness and sought a different kind of understanding than prose did.

As with organicism, Modern thinking on the difference between poetry and prose owes much to nineteenth-century theory. Those looking for precedent for Whitman's long line and the rhythms of his verse often cite prose works, such as translations of the Bible, or oratory. However, in nineteenth-century terms, these sources are all "poetic"—the types of utterances that nineteenth-century writers would be tempted to label as poetry anyway.[41] Complicating matters is the fact that these sorts of works often use patterns that approach the patterning typical of traditional verse. James Kugel's conclusions from his study of parallelism in the Bible are worth noting in this regard. Pointing out that there is no ancient Hebrew word for "poetry," Kugel argues that "what is called biblical 'poetry' is a complex of heightening effects used in combinations and intensities that vary widely" (94). While the patterning is unmistakable, Kugel demonstrates at great length that there is no "*system* comparable to those familiar to us from our own poetry" (250). Since the distinction between poetry and prose "correspond to no precise distinction in the Bible," Kugel concludes it "might be wiser" to simply speak of sections that are more rhetorical and those that are less rhetorical (302).

Kugel demonstrates that the assumption that the Bible must have a meter (even if it is lost to modern readers) stems from applying later categories on earlier writing and the notion that lyrical and beautiful passages simply must be poetry. What was a longstanding theory in biblical studies was applied more generally for poetry in the nineteenth century. The general thrust of the century was to define poetry modally. Thomas De Quincey's distinction between the "literature of knowledge," which informs its reader, and the "literature of power," which moves its reader, sums up what for many was the distinction between prose and poetry. Defining poetry as an exalted means of expression that moves its reader resulted in various writers deciding that prose works were poems. For instance, aside from the familiar dictum that a poem is a "meter-making argument," nothing in Emerson's essay "The Poet" prevents the classification of prose works as poetry. By mid-century, the modal definition of poetry was so prevalent that John Stuart Mill could confidently call the "vulgarest" definition of poetry "of all" was that it was meter that made writing poetry. Such a view, Mill asserted, was "one with which no person possessed of the faculties to which poetry addresses itself can ever have been satisfied" (994). In this way, Whitman was revolutionary not because he found meter dispensable, but instead because he actually dispensed with it.

In the Modern period, poets often considered the rhetorical flights that made prose works "poetic" suspect. Moderns wanted to discard what Pound called the "encumbrance" or "set moods, set ideas, conventions" (*Ezra* I.73). Poetry needed, Pound thought, not more prosaic poetic, but poetry with what Eliot called prose virtues. These include, Pound remarked in "Mr. Hueffer and the Prose Tradition in Verse," "clarity and precision" (*Ezra* I.248). In a letter to *Poetry,* Pound wrote

> Poetry must be as well written as prose. Its language must be a fine language, departing in no way from speech save by a heightened intensity (*i.e.*, simplicity). There must be no book words, no periphrases, no inversion. It must be as simple as De Maupassant's best prose, and as hard as Stendhal's. (*Ezra* I.148)

It is no accident that Pound comments on the need for poetry to have the virtues of prose in an article on Ford Madox Ford[42] because Ford shared Pound's opinion that Modern poetry had to embrace many approaches some would consider prosaic.[43] Criticizing poets who mistook "the obsolescent and sonorous for the beautiful and the interesting" (*Critical Writings* 158), Ford, like Pound, recommended clarity and precision, which he associated with prose.

As Wordsworth before them, when addressing the distinction between poetry and prose Pound and Ford often begin to talk about meter but then focus most of their talk on diction. Steele complains that Moderns in general "confused" meter and diction, ignoring the Moderns' own comment on the matter. "If you write a decasyllabic, eight-lined form," writes Ford, "a certain percentage of it must be false" (*Critical Writings* 161). "If you are using a symmetrical form," writes Pound, "don't put in what you want to say and then fill the remaining vacuums with slush" (*Ezra* I.121). Both were convinced that too much poetry was being written simply to fill out a line and achieve a smooth meter. The "slush" was wordiness inserted to make whatever the poet wanted to say stretch over the requisite number of syllables and consisted of "obsolescent" diction, corresponding to what Wordsworth (in the preface to *Lyrical Ballads*) found true of nine out of fourteen lines in Gray's "Sonnet on the Death of Mr. Richard West"—*merely* poetic diction. Although this greatly underestimates a good deal of traditional verse, it is not, as Steele implies, blind ignorance. Like Wordsworth, Pound and Ford esteemed direct simplicity.

The Moderns tended to discount linguistic differences between poetry and prose while insisting on modal distinctions. In this vein, Ford thought *vers libre* best suited for "the expression of fugitive moods" (162); he thought prose articulated more "conscious" expression ("Impressionism" 177). Lowes maintained, somewhat similarly, that prose stated truths while poetry suggested them. Flint said that poetry was writing in which "you feel the warmth of human expression and imagination" (qtd. in Glenn Hughes 77–78). Williams, too, implied a modal definition in a letter to Frances Sterloff: "A poet's task, in any age, is to listen to the language of his time, when it is impassioned" and to make from that "the essentials of his form, his form" ("Letter" 24).

With all this emotion, what was the need for prose? Pound said that prose virtues were necessary in shaping this feeling. Differentiating between the transparent statement, "Send me four pounds of ten-penny nails," from the subjective statement (Pound calls it an "utter cryptogram"), "Buy me the kind of Rembrandt I like," Pound asserted the poet's task was to say the latter "in the terms of" the former (*Ezra* I.199). Hence, he associates poetry with a greater subjectivity. In the same essay, Pound said, "[P]rose, unlike poetry, does not need emotion"; the prose writer shows the reader the "triumph of his intellect" whereas the poet brings the reader "upon the passionate moment" (*Ezra* I.200). Modally, he is not saying anything much different from De Quincey. Formally, though, a significant transposition has occurred: while the British Romantics used meter to help shape their verse and free it from mere subjectivity (and Whitman used "sympathy"), Pound argues for prose, or more precisely the "virtues" associated with prose, to do that job.

In saying that it was common in the Modern period to claim to be trying to write poetry with prose virtues, I am not saying that the Moderns actually melded the intrinsic qualities of prose and poetry, or even that prose and poetry necessarily have any intrinsic qualities. Anyone with even a cursory knowledge of literature can call to mind any number of prose works not exemplifying "prose virtues"—"book words," "periphrasis," and "inversion" are common in prose as well as poetry. While these distinctions between prose and poetry may not tell us very much about the actual difference between the two kinds of writing, they do imply an influential fiction of composition. The traditional duality of heart and mind (or imagination and reason, or inspiration and control) is in effect allegorized as an opposition between two modes of writing. Literalized, the supposed difference sanctions such heterogeneous poems as *The Cantos* and *Paterson;* more generally, it elevates contemporary diction and syntax while suggesting to the Moderns a way that a poet could achieve concision without resorting to traditional form. By claiming that their poetry was organic and evinced prose virtues, the Moderns sanctioned their departures from meter by asserting that such departures were the hallmarks of a more natural and precise poetry. Together, organicism and poetic modality with prose virtues are the two most prevalent myths that enabled Modern free verse.

CHAPTER TWO

The Loose Tradition in Verse from Cowley to Eliot

"[T]he development of metrical verse into free verse is still a mysterious one," Dennis Taylor comments. "On or about December 1910 human character changed, and so did our sense of metrical verse form" (209). Seeking to demystify that development by tracing the loose tradition in verse from Cowley to Eliot, this is my first demonstration that Modern free verse is indeed what Wesling and Bollobás call the "natural child" of traditional prosody. Indeed, Eliot's ghost-of-meter paradigm for free verse demands that it must be. The "mystery" is largely a result of how literary history has been construed, for Eliot's free verse extends a tradition of poetry underrepresented in anthologies and underappreciated by critics.

The Moderns are as much to blame as the academia for this situation. Taylor has the considerable authority of Virginia Woolf (in "Mr. Bennet and Mrs. Brown") for his date for the sudden change in sensibility. The contemporary name generally used for Modern verse, the New Poetry, encourages the view that Modern free verse was unprecedented, and critics have by and large accepted this view. Four major book-length studies of free verse are a case in point. Hartman's *Free Verse* argues that until 1912 or so, "no one cared to abandon so rich a prosodic tradition which ran from Chaucer through Shakespeare up to the Edwardian present" (5). Wesling's *The New Poetries* (1985) attends closely to the continuity between nineteenth- and twentieth-century aesthetic ideas, but describes the shift in practice as "a break, an earthquake, or explosion" (87). In *Missing Measures,* Steele similarly finds congruities between the governing aesthetic principles of nineteenth-century verse and those of free verse, but largely denies any continuity of practice. Harvey Gross's *Sound and Form in Modern Poetry* (rev. ed., 1964) does acknowledge that "the nineteenth-century movement toward greater prosodic flexibility culminated in the free-verse movement of the teens and twenties" (80), but goes on to argue that although "Browning, Whitman, and Hopkins forecast the three major prosodic developments of the modern period," he would "hesitate to call them influences" (96).

As the quotation from Gross helps indicate, those looking for precursors to free verse often focus on poets such as Hopkins, Dickinson, and Whitman. These three exceptions to the mainstream, smooth verse associated with Tennyson seem to prove the general contention that these early precursors to free-verse poetics were anomalies. All three poets were in some way isolated, and the sometimes hostile (or nonexistent) reception of their works shows that they were out of step with their era.

But even the corpus of Tennyson makes it clear that this view is inadequate. Formally, the Victorian poet laureate's works are varied and by no means uniformly smooth. Surely he was an exemplar of his age, but poets of the nineteenth century were no more single-minded than those of the twentieth. In a broader view of the century, Dickinson, Hopkins, and Whitman begin to look more and more representative. The "earthquake" Wesling perceives is largely a result of narrowly defining the past, in part due to the procedures of canonization. In the early part of this century, poets were valued because they were easily comprehensible under the received notion of Tennysonian (and Longfellowian) poetics; paradoxically, the later part of the century valued other poets because they did *not* ascribe to these poetics and were therefore "innovative" and "original." As noted in the previous chapter, polemicists on every side of the free-verse debate have largely accepted the contours of formal analysis as set forth by the propaganda, or perhaps *misprision,* of the Moderns.

In 1954 Robert Mayo published a watershed article arguing that many traits generally asserted as distinctively Romantic could be found in eighteenth-century magazine verse. Seeking out these connections has been a fruitful avenue of inquiry ever since. This chapter attempts to begin a similar line of inquiry for Modern free verse. In many respects, my approach mirrors that of another Romantic scholar, Stuart Curran. His study, *Poetic Form and British Romanticism* (1986), considers the way that such works as Coleridge's "Dejection: An Ode" and "Ode to the Departing Year" respond to the ode tradition. Curran argues that "Coleridge's recreation of his literary heritage," not his "self-paralysis," determined to a large extent the form of the poems (73). More fundamentally, Curran takes issue with the idea that poetic form is a spontaneous, unmediated eruption from conception to production. Chapter 1 shows that taking this view leads to considering each poem *sui generis,* a critical endorsement of a kind of organicism that does not (as Coleridge's did) include an inorganic component. Identifying the traditional aspects of a poem's form need not lead to a reductivist view that later poems merely imitate, or debase, earlier poems: "If we begin with the premise that genres underlie, motivate, and organize all literary discourse," Curran argues, "still we must immediately acknowledge that their function is dependent on their formulation" (5). In other words, poets modify tradition as much as they further it.

I will use conventional scansion. For this procedure I have the sanction of Eliot, who remarked in "Reflections on *Vers Libre,*" "Any line can be divided into feet and accent" (185). Although he questions the utility of conventional scansion for much of the free verse in "popular American magazines" (184), his ghost-of-meter paradigm indicates that his own poetry constantly moves toward and withdraws from traditional meter. To track Eliot's approaches to and departures from traditional meter, it is thus necessary to use traditional prosody. This chapter and the next will also argue that, while Eliot's rather gothic metaphor seems to imply that poets are haunted sub- or unconsciously by tradition, he himself used the procedure consciously to build meaning and rhythm into his verse.

This survey of precursors begins at a time fitting to Eliot, the seventeenth century. It was the irregular, "Pindarique" odes of Abraham Cowley that introduced the nexus of ideas that came to comprise the poetic of "Prufrock," especially the concepts of organic form and the sublime. Further, Cowley's practice—his use of rhyme, his lineal decorums, and his contextual prosody—anticipates the approach that characterizes "Prufrock." Even the contemporary reception of Cowley anticipates the contemporary reception of Modern free verse.

It cannot be argued that the connection between Cowley and Eliot is accidental, because, as I shall establish, Cowley's ideas and procedures persisted in a continuing tradition that includes such prominent writers as William Collins and Matthew Arnold. To clear myself of the charge that my attempt to trace the history of free verse has forced me to scour the library for obscure authors and unread works, I will focus on easily available works by authors that were well known in Eliot's day.

Although Cowley knew that Pindar's stanzas were (by Cowley's standards at least) regular, in the preface to his *Pindarique Odes* (1688) he defends the irregularity of his own odes on the grounds that he was following his source. Cowley tells his readers that the difference between Pindar's and Cowley's cultures coupled with the rhapsodic nature of Pindar's poems meant that a word-for-word translation would only convince a reader that "*one* Mad man *had translated* another" (155). Cowley criticizes smooth-verse translations of Pindar as inadequate for the powerful and wide-ranging odes. His own odes, Cowley explains, are *"Imitating"* Pindar, an approach he feels is superior to translation. Thus, Cowley did not aim to English Pindar's words or versification, but instead to replicate the Greek poet's spirit.

Whether or not Pindar would find Cowley's odes comparable to his own is a question I will not entertain here. Of interest for this survey is that Cowley was motivated by the idea that Greek poetry contains beauties not reproducible in conventional versification. Moreover, Cowley's Pindarism implies a concept of formal adequacy that goes much farther than that offered in, say, Aristotle's *Poetics* or later poets such as Pope and Johnson. That is, he is not searching for a form that convention deems proper for the matter; he wants a form that *in itself* reflects the matter. He is not bringing Pindar to English verse form, but bringing English verse form to Pindar. When Pindar dilates, then, so should the form. Although Cowley does not use the word, his poetic is organic. Cowley anticipates Whitman's idea of the "free growth of metrical laws," and Whitman's trope of poet as translator.[1]

Formally, Cowley's irregular odes differ from more traditional verse in three ways: the lines are not of a uniform or predictable length; the stanzas are not of a uniform or predictable length; the rhymes are not predictable. Under this definition, Cowley's oft-anthologized "Of Wit" does not qualify as irregular, because each stanza is formally identical.[2] Less regular is the first ode in *Pindarique Odes,* "First Olympique Ode." It begins with stanzas of seventeen, eighteen, nineteen, and thirteen lines long; its rhyme schemes are AABBCCDDDEFFEGHH, AABBBBBCCDDEEFFGGHH, ABBAAACCCDDDDEEEFFFF, and AAAABBBBCCDDEE;[3] and it mixes mostly pentameter and tetrameter lines, with some trimeter, Alexandrines, and seven-foot lines. In other poems Cowley uses monometer and octometer. Oddly, in "First Olympique," Cowley uses more seven-foot lines than six-foot lines, as if deliberately avoiding the traditional longer line, the Alexandrine.

Despite their eccentricity, though, Cowley's odes exhibit significant coherence. For example, the lines are usually iambic, with some trisyllabic substitution (or, perhaps, unmarked elisions)[4] and inverted feet. Cowley was interested enough in regular meter to use such meter-keeping elisions as "o'er," "vig'rous," and "poy'snous." He also used contractions to maintain an iambic pace. Furthermore, every line rhymes, almost always with the line next to it; he rarely uses rhymes more distant than ABBA. Finally, most lines are either tetrameter or pentameter, with trimeter the third-most-frequent line. Thus, though the line lengths were mixed unpredictably, a reasonably well read seventeenth-century reader would be acquainted with the various meters.

Still, Cowley's irregular odes do not observe a principle important to other writers. I have already noted that Johnson complained that Cowley's poems did not afford the "great pleasure" arising when an Augustan reader is offered and has satisfied a metrical contract. In a traditional contract, a reader may be sure that a poem set

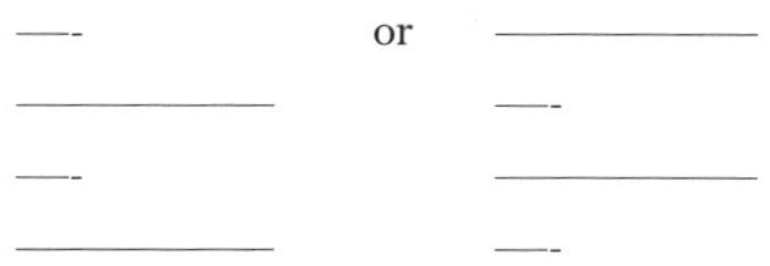

will rhyme ABAB; an ABBA stanza will likely look like one of these two ways:

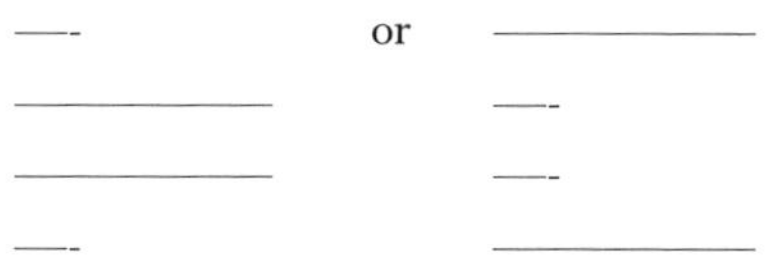

Thus, not only do line lengths recur regularly, but also the rhymes correspond with their recurrence. However, in Cowley's "To Mr. Hobs," a reader confronts lines that look like this:

Line lengths crop up irregularly, and lines of similar length do not always rhyme: the above lines rhyme ABBBAACCC, not ABACDACDD as the typography suggests. In short, there is no predictable pattern. Consequently, Cowley's readers, as Alan Golding said about readers of free verse, cannot relax.

The poet himself acknowledged the difficulty of his metrical contract. "For as for the Pindarick Odes," Cowley wrote in the preface to his *Poems,* "I am in great doubt whether they will be understood by most Readers"(10):

> The Figures are unusual and bold, even to Temeritie, and such as I durst not have to do withal in any other kind of Poetry: The Numbers are various and irregular, and sometimes (especially some of the long ones) seem harsh and uncouth, if the just measures and cadencies be not observed in the Pronunciation. So that almost all of their Sweetness and Numerosity (which is to be found, if I mistake not, in the roughest, if rightly repeated) lies in a manner wholly at the Mercy of the Reader. (11)

This is strikingly similar to free-verse theory's insistence on the need for a competent reader. When Cowley insists on the "just measures" of his "Numerosities," he is insisting on a musical harmony that a subtle reader can hear. If he had lived in the twentieth century, he likely would have added that this harmony avoided the metronome of traditional versification. Cowley directs his reader to his poem "The Resurrection" for further amplification. That poem concludes,

> Stop, stop, my *Muse,* allay thy vig'rous Heat,
>   Kindled at a *Hint* so Great.
> Hold thy *Pindarique Pegasus* closely in;
>   Which does to *Rage* begin,
> And this steep *Hill* would gallop up with violent course,
> Tis an unruly and a *hard-mouth'd* Horse,
>   Fierce and unbroken yet,
>   Impatient of the *Spur* or *Bit.*
> Now *praunces* stately, and anon *flies* o'er the place,
> Disdains the *servile Law* of any settled *Pace,*
> *Conscious* and *proud* of his own *natural Force,*
>   'Twill no *unskilful Touch* endure
> But flings *Writer* and *Reader* too that *sits* not *sure.* (17)

Cowley here reinterprets poetry's traditional equine symbol and its corresponding pun on poetic feet[5] as irregular and wayward, arguing that the Pindaric strain unleashes the "*natural Force*" of poetry. The reader, like an accomplished horseman, must learn how to anticipate and adjust to the rhythm. Comparably, "The Praise of Pindar" appeals to the organic:

Pindar's unnavigable Song
Like a swoln Flood from some steep Mountain pours along;
The Ocean meets with such a Voice
From his enlarged Mouth, as drowns the Ocean's noise.

So *Pindar* does new *Words* and *Figures* roll
Down his impetuous *Dithyrambique Tide,*
Which no *Channel deigns* t'abide,
Which neither *Banks* nor *Dikes* control. (15)

Cowley implies that traditional form is inadequate for poetic inspiration of Pindar's magnitude, again assuming that form ought to mirror, not just garb appropriately, what it seeks to express.

Norman Maclean points out that Cowley wrote during a time when, through new translations of Longinus, the theory of the sublime gained wide currency. Sublime theory shared Cowley's endorsement of roughness, because, Maclean explains, "the language of the sublime is an impassioned disruption of the normal mode of expression; and irregularity (even error) Longinus not only condones but views as a mark of writers with more than human inspiration" (421). Alliance with such an influential theory helped ensure the continuing presence of the ode in subsequent centuries and is a persistent rationale for looser versification.

Maclean also identifies a corollary to the equation between irregularity and sublimity: the sublime tends to appear in fragments. Cowley's odes are not to be read as uniform effusions of the sublime, but instead as longer poems interspersed with sublime patches. This attitude suggests a procedure of reading on a linear level. An ideal reader must attend to context constantly in order to determine disruption. I have noted that Cowley's verse is consistently iambic, but line length varies significantly. Consider this from "The Resurrection":

Begin the *Song,* and strike the *living Lyre;*
Lo how the *Years to come,* a numerous and well-fitted *Quire,*
All Hand in Hand do decently advance,
And to my *Song* with smooth and equal measures *dance.*
Whilst the *Dance* lasts, how long so e'er it be,
My *Musick's* Voice shall bear it company.
          Till all *gentle Notes* be drown'd
          In the *last Trumpet's* dreadful sound.
That, to the *Spheres* themselves, shall *Silence* bring,
          Untune the *Universal String.*
          Then all the wide extended *Sky*
          And all th' *harmonious Worlds* on high,
          And *Virgil's* sacred *Work* shall die;
And he himself shall see the one *Fire* shine
Rich *Nature's* ancient *Troy,* though built by *Hands Divine* (182)

Of the first six lines, lines one, three, and six are in smooth iambic pentameter; line five contains an inversion at the beginning but settles down into iambic pentameter thereafter; line six is a regular alexandrine; and line two, with perhaps seven feet, is arguably smooth.[6] The lines describing smoothness are themselves smooth, and the lines mentioning number are numerous inasmuch as they contain more feet than the rest of the lines: this passage thus establishes a "normal mode of expression" as iambic pentameter and a further decorum of proceeding in couplets.

Thus, when the lines shrink, the disruption should indicate a growing sublimity, and indeed when the lines shorten the poem shifts from describing earthly music to the music of the spheres and from the daily to the apocalyptic. Further, line nine, which begins on the left margin, is made to rhyme with line ten, five spaces in. Typographically, the poem announces a break but the rhyme insists on convergence, and a triplet then further disturbs the "normal" manner of proceeding. The reader is seemingly encouraged to take the reintroduction of the concluding pentameter/alexandrine couplet as a result of the preceding prosody—the norm is reconstituted with an infusion of the sublime. And the line describes a reconstitution, a new Jerusalem aestheticized (presumably for Virgil's sake) as a new Troy.

When they comment on their own form, poems like this encourage readers to make connections between the form as it appears on the page and what the poem is saying at that moment. That is to say, these poems imitate ideas prosodically. Since these are not *inevitable* connections (it seems nonsensical to insist that octosyllabic couplets are intrinsically sublime), they can be described as allegories of lineal form brought to readerly attention by self-reflexivity. Readers have long been accustomed to reading Pope searching for lines where sound echoes sense, but Cowley's "Pindarique" odes often seek to imitate *ideas* and not *sounds*. Furthermore, Cowley's poetic differs in its contextual prosody. Pope's effects tend to be consistent from poem to poem and within a poem. However, in the passage just cited iambic pentameter indicates one sort of discourse in the beginning and another at the end. These allegories of form often do not carry from one poem to the next. For instance, "The Praise of Pindar" concludes

> Lo, how th'obsequious *Wind,* and swelling *Air*
>
> The *Theban Swan* does upwards bear
> Into the *Walks* of *Clouds*; where he does play,
> And with extended *Wings* opens his liquid way.
> Whilst, alas, my *tim'rous Muse*
> *Unambitious* Tracks pursues;
> Does with weak unballast Wings,
> About the *mossie Brooks* and *Springs*;
> About the *Trees* new-blossom'ed *Heads;*
> About the *Gardens* painted *Beds;*
> About the *Fields* and flowry *Meads;*
> And all *inferior beauteous things;*
> Like the laborious *Bee,*
> For little drops of *Honey* fly,
> And there with *humble Sweets* contents her *Industry.* (15)

James Taafe remarks that the "poem modulates beautifully" at the end (64). In "Praise" pentameter/tetrameter pairs of lines signal sublimity; when the speaker describes his own experience, he does it in simpler octosyllables, the line of Chaucer's early poetry (and quite a bit seventeenth- and eighteenth-century descriptive poetry). It is as if the speaker's more humble experience cannot fill out the more expansive Pindaric line, and so it establishes a narrower compass. Note, too, the suitable ending—tetrameter followed by trimeter, tetrameter, and a final line filling up the gap left by the trimeter line and adding another foot for concluding polish. Again, the reader must pay attention to a changing context in order to comprehend a changing norm.

Cowley's poetics, then, complicate the meter. Overall, there is an iambic progression and the general rules that every line will rhyme and that line lengths should shift as the speaker's attention shifts. There is also a local patterning to govern blocks of poetry of similar lineal form. What keeps Cowley's form familiar, however, is the fact that the local patterns often conform to existing norms. Thus, "The Praise" moves into a descriptive line when it shifts to descriptive poetry. Sometimes, the "organic" movement of a poem involves little more than moving from one traditional lineal decorum to another.

A poetry driven by the notion that faithful translation of poetic inspiration necessitates the poet to supersede the normal conventions of verse; one that insists that form must represent, not just be appropriate for, its subject; that maintains that its lack of symmetry is evidence of greater, more organic poetry; that demands more of its reader while promising greater transport; and that uses contextual prosody: it is no wonder Maclean remarks that the ode "was the 'free verse' of the neoclassical period," though he adds that it "attracted scores of writers who aspired to the heights of poetry because of the difficulties of prose" (424). Maclean was right in a way he perhaps did not intend. The irregular ode *was* the standard-bearer of the tradition that led to free verse. His contention that Cowley encouraged writers to create poetry because prose was too difficult to write is unprovable and probably false.

Another striking similarity between the ode and free verse is the ode's reception. I have already noted Dr. Johnson's complaint about irregularity. In his edition of Cowley's verse, Thomas Sprat concedes that "the irregularity in numbers" of the odes may "disgust" some readers. Nevertheless, he explains, patient readers will find

> that the frequent alteration of Rhythm and feets affect the mind with a more various delight, while it is soon apt to be tyr'd by the settled pace of any one constant number. But that for which this inequality of number is chiefly to be preferr'd, is its near affinity with Prose: From which all of her kinds on English Verse are so far distant, that it is seldom found that the same man excels both ways. (xxvi)

Thus, Cowley's odes are superior because they have prose's rhythmic variety while remaining poetic. In his life of Cowley, Johnson seized on Sprat's assertion as evidence that the poems were faulty: such "lax and lawless versification," he said, were due to, among other things, the "laziness of the idle" (324). This anticipates later judgments by Max Eastman (and Norman Maclean). These readers do not seem to share Sprat's high opinion of prose rhythm,[7] nor do they perceive, or are not impressed by, the formal allegories Cowley's verse provides. In faulting the lack of smoothness in Cowley's verse, however, such critics create an allegory of their own, one that posits that adherence to certain rules of versification is tantamount to adhering to the rules of a stable society and the Protestant work ethic. For his part, Cowley claimed that the apparent disorderliness gave his poems a greater harmony. His remarks on rhyme show how this could be.

Cowley's basic theory in some ways contradicts the traditional approach to rhyme typical of a poet such as Pope. W. K. Wimsatt's essay, "One Relation of Rhyme to Reason" (1944), is perhaps the clearest statement of conventional rhyme theory. Noting that the languages from which English borrowed the technique of rhyme were more greatly inflected than English, Wimsatt argues that poetry in those languages tends to rhyme words with the same inflectional ending. Thus the endings, not the roots, rhyme. But in an analytical language like English, the roots are usually rhymed.[8] Because of this, inflectional languages tend to rhyme words that fulfill "closely parallel functions" in the sentence, whereas analytical languages bring together "different parts of speech" (160). As a result, English poets often use rhyme to indicate differing concepts being brought together. Wimsatt quotes Pope's *Essay on Criticism* to model rhyming antithesis:

> Some are bewilder'd in the Maze of Schools,
> And some made Coxcombs Nature meant but Fools (ll. 26–27)

Of course, Pope often uses rhyme for the opposite effect: *Essay on Criticism* also rhymes "light" with "right" (and "bright"), "exprest" with "drest," "fit" with "wit," "strife" with "wife," and so on. Indeed, a poet's characteristic rhymes often say volumes about the nature of that poet's vision—Hopkins, for example, several times rhymes "God" with "rod" (and "trod"). Thus, rhyme is an accidental feature of language that poets use intentionally to help poems cohere semantically and aurally. Wimsatt chooses Pope to illustrate conventional notions of rhyme because Pope's poetic—regular rhythm, poems proceeding a couplet at a time, end-stopped lines—tends to highlight the device. Pope does not rush the reader past rhymes with enjambment and generally focuses his wit on the rhyme. In a sense, he saves his punch line for the end.

Cowley and looser poetry in general use rhyme differently. Consider these lines from "Ode. Upon Liberty," a poem in which Cowley explains the "Pindarique way":

> The matter shall be Grave, the Numbers loose and free,
> It shall not keep one settled pace of Time,
> In the same Tune it shall not always Chime,
> Nor shall each day just to his Neighbor Rhime,
> A thousand liberties it shall dispense,
> And yet shall mannage all without offence;
> Or to the sweetness of the Sound, or greatness of the Sence (391)

Lines previous to the ones quoted established a couplet/quatrain pattern. But the rhyme for "free" is five lines away—unusually far for Cowley—and then there are two consecutive triplets to disrupt the pattern further. Triplets discourage the kind of comparison and antithesis common in Pope. The poem argues that despite this irregularity, both "Sound" and "Sense" will be successfully managed. The poem aspires to a higher, looser unity. Compare in this regard this couplet from "Of Wit":

> In a true piece of Wit all things must be
> Yet all things there agree (18)

The verse insists on the notion (and provides an example of it) that even numerically unequal lines, if they are mediated by the poet's skill and superior inspiration, can attain harmony.

The typography of the odes underscores their formal coherence. These lines from "The Muse" rhyme a monometer line with an alexandrine:

> Nor dost thou only *dive* so low
> But *Fly*
> With an unwearied *Wing* the other Way on high (18)

"Thou" is the Pindaric muse. The setting of the poem helps give a sense of balance to numerically unequal lines. Visually, the poems avoid the boxy symmetry of sonnets and Spenserian stanzas, yet appear balanced along a vertical axis.[9] Seventeenth- and eighteenth-century odes were almost always printed in this way. Though this typography may have been the printers' and not the poets' idea, the fact remains that the received ode visually suggests a kind of various harmony.[10]

Cowley's odes, despite their formal irregularities, always insisted on an overarching unity. The odes of later writers, such as Thomas Gray and Collins, started to question this integrated synthesis both formally and semantically. My concern here is with irregular odes, and hence my focus on Collins, because Gray did not write any truly irregular odes. "The Bard," which Gray designates as Pindaric, is symmetrical and regularly repeats stanza lengths and rhyme schemes. Although it mixes line lengths, the pattern is identical among stanzas. Still, whether readers can remember and anticipate an ABABCCDDGFGFII rhyme scheme, or notice that the first line of each strophe scans / U / U / U / U, the second line, U / U / U / U /, the ninth line like the first, and so forth, is questionable. I have not seen it commented upon, though most critics today do not seem to scan poetry.[11] Perhaps an age more concerned with "numbers" could detect such regularity, but it seems likely that Gray's ode reaches its symmetry because Gray's poetic demanded it. I suspect most readers experience the poem as irregular.

Though most of Collins's odes are regular, two deserve mention. The first is "Ode to Evening," which does not rhyme. Of course, the example of Shakespeare and Milton had accustomed English readers to unrhymed narrative verse, but, as Collins's friend and editor, John Langhorne, remarked, "for the lyric muse, it seemed still a stranger of uncouth figure." Nonetheless, Langhorne found classical precedent, which he said "in some degree reconciles us to the want of rhyme, while it reminds us of those great masters of antiquity, whose lines had no need for this whimsical jingle of sounds" (138).[12]

However unusual, the poem is in many respects quite regular. It proceeds by alternating two lines of iambic pentameter with two lines of iambic trimeter, with some lines beginning with inverted feet and some trisyllabic substitution (or unmarked elision) for polysyllables such as "Pastoral" and "ethereal." Otherwise, the poem is metrically smooth. Although Collins eschews rhyme, the poem's grammar progresses as if he did not. For example, the poem uses three colons, three exclamation marks, and four periods, all occurring on the second of either a pentameter or trimeter pair. Collins freed himself from rhyme, but not from rhyme's decorum. He may have been writing a modified blank verse, yet he was still thinking in terms of couplets.

Like Gray, Collins wrote poems that may seem irregular but are not. "Ode to Fear," for example, sandwiches five iambic pentameter quatrains between twenty-six-line coupleted strophes.[13] Four lines in, both strophes contain a trimeter couplet. Again, I doubt that a reader not specifically looking for these types of agreements will notice them. Richard Wendorf notes that "most argue" that there is a "structural imbalance" (41) in Collins's "Ode on the Poetical Character," but the lineal structure is decidedly balanced: two 22-line sections which begin with four iambic tetrameter couplets before breaking into an ABCBADDACEEFFC rhyme scheme around a thirty-two-line section. Counters will also notice that the fourteenth line in each stanza has a feminine rhyme. Similarly, the strophes of Collins's "Ode to Liberty" rhyme AABCBDDEFE-FGHGH IJIJJKJKK with corresponding line lengths 44555445556444445445546, with feminine rhymes occurring in the same positions. Like Gray, then, Collins tends to balance his liberties. It seems probable that he wrote one stanza then matched up the rest; whatever the case, this is powerful evidence that Collins was very concerned about his numbers. But, to return to Hartman's comment, if a prosody is not shared, is it a prosody? As with "The Bard," a metrical contract this complicated is not likely to be recognized by a reader.

Collins's truly irregular ode, "The Passions," exhibits both his sense of balance and important innovations. The title indicates the sanction for the irregularity—the form matches the presumably ungovernable emotions described. The ode begins with six iambic tetrameter couplets and three iambic tetrameter quatrains, moves to a long irregular middle section, and ends with twelve iambic tetrameter couplets, thus beginning and ending with expectable lines. The stanza beginning "But thou, O Hope" rhymes ABBCDCEEAFEFGGHIJJK-LLMH. Worth noting are the two very distant rhymes for A and H (the beginning and end rhymes, by the way) and the fact that I has no rhyme. Similarly, the section beginning "With Eyes uprais'd" rhymes ABCACDEEBFGGHF again featuring a distant rhyme (B) and a line without a rhyme (D). These sections are also numerically diverse, mixing pentameter, tetrameter, and trimeter lines. I believe Cowley never left a line unrhymed nor ever put a rhyme so distant. Thus Collins created not only an unrhymed ode, but also odes that a reader is likely to experience as rhyming less than they actually do.

Of course, picking out the unrhymed lines is difficult, even in the rhyme schemes I have typed out above. The point is that even though Collins in many ways is more regular than Cowley, he further destabilized the ode by placing more of its structure into the unexpectable category. The increasing formal instability reflected the poem's thematic concerns. Curran argues that the odes of Gray and Collins represent a significant change in the character of the ode, radically internalizing the form's statement. "The intrinsic paradox of the English ode," he writes, "is that, almost from the first, the Horatian voice was invested with a Pindaric form." He continues:

> the Horatian meditative presence, its contemplations built through a sequenced and associational logic, becomes a meditating presence standing above sequence, forced to interpose, or to create within itself, a synthesizing order—an epode—upon the universal strophe and antistrophe of experience. (71)

In effect, English poets tended to allegorize the traditional turns of the ode's argument (i.e., the strophe, antistrophe, and epode) as representing turns of the individual mind. By the nineteenth century, Curran argues, the ode had emerged as a "dramatic, self-reflexive, and dialectical form" (66). The irregularities and unusual harmonies represent the difficulties of coming to grips with experience while they continue the tradition that form should mirror the thing it describes. And more and more, the thing described was the mind of the poet. "The driving force to contain polarities is the imaginative sympathies of the poet," Curran maintains, "who is personalized to the extent that he presents himself as fulcrum and mediator for the ode's dialectical claims" (64). In a sense, Collins intermixed an unrhymed line or two, or shunned rhyme entirely, because he had the faith that the poem would otherwise cohere. Later poets were more apt to question stability, aesthetic and otherwise. Paul H. Fry links this formal decorum to poststructuralist thought. "Not only is the ode . . . a vehicle for ontological and vocational doubt," he contends, "but it also raises questions more steadily than any other poetic mode about the aesthetic shibboleth of the unified whole" (1). Again, the self-reflexivity of the poems encourages a formal allegory, this one without the ultimate regularity Cowley assumed. Simply put, the form of the ode became associated with themes of uncertainty, prosodically enacting a crisis of what is labeled "closure" today.

By the beginning of the nineteenth century, the loose verse tradition that emphasized surprise and tolerated irregularity competed with the regular tradition. Both poetics sought harmony, but endorsed antithetical philosophies of rhyme: Pope brought together ideas that "belonged" together or used rhyme to show how human flaws brought together things that should not be yoked, while Cowley claimed greater harmony because he could harmonize unlikeness.

I have shown that Romantics such as Coleridge and Shelley helped further the aesthetics that led to Whitman's break with meter; in effect, they tended to be theoretically revolutionary but relatively conservative in practice. There are other indications of a loosening of, but not disregarding of, the traditional strictures of smoothness. As early as 1793, Frank Sayers wrote, "[T]here appears no natural incapacity in the English language to admit of a more general introduction of unrimed measures" (129).[14] After the turn of the century, William Cullen Bryant wrote in praise of trisyllabic substitution, saying the extra unstressed syllable's "spirited irregularity relieves and refreshes" a reader caught in "a dead waste of disyllabic feet" (64). Neither writer called for free verse by any means, yet both favored greater prosodic variety. In the nineteenth century, the most various form was the ode.

Although the Romantics transformed the meditative quality of the English ode so that it became more inward and personal, they continued its formal traditions. Thus, Keats's "Ode to Psyche" has two unrhymed lines that, as in Collins, tend to get lost in the overall rhyming structure.[15] It perhaps goes without saying that Keats's odes show the anxiety over resolution that such unstable poetics suggest. Wordsworth's familiar "Intimations of Immortality" leaves no line unrhymed, but continues the tradition of contextual prosody in which form is made to reflect the idea expressed. Thus when the poem looks at the world through the eye of a child, the lines are irregular and short:

> The earth, and every common sight
>   To me did seem
> Appareled in celestial light (ll. 2–4)

This decorum is repeated later when the speaker reexperiences childhood joy:

>   And all the earth is gay;
>   Land and sea
>   Give themselves up to jollity,
>   And with the heart of May
>   Doth every Beast keep holiday;—
>   Thou Child of Joy
> Shout round me, let me hear thy shouts, thou happy Shepherd-boy! (ll. 29–36)

When proceeding to statement, such as in the famous ending,

> Thanks to the human heart by which we live,
> Thanks to tenderness, its joys, and fears,
> To me the meanest flower that blows can give
> Thoughts that do often lie too deep for tears. (ll. 200–204)

the poem modulates to longer, more regular lines. Shorter lines, then, focus on natural vitality; longer lines can bear the heavier weight of philosophy.

Something similar occurs in Coleridge's irregular odes. Consider lines twenty-seven through thirty-four from "Ode to the Departing New Year":

> From every private bower
> And each domestic hearth,
> Haste for one solemn hour;
> And with a loud and yet louder voice,
> O'er Nature struggling in portentous birth,
> Weep and rejoice! (ll. 27–32)

Prosodically, the lines build up to a ponderous iambic pentameter before letting loose with a dimeter. Meter also is used contextually in the first three stanzas of "Dejection: An Ode." Thus, the trimeter in stanzas I,

> Or the dull sobbing draft that moans and rakes
> Upon the strings of this æolian lute
> Which were far better mute.
> For lo! the New-moon winter bright! (ll. 6–9)

II,

> Which finds no natural outlet, no relief
> In word, nor sigh, nor tear—
> Oh Lady! in this wan and heartless mood (ll. 22–24)

and III

> My genial spirits fail
> And what can these avail
> To lift the smothering weight off my breast? (ll. 39–41)

all indicate a step away from a silence that, in turn, sparks a more numerous effusion.

These poems continue key elements of the looser tradition: "organic" form, visual balance, sublimity (or aspirations to it), and an overall shift from the poetics of satisfying expectation to one that values surprise. Nevertheless, it was during the Victorian era that verse strongly resembling free verse flowered.

Matthew Arnold nowadays has such a reputation as a spokesman for Victorian values that it is often forgotten that he promoted looser versification. When Margaret Holley comments that "the music and authority of the sustained iambic voice seem to assure us, as Matthew Arnold did, that poetry's elevation and beauty will continue to sustain us" (189), she is thinking of Arnold's essays and not his poetic practice. Though Arnold sometimes appears in laundry lists of precursors to free verse, his participation in a larger tradition of verse, one consistent with the prosodic ideas in his essays, is not generally understood.[16] "Dover Beach" provides an example of the continuity of the linear decorums, rhyme, and contextual prosody of the loose tradition.[17] The poem proceeds from a similar notion of organic form and an evolved conception of the sublime. In addition, his poetry received the same kind of contemporary reception as Cowley and the Moderns.

The title of "Dover Beach" announces no genre,[18] but its form does. Four stanzas—fourteen, seven, seven, and nine lines long—the last disrupts any chance of pattern; a predominantly iambic movement; a mix of predominantly pentameter and tetrameter lines with some trimeter and one line in dimeter;[19] a complex nonrepeating rhyme scheme; little or nothing in the way of transitions: "Dover Beach" is an irregular ode. In addition, the poem thematically evinces the same concern with resolution as do Romantic odes.

Moreover, Arnold clearly understood the theory of rhyme. In his essay, "On Translating Homer," Arnold faults Pope's heroic-couplet translation of the *Iliad* not because the pressing need of rhyme forces the translator to invent and falsify, but because "rhyme inevitably tends to pair lines which in the original are independent" (*On the Classical* 106). He expands upon this idea:

> Rhyme certainly, by intensifying antithesis, can intensify separation, and this is precisely what Pope does; but this balanced rhetorical antithesis, though very effective, is entirely unHomeric. (*On the Classical* 107)

He characterizes the heroic couplet as a "simple system of correspondences" (*On the Classical* 142) and the Spenserian stanza as an "intricate series of correspondences" (*On the Classical* 143). These "correspondences" are of sound and sense.

Given this theory of rhyme, the rhyme scheme of "Dover Beach" should be significant. The first stanza rhymes ABADCBDCEFCGFG. Noteworthy is the stretch BADC—four lines without a rhyme, and the poem's grammar further separates the rhymes.[20] That is to say, the logic of the grammar does not coincide with the appearance of the rhymes. Further one line, E, has no rhyme. Paull F. Baum points out that a rhyme for E can be found in the third stanza, and thus concludes the stanzas are "interlinked" (94), but a rhyme twenty-eight lines away is such a tenuous connection that a reader is not likely to hear it. It seems to me that the third stanza harks back not very successfully to the first. The second stanza's rhyme scheme, ABACBC, is fairly orderly, as is that of the fourth stanza (ABBACDDCC). In the third stanza, with a rhyme scheme ABCDBADC, the reader proceeds four lines before arriving at the first "correspondence." Overall, the poem several times threatens to fall apart disharmoniously.

In addition, "Dover Beach" uses many significant rhymes. The poem rhymes "bay" with "spray," "shore" with "roar," "strand" with "land," and "ago" with "flow." Many before me have noted that the first rhyme goes from darkness to light ("night" / "light"), while the last goes back to darkness ("light"/ "flight" / "night"). This sense of rhyme is a significant departure from the practice of Cowley and Collins, who tend to use rhyme more as a cohering device than as a means of comparison and antithesis. In a sense, Arnold uses Collins's form with Pope's sense of rhyme, a sense problematized by distance and irregularity. Thus the poem's possible off rhyme, "Faith" and "breath," seems significant. The words sound close enough to rhymes that I "counted" them, though they are not even eye rhymes. To my ear, "The Sea of Faith" comes close to but does not concord with "the breath / Of the night-wind." The rhyme scheme seems to want it to, even insist on it, but the two do not harmonize.[21] It goes without saying that the failure of the rhyme allegorizes a significant theme of the poem, suggesting a similar failure of a faith to harmonize the world.[22]

Thus Arnold's use of rhyme destabilizes a form already committed to irregularity by questioning some of the ways the form usually coheres. The same crisis is evident in the typography. Unlike other irregular odes considered thus far, the lines are not centered. It is sometimes suggested that the jagged edge suggests the undulating pattern that waves make on a beach, perhaps the "ebb and flow" the poem mentions. However, the nontypographical irregularities were no invention of Arnold; they were part of the tradition. The salient point is that the unequal stanzas offer no compensatory typographical balance with centered lines, just as the speaker searches for compensation and order and perceives none.

"Dover Beach" also modifies what may be called the "Pindarism" of the ode. Although Arnold listed Pindar as one of the masters of the "grand style" he thought poets should aspire to,[23] "Dover Beach" does not emulate the enthusiastic emotion typically attending English Pindaric verse. Readers of the odes of Cowley, Collins, Keats, and Coleridge customarily encounter sudden ejaculations and spates of exclamation marks. "Dover Beach" certainly does not lack emotion, but the governing feeling, it seems to me, is one mingling melancholy and regret. Some of this may be ascribed to Arnold's differing notion of sublimity. In the preface to *Merope,* Arnold said that a tragedy ought to produce in the reader "a sentiment of sublime acquiescence in the course of fate, and in the dispensations of human life" (*On the Classical* 59), redefining the sublime as submissive rather than active and inspired.

As I have explained, loose poetry often claims organicism as its central principle, and Arnold subscribes to this idea as well. Like Coleridge, he cites German aesthetics to authorize his own view: quoting Goethe approvingly, Arnold said that true art is "*Architectonicè* in the highest sense, that power of execution, which creates, forms, and constitutes" (*On the Classical* 9). It is not a numerical regularity of parts, but a "unity and profoundness of moral impression" (*On the Classical* 12). In fact, Arnold constantly champions the looser tradition in his prose. In "The Study of Poetry," he explains that a "nation may have versifiers with smooth numbers, and yet may have no poetry at all" (*Essays* 21); thus, since Pope and his kin valued "regularity, uniformity, precision," their poetic necessarily involved "some repression and silencing of Poetry" (*Essays* 29). He defends Chaucer against the charge that his "fluidity" depended on "a free, licentious dealing with language, such as is now impossible" (i.e., the addition or nonaddition of a sounded final *e*): "It is true that Chaucer's fluidity is conjoined with liberty," he argues, but it is "admirably served by it . . . we ought not to say it was dependent on it" (*Essays* 23). Far from equating license with laziness or moral turpitude (as, say, Pope and Johnson do), Arnold finds it an avenue of True Poetry.

Regarding his own verse, Arnold told his sister not to worry about making his poems "square in all their parts" (i.e., symmetrical and balanced) because they are "fragments" (*Poetry and Criticism* 524); such fragmenting is consistent with the sort of Longinian sublime that informs the irregular ode. Five years later, he remarked,

> People do not understand what a temptation there is, if you cannot bear anything not very good, to transfer your operations to a region where form is everything. Perfection of a certain kind may there be attained, or at least approached, without knocking yourself to pieces, but to attain or approach perfection in the region of thought and feeling, and to unite this with a perfection of form, demands not merely an effort and a labour, but an actual tearing of oneself to pieces. (*Poetry and Criticism* 526)

With such close relation between poet and form, it stands to reason the resulting poem would not conform to mechanic laws. Notwithstanding, Arnold's figure proposes transmutation, not following personal whim. In this respect he shares his Romantic precursors' reluctance to chuck conventional verse form entirely. Consider, for example, his remark made in 1853 that the "boundaries, and wholesome regulative laws" of poetry are ever at odds with "Caprice" (*On the Classical* 15). This all adds up to a mixed poetic envisioning a constant battle among three contrarieties: received form, "Caprice," and the poet's sentiments, the last of which, Arnold claims, are as much a part of form as the first two elements.

This uneasy mixture is evident in "Dover Beach." Metrically, the poem is most iambic when describing either thoughtless regular motion, as the way the waves

    /   /   /   /   /
    Begin and cease, and then again begin

or an unrealizable ideal,

                                 /   /
                          the world, which seems
    /   /   /   /   /
    To lie before us like a world of dreams

It ends with capricious inverted feet and extra unstressed syllables:

    /   /   /   /   /
    Swept with confused alarms of struggle and flight
         /   /   /   /
    Where ignorant armies clash by night.

Further, whereas exclamations in Collins and Cowley indicate junctures of special inspiration, they appear in "Dover Beach" when the speaker cries out to his beloved. Thus Arnold replaces the extrahuman (and sure) muse with a human (and uncertain) lover, in doing so replacing divine connection with human desire.

I have shown that the enemies of twentieth-century free verse often said that free verse was nothing but chopped-up prose and that seventeenth- and eighteenth-century critics made similar comments about irregular odes. Nineteenth-century readers reacted in the same manner. In 1849, Charles Kingsley found some of Arnold's poems "nervous and picturesque prose cut up into scraps" (46); in 1875, William Adams thought the poems bore "a suspicious resemblance to the baldest prose" (166); I have already cited Harriet Martineau's complaint that Arnold's poetry did not keep its metrical contracts.

A list of detractors to Arnold's verse could go on for quite a while, but one more comment is significant for my purposes. In 1850, William Michael Rossetti told readers of *Germ:*

> Seldom indeed, it appears to us, is the attempt to write without some fixed laws of metrical construction attended with success; never, perhaps, can it be considered as the most appropriate embodiment of thought. The fashion has obtained of late years; but it is a fashion and will die out. (61–62)

It is not surprising that the sibling of Dante Gabriel and Christina Rossetti should find irregular poetry wanting; strikingly, Rossetti does not find Arnold an isolated case. In the year 1850 Tennyson reigned in Britain as did Longfellow in America. Nor can we look for the usual suspect, Whitman, here, for *Leaves of Grass* would not appear for five more years, and anyway Rossetti championed Whitman. Though Rossetti does not further specify, I suspect he is referring to a group of poets later satirized by William Aytoun as the "Spasmodics." Philip James Bailey's *Festus* (first published in 1839) started a fashion of epic (or epical) poems written in the style of what may be called Byronic Manfredism. John Westland Marston's *Gerald* (1842) is typical. Mark Weinstein points out that the titular character is described as "'the kingly eagle' who dwells on the 'rock's peak in solitude'" (78) and the poem is long, diffuse, loosely organized, and very rhetorical. Elizabeth Barrett Browning's *Aurora Leigh* and Tennyson's *Maud* are generally thought to have been influenced by the so-called Spasmodics.

The bulk of a Spasmodic epic is generally written in blank verse, but the poem usually mixes in other meters, as does the great ur-spasmodic work,

Manfred. Though these poems are not irregular odes, they do introduce a greater degree of unpredictability than traditional verse for essentially organic reasons. Rossetti's comment thus indicates the prevalence of the less regular versification, a practice also evident in the liberties and virtuosity of Browning and Tennyson. In fact, a good many irregular poems appeared in nineteenth-century literary magazines by poets other than transcendental poets like Whitman, Emerson, Cranch, and Adah Isaacs Menken.[24] Even Longfellow has a relatively loose poem, "The Building of a Ship." Clearly, Rosetti's disapproval did not stem the tide of poetry in the loose tradition—by the end of the century, there was quite a bit of it. For example, C. E. Andrews and M. D. Percival's *Poetry of the Nineties* (1926) collects such loose poems as "Red Night" by Laurence Binyon, "The White Peacock" by William Sharp, and "Across a Gaudy Room" by "Michael Field."[25] Looseness could lead to poems that seem to depart from meter altogether. For example, consider these lines from Mary Eliza Tucker Lambert's *Loews Bridge:*

> Down, down from Romance's perch, my muse,
> Wipe Fancy's dust from off thy shoes:
> Let good and pure rest for a while,
> Portray realities of guile.
> Guile? Say, is there real guile on earth?
> And should we be judged
> By sins—not weakness?
> God forbid!
> Mortals we are, conceived in sin—
> None, none are pure, all "might have been"
> Had woman's heart been made of stone.

The poem rhymes most of its lines and is usually in meter, and this same comment could be made for Mary Weston Fordham's *Uranne* of thirty years later, whose prosody seems to be loose syllabics more than anything else.[26] In the introduction to a reissue of Fordham's poetry, Joan R. Sherman calls it "attractive free verse" (xxxi). Though a reader of today may be tempted to ascribe the form of these poems to poor versification, such judgments need to be tempered by the fact that these poems do not aspire to regularity.

Especially significant to this study is the fate of the irregular ode. The form continues in the crisis poem, as in Francis Thompson's "The Hound of Heaven" and William Vaughn Moody's "Ode in a Time of Hesitation," but it began to appear in other modes. Moody uses it to meditate on his past, first in "The Daguerreotype" and again in "A Prairie Ride":

Now for many nights and days,
The hills of memory are mutinous,
Hearing me raise
Above all other praise
That autumn morn
When league on league between ripe fields of corn,
Galloping neck and neck or loitering hand in hand,
We rode across the prairie land
Where I was born.

Compare the opening to Henry Timrod's "The Cotton Boll":

While I recline
At ease beneath
This immemorial pine,
Small sphere!
(By dusky fingers brought this morning here
And shown with boastful smiles),
I turn thy cloven sheath,
Through which the soft white fibre peer (206)

and this from William Gilmore Simms's "The Lost Pleiad":

Not in the sky,
Where it was seen—
Nor, on the white tops of the glistering wave—
Nor in the mansions of the deep—
Heavens green,
In its enamell'd caves of mystery—
Shall the bright watcher have
A place—nor how once again proud station keep! (363)

and from Richard Hovey's "Evening on the Potomac":

Far away,
The river melts in the unseen.
Oh, beautiful Girl-City, how she dips
Her feet in the stream
With a touch that is half a kiss and half a dream! (561)

My point is that by the end of the century the irregular ode form had blended with the type of descriptive poetry an eighteenth-century poet would likely have put into iambic tetrameter or pentameter couplets. The poems quoted above are not particularly crisis poems. They do not swing back and forth "Pindarically," do not exhibit much anxiety, nor question particularly the subjectivity of their speaker. In the fashion of their day, the poems are ultimately religious and moral.

In this respect, Sidney Lanier's choice for *subject* for his irregular poem, "The Marshes of Glynn," is conventional. Though the poem seeks to put into practice the musical (or quantitative) principles Lanier would expound in *The Science of English Verse,* choosing a rural setting for an irregular poem would not have struck a contemporary reader as odd. The poem is most irregular when describing the action of the water. Thus,

Bending your beauty aside, with a step I stand
On the firm-packed sand,
Free
By a world of marsh that borders a world of sea. (413)

and

About and about through the intricate channels that flow
Here and there
And everywhere
Till his waters have flooded the uttermost creeks and low-lying lanes (415)

When the poem makes statements, the lines grow more regular:

God out of knowledge and good out of infinite pain
And sight out of blindness and purity out of a stain.

As the marsh-hen secretly builds on the watery sod,
Behold I will build me a nest on the greatness of God (414)

This principle governs most of the irregular poems of the period. Generally short lines, or short lines mixed with longer ones, describe first-hand observation, while longer lines in more regular sections are used for moral and religious explanations. Thus, the second section of "The Cotton Boll" begins this way:

Yonder bird
Which floats, as if at rest,
In those blue tracts above the thunder, where
No vapors cloud the stainless air,
And never sound is heard

Isolated on its own line, "Yonder bird" seems to imitate the sensation of viewing the bird. Like the bird, the word is alone. When the speaker apostrophizes the natural world—while doing so categorizing and renaming in human terms—the lines lengthen out:

Ye Stars, which, though, unseen, yet with me gaze
Upon this loveliest fragment of the earth!
Thou Sun, that kindest of all thy gentlest rays
Above it, as to light a favorite hearth!
Ye Clouds, that in your temples in the West
Seen nothing brighter than its humblest flowers!
And ye Winds, that on the ocean's breast
Are kissed to coolness ere ye reach its bowers!

The ejaculation is a second occasion for very short lines. "And lo!," for example, is a single line in "The Cotton Boll." This decorum is consistent with the practice of Wordsworth and Coleridge.

Thus, in a century where the iambic line was already being loosened by the general favor for occasional trisyllabic substitution, a significant minority of the poets were perpetuating the looser tradition to the extent that, by the turn of the century, a poet need not claim special emotion, sublimity, or crisis to justify irregularity. Most of the poems just quoted are thematically conventional, ending with sentiments meant to provide moral and religious uplift—a sentimentalization, perhaps, of Arnold's acquiescent sublime.

Further, the strophe-antistrophe-epode movement of the ode gradually faded away to a general meditative drift. The poems also seem less interested in balance, possibly because their speakers are less unbalanced. These poems do not use typography to suggest equipoise. My sense is that the poets seemed to consider irregular-looking lines carefree, perhaps freed from the constraints of city life, since so many of these poems have pastoral settings. Finally, when the poems get around to moral and religious statement, they almost always did so in iambic pentameter.

Because it was written early in the Modern period and widely admired, T. S. Eliot's "The Love Song of J. Alfred Prufrock" is a particularly telling poem to examine when studying the relation between traditional and free verse. The poem was written according to a poetic that I have shown evident in "Dover Beach."

The sensibility of "Prufrock" is so odd that most assume the form is deliberately odd to mimic it. For example, Jewel Spears Brooker claims that Eliot's poems "can be thought of as a series of experiments by a scrupulous artist searching for form in a formless era" (140). Most consider the poem a monologue and usually stress its difference from traditional verse. Angus Calder's comment is typical of this approach. "Prufrock," he argues, "is a dramatic monologue of a kind, but, under Laforgue's influence, like no predecessor in English. Its jazzy rhythm and pleasurable word play aerate it with a levity of popular song" (30–31).

Others, however, find more precedence. David Spurr, for example, is not alone in locating the poem in the tradition M. H. Abrams calls the Greater Romantic Lyric, of which Shelley's blank-verse poem "Mont Blanc" is an example.[27] Gregory Jay comes closer to my approach when he calls the poem a "crisis ode" (his nomenclature, he tells his reader, comes from Harold Bloom), but like Spurr he compares the poem to "Mont Blanc" (94) and is interested in ideas and not lineal form. These studies have much to say about the philosophical precedents of "Prufrock," but do not do very much to elucidate the form and tend to locate the poem in a Romantic tradition without considering a good deal of intervening poetry.[28]

The poem clearly participates in the irregular ode tradition. My introduction noted that many of its lines are iambic; both Helen Gardner and M. Martin

Barry, after scanning all of "Prufrock" and many of Eliot's early poems, determined that as a whole the poems are largely iambic.[29] For just "Prufrock" Barry finds about 30 percent of the lines are in iambic pentameter, about 45 percent are iambic but not pentameter, about 14 percent pentameter but not iambic, and about 11 percent are neither (135). Eliot uses a lot of trisyllabic substitution, often with articles supplying the extra syllable, a liberty frequently taken in the nineteenth century. "Prufrock" varies its line lengths from trimeter to heptameter, and its first four stanzas rhyme AABCCDDEEFGG AA AABCDEFD ABCABDEDFGGF, so that there are irregular lines, irregular rhymes, and irregular stanzas, just as in other irregular odes. As Curran said about readers of Coleridge's odes, readers of "Prufrock" should be aware that much of the poem's eccentricity comes from its participation in tradition. Further, I have shown that the irregular rhymes and line lengths that Calder finds "jazzy" occur in many poems that predate jazz.

While formally adhering to the traditional decorum of the irregular ode, the poem increases its liberties. Though most lines rhyme, a good many do not, and halfway through the poem two stanzas have no rhymes. Thus, the poem increases the sense of instability—that is, compared to most previous poems, it has a higher degree of noniambic lines and more lines that do not find a rhyme. Generically, the poem surely recalls crisis odes such as "Dover Beach." While the speaker of "Dover Beach" calls to his lover for some stability in an otherwise arbitrary or tragic world, J. Alfred Prufrock does not find potential solace in a lover's embrace. Instead, he ends his lamenting with an erotic fantasy of drowning in the real world. "Prufrock" is a "Love Song" inasmuch as it is about the failure of love in the modern world.

The poem does more than continue the crisis ode tradition. George Williamson and many others note the presence of the "mock-heroic" in the poem (51). The love song tradition is not the target of the poem, because the poem does not in the least resemble traditional love songs. Instead, the poem mocks the carefree, pastoral, late nineteenth-century irregular ode. Compare the opening to "Prufrock" with the opening to Sir Lewis Morris's "Ode on a Fair Spring Morning," written about 1872:

> Come friend, let us forget
> The turmoil of the world a little while
> For now the soft skies smile;
> With the dew the flowers are wet.

> Let us away awhile
> With fierce unrest and carking thoughts of care. (148)

Both poems begin with a short line (as do so many of the pastoral irregular odes) and call out to the reader. Further, "Prufrock" relates to "Fair Spring Morning" in the ways mock poems usually relate to the traditions they critique. The poems are in the same form, but the mock poem overturns the values of its target. Prufrock cannot forget his cares, and while Morris goes on to invoke God for consolation, Prufrock only hears an "eternal Footman" snickering. "Prufrock" substitutes urban gritty reality for Morris's easy pastoralism, and in this respect resembles Jonathan Swift's "Description of a City Shower." The dynamism of "Prufrock" in part stems from its operating on two generic levels at once: it perpetuates the crisis ode while mocking the pastoral ode. I do not mean to argue that Eliot had "Fair Spring Morning" in mind (I doubt it, though I took the quotation from Morris from the *fourteenth* edition of his works), but rather that Eliot satirized that tradition.

The manner in which "Prufrock" modifies the pastoral ode's formal conventions underscores the poem's gravity as a crisis poem. I have shown that short lines were often used for isolating bits of first-hand observation and ejaculations. Lines with three or fewer feet in "Prufrock" include "Do I dare," "Disturb the universe," "So how should I presume?," "And how should I begin?," "That is not it, at all," and "Almost, at times, a Fool." Timrod says with his short line, there is a bird, something solid and certain, and as yet unmarked by the poet's rhetoric; conversely, "Prufrock" uses short lines to describe particularly uncertain sensations. Further, the description of fog, which Lanier would have handled in short irregular lines, Eliot does in longer lines, in a passage I have always felt to be a periphrastic parody of Sandburg's "Fog." "Prufrock" offers nothing free from the poet's rhetoric; disrupted passages indicate not sublimity but growing uncertainty.

As the poem questions the decorum of line length, it also enacts a crisis in rhyme. Although most lines rhyme, disturbing this coherence is the fact that often words rhyme with themselves. "All" rhymes with "all" four times, "time" with itself twice, "window-panes" with itself once, and "while" with itself once. "Universe" is also made to rhyme with "verse," a rhyme that does not obey the rule that the initial consonant should vary in such a rhyme. For irregular odes, rhyming this way constitutes a serious breach in decorum. Cowley, in a note to the ode "To Dr. Scarborough," apologizes for rhyming "find" and "refin'd," explaining that he does not "allow" such a rhyme in English (though the French "delight" in them) except in the "free kind of poetry" of the Pindaric ode, and then "hardly at all without a third Rhyme to answer both." He goes on, "There can be no Musick with only one Note" (200). Rhyming a sound with itself is not a concord but a monotone in Cowley's view. In terms of conventional rhyme theory, rhyming a word with itself is not harmonizing two ideas. It is just the same thing again. Add to this fact that "me" and "tea" rhyme twice, as do "all" and "shawl" (and, of course, "go" and "Michelangelo"). There are other repeating phrases, notably "overwhelming question," which occurs near the beginning of the poem and then again at the end, both times at the end of a line and both times without an interstanzaic rhyme. A triplet amongst quatrains and couplets often gives the sense of abundance; sounds according only with themselves provide a feeling of constriction in a poem of failure like "Prufrock." This constrictive feeling may seem at odds with the poem's penchant for jumping without transition from idea to idea, and also with its sudden, odd metaphors.[30] The sounds of the poem seem to suggest that, despite the speaker's powers of invention, he ends up saying the same thing over and again.

The way that "Prufrock" approaches and then evades regular meter and rhyme demonstrates that what Eliot called the "ghost of meter" haunts the poem. Obviously a generic ghost haunts "Prufrock" and a good deal of Eliot's early poetry. Indeed, the entire loose tradition depends upon such a ghost: the reader is supposed to read the poem's irregularities through the spectacles of iambic pentameter, a procedure further emphasized when so many of the poems regularize into iambic pentameter when making moral or religious statements. Popean aesthetics and the metrical contract emphasize that divergence from the norm indicates special prominence. Loose poetry, by claiming special inspiration, argues in effect that the whole poem is especially prominent. Readers are thus in an atmosphere where things are not the way they are "supposed" to be. The reader must use contextual prosody to determine extraspecial prominence.

If we classify "Dover Beach" as traditional verse and "Prufrock" as free verse, then we must conclude that the distinction between the two kinds of poetry is a matter of degree and not of type. Both have lines of irregular length, a largely iambic progression, unrhymed lines, and irregular stanzas. Eliot just has greater diversity and repeats his rhymes more frequently ("Dover Beach" repeats its "light"/"night" rhyme).

This discussion has centered on Eliot's participation in an English and

American tradition. However, Eliot himself told Donald Hall that his inspiration was not Arnold and Sir Lewis Morris but Jules Laforgue:

> My early *vers libre* of course was started under the endeavor to practice the same form as Laforgue. This meant rhyming lines of irregular length, with the rhymes coming in irregular places. It wasn't so *vers* as *libre,* especially the sort that Ezra called "Amygism." (208)[31]

I do not mean to discount Laforgue's influence on Eliot; *Prufrock and Other Observations*' Dandyism and many other traits are Laforguian. But as Eliot acknowledges that Laforgue influenced his own verse, he seemingly forgets that Laforgue himself was influenced by a number of other writers. The French poet did not invent free verse; before embarking on his free poems, he translated Whitman. Further, though France did have its crisis in the line in the nineteenth century, it was not a French aberration but a *zeitgeist.* Referring to a letter in which Laforgue explained his *vers libre* by saying that he had forgotten about rhyme, the number of syllables, and the other conventions of French poetry, Léon Guichard remarks, *"Laforgue aurait plutôt dû écrire: J'essaie d'oublier de rimer. J'essaie d'oublier le nombre des syllabes, . . . etc"* (160; orig. ellipsis). In other words, Laforgue, because he could not "forget," was, like Arnold and Eliot, haunted by traditional verse form. Laforgue's innovations should not obscure the fact that he was in this respect a fellow traveler.

A full accounting of Eliot's versification would include examination of his verse in traditional form, as well as in the short-line and long-line genres of free verse. Since this chapter is concerned with the poetry using the ghost-of-meter approach, I will conclude with a few comments regarding his use of form in his two important poems, *The Waste Land* and *Four Quartets.*

In chapter 1, I argue that Eliot's organicism amounted to a recipe for heterogeneous poetry. His fiction of composition was that at moments of "intense" writing, the poet writes unfettered free verse; at other times he slips into meter and rhyme. Central to this poetic, then, is the notion of a tangible separation between inspired and less inspired writing. The poet relies on tradition, it might be said, when he cannot find his own feet. However, Eliot's poetry shows that he often used rhyme and meter to signal the dispiritedness of the characters and situations described. The poetry itself does not seem to be uninspired.

Certainly no poem of Eliot's more manifests his heterogeneous poetic than *The Waste Land.* The poem constantly insists on its amalgamation through the use of italics, quotation marks, indentation, section titles, small capitals, parentheses, the incorporation of languages other than English, spaces between lines, and shifts in punctuational practices. Though considering a poem as a collage is common enough in Modern poetry, no poem is more eager to alert its reader to its assembled status. There is more typographical variety in the first ten lines of *The Waste Land,* for example, than in all of Marianne Moore's "Marriage" (which, Moore explains in a note, consists of "statements that took my fancy which I tried to arrange plausibly" [270]).

These typographical boundaries tend to emphasize juxtapositions that often give the reader a sense of degeneration. For instance, line 124 quotes from *The Tempest,* a play with imagery regarding water, regeneration, and art, which are all prominent themes in *The Waste Land.* A few lines later thereafter, the reader comes across,

> O O O O that Shakespeherian Rag—
> It's so elegant
> So intelligent (ll. 128–30)

The connection between the twentieth-century rag and the Renaissance play seems to be that there is only a surface connection. Northrop Frye argues that in *The Tempest*'s epilogue, "Prospero hands over to his audience what his art has created, a vision of society permeated by the virtues of tolerance and forgiveness" (1370). Nobody argues that the Shakespeherian Rag offers anything more than a temporary anodyne.

Similarly, when Tiresias looks with epic vision upon the "violet hour" that "brings the sailor home from sea" (ll. 220–21), a reader might be expected to think of any number of Greek sailor-heroes, preeminently Odysseus struggling through various obstacles to reunite with his faithful wife. However, Tiresias's eye rests on a typist "home at tea-time" engaging in a meaningless, passionless tryst with a carbuncular clerk. When Odysseus returns home, his union with Penelope brings him personal fulfillment and restores moral order to his society. The typist feels no such fulfillment, and her anomie indicts her society. The sense that something has fallen off is unmistakable.

With the pervasive sense of twentieth-century decay throughout the poem, it is appropriate that it ends with its most polyglot passage:

> London Bridge is falling down falling down falling down
> *Poi s'ascose nel foco che gli affina*

Quando fiam uti chelidon—O swallow swallow
Le Prince d'Aquitaine à la tour abolie
These fragments I have shored against my ruins
Why then Ile fit you. Hieronymo's mad againe.
Datta. Dayadhvan. Damyata.
    Shantih shantih shantih (ll. 427–34)

The last words of the poem are its most ancient. Eliot glosses the Sanskrit words on line 433 as "give, sympathise, control" (54), and the final line as "The Peace which Passeth understanding" (55), suggesting that the personal and moral qualities of line 433 will bring about the sense of peace so lacking in the rest of the poem.

Sanskrit is an especially appropriate choice. Anyone who has studied the language, as Eliot did, knows that it was the study of Sanskrit that allowed philologists to piece together the family of languages now known as Indo-European. In addition to being very ancient, Sanskrit is very pure. Since it is the language of many religious works, including the national epics *The Mahabharata* and *The Ramayana,* ancient Indian scholar-priests were interested in studying and conserving the language so as to retain a full understanding of these texts. As a spoken language of daily intercourse, Sanskrit evolved into such languages as Urdu, Bengal, and Hindi; written, Sanskrit was frozen and codified by the grammarian Panini around 400 BC. Unlike most ancient languages, there exists a relatively full grammar of the language (probably the most complete grammar written before the nineteenth century) produced during a time when it was something like a living language. Thus, not only is Sanskrit free of twentieth-century corruption, and of Western corruption, Sanskrit is free even of Indian corruption, indeed, free of the corruption of most of recorded history. For the conclusion to his poem, Eliot did not return to the wells of English poetry undefiled, he returned to what an early twentieth-century philologist would have considered the wells of language undefiled. Sanskrit was the key that unlocked the Babel that succeeded it, and *The Waste Land* seems to offer the language as a possible solution to modern dissipation.

What does all this have to do with the line? First, the conclusion to *The Waste Land* suggests that resolution cannot occur in traditional English lineal form. The final lines juxtapose a nursery rhyme, and poetry in Italian, French, Early Modern English, contemporary English, and Sanskrit. That adds up to five separate prosodic systems, each controlling different aural features. If progression through an abbreviated course in comparative literature is necessary to achieve profound peace, then one meter is inadequate.

Second, it suggests that Eliot considers English lineal form within a historical continuum, as one mode that is possibly outdated. Barry and Gardner have scanned *The Waste Land* and found it largely iambic, but where the poem is most iambic is telling. Sometimes, the poem ranges fairly far from the iambic pentameter norm. Describing the freedom of youth and the mountains, meter's ghost seems fairly well concealed behind its arras:

> And when we were children, staying at the archduke's,
> My cousin's, he took me out on a sled,
> And I was frightened. He said, Marie,
> Marie, hold on tight. And down we went.
> In the mountains, there you feel free. (ll. 13–17)

You can force this into iambics, of course, but the conversational tone seems to call for a less regular pattern of accents. More obviously strict iambics attend descriptions of mechanical action, similar to the use of meter in "Dover Beach." For example, part I juxtaposes a loosely metrical line about sighing with a more rigid one about walking mindlessly:

> Sighs, short and infrequent, were exhaled,
> And each man fixed his eyes before his feet. (ll. 64–65)

The alliterating *f*'s help emphasize the regular stresses of the second line. Likewise, meter brings the sense of constriction when the poem moves from the depiction of the sea to the narrow life of the typist. I suspect some readers might disagree with my scansion of the first two lines, but the second two seem unmistakably iambic:

> / / / / /
> At the violet hour, the evening hour that strives
> / / / / /
> Homeward, and brings the sailor home from sea,
> / / / / / /
> The typist, home at tea-time, clears her breakfast, lights
> / / / /
> Her stove, and lays out food in tins. (1.220–23)

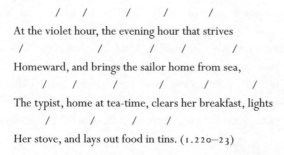

Again the alliteration, here repeating *t*'s that I have always supposed mean to imitate the sounds of typewriting, helps highlight the regularity. Similarly, when she reflects on her affair, her thoughts and actions are put into quatrains:

> She turns and looks a moment in the glass,
> Hardly aware of her departed lover;
> Her brain allows one half-formed thought to pass:
> "Well now that's done: and I'm glad it's over."
> When lovely woman stoops to folly and
> Paces about her room again, alone,
> She smoothes her hair with automatic hand,
> And puts a record on the gramophone. (1.249–56)

It does not seem that Eliot himself is not inspired in these lines. Instead, the regularity[32] seems to suggest a thoughtless following of form. Of special interest is the stressed "and." The prominence of the connective is entirely a product of lineation, the conventions of meter, and the exigencies of rhyme—it is not a word a nonliterary character would likely stress in that context. The pointless prominence of "and" reflects the typist's "automatic" adherence to pattern, with her self-consoling "hand" moving as mindlessly as the tone-arm on a gramophone. The lines also suggest a falling off from the decorums typical of the age that produced *She Stoops to Conquer.*

Rhyme in the passage seems to imply closure and resolution, but of course is used ironically to suggest a harmony the typist does not feel. The subsequent description of Elizabeth, Leicester, and other lovers likewise refers to the philosophy of rhyme while using meter significantly:

> "Trams and dusty trees.
> Highbury bore me. Richmond and Kew
> Undid me. By Richmond I raised my knees
> Supine on the floor of a narrow canoe."

> "My feet are at Moorgate, and my heart
> Under my feet. After the event
> He wept. He promised 'a new start.'
> I made no comment. What should I resent?"

> "On Margate Sands.
> I can connect
> Nothing with nothing.
> The broken fingernails of dirty hands.
> My people humble people who expect
> Nothing." (ll. 293–305)

The three stanzas enact a progressive breakdown of rhyme and meter. The stanzaic division suggests, in fact, the ruins of a sonnet. The first quatrain offers true rhymes and something approaching regular meter. In the second, the enjambment becomes harder, making it difficult to read according to the line breaks of the stanzaic form. The internal rhyme, "comment," further disturbs the rhyme scheme. By the third stanza, the line has broken in two. The only rhyme for "nothing" is itself. Lines describing sexual union might be expected to be especially cohesively yoked to provide a sense of harmony, but Eliot's speaker here can only connect "nothing" with "nothing." There is no progeny, no continuing love; there is just mutual emptiness.

Thus, while in "Reflections on *Vers Libre*," Eliot offers the ghost-of-meter paradigm to explain the way that tradition rather subconsciously influences the way a poet composes, in *The Waste Land* it emerges as a conscious device signaling how a passage is to be understood. Eliot seems to feel that iambic form is ornamental and mechanical. If a reality is appropriately described by the form, then there is something wrong with that reality. As I argued, if the conclusion of *The Waste Land* offers a solution to the problems the poem addresses, then the appropriate vehicle is not iambic pentameter.

The Sanskrit in *The Waste Land* is not the only manifestation in Eliot's poetry of a desire for a language not subject to corruption. *Four Quartets* has a similar theme. Words, the speaker says,

> strain,
> Crack and sometimes break, under the burden,
> Under the tension, slip, slide, perish,
> Decay with imprecision, will not stay in place,
> Will not stay still. (121)

Later in the poem, he calls language "shabby equipment always deteriorating" (128). At no time does Eliot consider the positive aspects of the change inherent in living languages—innovation and new combinations. *Four Quartets* seeks the Word, the "still point of the turning world" (119), as an antidote to ceaseless decay.

Also like *The Waste Land, Four Quartets* often separates its modes of articulation typographically. The range of voice is more restricted in the later work, however. There are two main modes. The first is in a line that visually suggests blank verse, but is not particularly haunted by meter, such as in the opening lines:

> Time present and time past
> Are both perhaps present in time future,
> And time future contained in time past.
> If all time is eternally present
> All time is unredeemable.
> What might have become abstraction
> Remaining a perpetual possibility
> Only in a world of speculation. (117)

The lines are lightly enjambed with key words repeated. Here, "time" appears seven times. Noticeable, too, is the level of abstraction in this meditative voice. For each of the four quartets, the first, third, and fifth sections are written in this way.

The second and fourth part of each quartet contain more rhyming, metrical poetry.[33] The beginning of part II of "Burnt Norton," for example, rhymes ABACCBDCBBDEEEC in fairly regular iambic tetrameter. The lines argue that human, natural, and celestial worlds are conjunct. The irregularly rhyming lines enact the notion that these connections are unpredictable but perceivable. Parts II and IV also use relatively more concrete, figurative language and are less tentative in making assertions. Even when addressing the unknown, the more metrical sections tend to have a decisive air. The Ballad of the Bleeding Surgeon that begins "East Coker," part IV, for example, tells us what we feel:

> The wounded surgeon plies the steel
> That questions the distempered part;
> Beneath the bleeding hands we feel
> The sharp compassion of the healer's art
> Resolving the enigma of the fever chart. (127)

Part IV of "Little Gidding," is equally unequivocal:

> Who devised the torment? Love.
> Love is the unfamiliar Name
> Behind the hands that wove
> The intolerable shirt of flame
> Which human power cannot remove.
> We only live, only suspire
> Consumed by either fire or fire. (144)

When words do repeat, they are often modified so that the reader feels that there has been some sort of progression. In the sort-of sestina of part II of "The Dry Salvages" (six stanzas rhyming intrastanzaically ABCDEF), the words of stanza one repeat in stanza six with a notable difference. The first stanza concludes,

> The prayer to the bone on the beach, the unprayable
> Prayer at the calamitous annunciation? (131)

Stanza six ends,

> The bone's prayer to Death its God. Only the hardly, barely prayable
> Prayer of the one Annunciation. (132)

There is a clear variance between a prayer that is barely prayable and one that cannot be prayed at all, and an annunciation and the capitalized announcement of the Incarnation to the Virgin Mary.

Thus, unlike *The Waste Land* where rhyme and meter signal satire and thoughtlessness, in *Four Quartets* traditional lineal form is often the site for the assertions the speaker wishes to make. However, like some of the parables of the Bible, the language of these assertions is often metaphoric, perhaps hermetic. Compare, in this regard, the straightforwardness of the beginning of section V of "Little Gidding":

> What we call the beginning is often the end
> And to make an end is to make a beginning.
> The end is where we start from. (144)

Far from the visions of the more metered sections, the odd-numbered prosy sections often assert that words have antithetical meanings—above, for example, the reader is told that the "end" is a "beginning," and in other parts of the poem readers find out that the past is the present, the sea is land, arriving is leaving, and so forth. It is not so much that opposites are reconciled as it is that different denotations and connotations of words are compared. Thus,

> We shall not cease from exploration
> And the end of all our exploring
> Will be to arrive where we started
> And know the place for the first time. (145)

Clearly there is some play between "end" as conclusion and "end" as goal, and "know for the first time" seems to imply a greater knowledge, not just "having an acquaintance with" as the word colloquially denotes. Throughout these sections of *Four Quartets,* the reader confronts these equivocations, and, to make meaning, must provide abstract meanings for the words. The word *place,* above, for example, clearly occupies intellectual and spiritual space. In this way, the poem encourages the reader to think abstractly, in a manner generally associated with philosophy and theology.

In *The Waste Land,* the traditions of English verse stand for the traditions of Western culture that wasted the land. After Eliot became an Anglican, he was no longer convinced that Western culture offered nothing to humanity. The even-numbered, more metrical sections of *Four Quartets* do not depict degeneration and they do not satirize. In fact, they focus on the Mysteries the odd-numbered sections seek to understand. Still, assuming that the poem seeks closure and that the end of each section is especially significant, it seems that Eliot finally comes down on freer versification as a more appropriate vehicle for human understanding. True to his ghost-of-meter paradigm, the best repository for value and for human inspiration is verse written during those times when the poet/speaker is evading the traditions of English verse.

CHAPTER THREE

The Haunting of Wallace Stevens

I begin with one more precursor to "Prufrock," a poem entitled "Ode." The first stanza reads,

A night in May!
And the whole of us gathered into a room
To pack and bundle care away
And not to remember that over the dark
The sea doth call
Doth call from out an upward-rising day
For us to follow and to mark
A patient workman by the city wall
A night in May!
A night in May! (*Souvenirs* 63–64)

"Ode" observes the decorum typical of irregular odes: the short lines describe natural vitality in a way that is supposed to be unmarked by the poet's rhetoric, the poem invites the reader to leave cares behind so as to appreciate the natural world, and so forth. What makes this thoroughly conventional poem apropos is that a young Harvard undergraduate named Wallace Stevens wrote it. Though most of Stevens's apprentice verse consists of sonnets and poems in traditional form, it is appropriate that Stevens should, near the beginning of his career, participate in the tradition that led to the kind of free verse he tended to write.

This chapter focuses on the way that traditional form haunts the poetry of Wallace Stevens. Although my estimation that Stevens is more interesting prosodically than Eliot is subjective, the case that Stevens wrote more consistently in the genre is undeniable. Eliot's "Prufrock," as well as other poems written similarly (such as "Portrait of a Lady"), are historically important for helping establish one approach to free verse. At the time "Prufrock" was published, Stevens was largely known as the author of such blank-verse poems as "Sunday Morning" and "Le Monocle de Mon Oncle." However, Eliot wrote comparatively little poetry in this genre. If his plays, light verse, poems in stanzaic form and in other genres of free verse are excluded from his corpus, there are fewer than fifty pages of poetry left. Performing the same operation on Stevens leaves over six hundred pages of verse.

Although Eliot and Stevens are in many respects quite different, I am not the first to notice formal similarities. Both were capable of exploiting, in Hugh Kenner's phrase, "the authorized sonorities of the best English verse, circa 1870" (*Homemade* 6); Eleanor Cook, Taylor, and Gross might dispute the date, but all point out that both Eliot and Stevens mastered traditional form.[1] The two poets did not know each other, did not correspond, and did not have the same circle of friends. Their similarities stem from the fact that they were writing the same genre of free verse.

Though there is no dearth of comment on Stevens's poetry, few have spent much time on his prosody. Stevens's comments on his own work, which tend to paraphrase what he was trying to "say" in this or that poem (usually with the disclaimer that the poem in question means much more than his paraphrase), seem to have dissuaded many from attending too closely to his practice. Still, those looking at structure in any sense of the word by and large agree that Stevens's poems are a mixed bag. Differing poems are written very differently and often seem to argue antithetical philosophical positions. Readers have sought for a method for determining which lines are parodic and which are meant to be satisfying. Describing Stevens's practice for an ultimately interpretive purpose is an important concern for such critics as Marie Borroff, Irving Ehrenpreis, Hollander, Cook, and Helen Vendler, and it is one of my aims here.

Those interested in lineal form generally share Joan Richardson's view that "While other poets in [Stevens's] circle—like William Carlos Williams, Mina Loy, Alfred Kreymborg, and Walter Arensberg—experimented with new rhythms and meters, Stevens held on to familiar sound and the traditional forms" (446). Those who have looked more carefully, Taylor, Justice, and Gross particularly, have settled on a ghost-of-meter paradigm: Taylor (after quoting Eliot) finds ghosts of "sonnets, quatrains, blank verse, terza rima" (220) floating around in Stevens's canon; Gross finds that in "Notes toward a Supreme Fiction," "The rhythm of blank verse surges forward at times, then fades and dissolves into other cadences" (*Sound* 242); Justice argues that Stevens's later line became "in essence 'free,' without quite losing touch with its source in the old heroic line" (65). Though these assessments have much truth in them, they are too often informed by an ahistorical or otherwise oversimplified notion of lineal form. It is hasty and inaccurate to conclude, as for example William Bysshe Stein does about "Peter Quince at the Clavier," that a poem in meter and rhyme is necessarily satiric.[2]

The Moderns always claimed for themselves a new sensibility, often a sensitivity to subjects and aesthetic issues that they felt previous generations misunderstood, ignored, or took for granted. This emphasis on the "new" was realized in many ways on the lineal level. For example, when E. E. Cummings and poets like him started experimenting with capitalization by not capitalizing according to traditional rules, they were reconsidering and building into a meaningful device one aspect of lineal form most poets took for granted. A reader of Pope should think nothing of the fact that the first letter of each line of *The Rape of the Lock* is capitalized, but if Cummings capitalizes the first letter of a line, the reader knows Something is Up. In this way, Cummings resensitized his verse to capital letters.

In the teens and twenties, poets such as Stevens—aligned both by reputation and choice to the New Poetry—similarly reconsidered other traditions of verse. In the same way that Cummings did not "reject" capital letters but used them to indicate prominence, so Stevens reconsidered rhyme, meter, and alliteration. Stevens used and evaded traditional versification to construct what amount to formal allegories of freedom and constriction, of speakers responsive to the actual world and of speakers intent on following predetermined patterns.

Traditional form's haunting of Stevens is evident in his use of alliteration. In the way that Cummings reconsidered capitalization, Stevens reconsidered alliteration, a device distinguished by the fact that it is common in all phases of English poetry, from Old English to today's free verse. Readers familiar with the way that poets often use sounds to echo the sense will find these lines from "Infanta Marina" very familiar:

> The rumpling of the plumes
> Of this creature of the evening
> Came to be sleights of sails
> Over the sea. (7)[3]

The m's and p's are meant to echo the tousling plumes of the first line, and the s sounds of the last two lines are traditionally supposed to sigh like the wind. Similarly, of the thirteen words in Stevens's short poem, "To the Roaring Wind," six have significant *s* sounds. *Harmonium,* Stevens's first book, is replete with other mimetic sounds as well. In "Indian River," for example, the clinking of nets against boats in the sea can be heard in the interplay of the consonants in the anapestic rhythm of "jingles the rings in the nets around the racks by the docks" (112).

But Stevens controls his sounds for more than echoic effects. "The Load of Sugar Cane," for example, begins with a load of *g*'s:

> The going of the glade boat

The *w* tucked in the second word (i.e., go-*w*ing) is made explicit in the second line:

> Is like water flowing

There is an aural link between the action of the glade boat and the action of the water, which after all is what the poem has just said. Line three repeats line two to further the aural link, then the next line connects back to the *g*'s of the first line with "*g*reen saw-*g*rass," which links with *g*lade boat, which was already linked with the water. The *r*'s of the "g*r*een saw-g*r*ass" then link with "*r*ainbows" of line six, and line seven repeats line six, so that the poem is all linked up and floating along placidly at this point. In this way, the poem makes connections using aural correspondences in a way that does not mimic natural sound.

Line eight disrupts the quiet repetitions:

> That are like birds,
> Turning, bedizened,
>
> While the wind still whistles
> As kildeer do,
>
> When they rise
> At the red turban
> Of the boatman. (12)

The diction changes a bit and after a context largely of *r*'s and *w*'s, the *b*-*d*'s explode. The wind whistles, an imitative sound that also seems to pick up the *w* sound of the previous lines and pairs it with a less euphonious short *i* sound. Note too, that "kildeer" has the same loud *d* sound that "bir*d*" does—and a kildeer's name imitates its call. The poem ends up in the boat with the red vibrancy (and unusual, unexpected rhyme) of the boatman with his turban. In all, the poem is balanced on the fulcrum of the bird and its sound, which act as transforming agents.

What is the poem about? It is about a boat and bird and a boatman if you stick to the poem's images. In an important sense, the poem is about the way that sounds, like the red turban, create a new ordering of reality; the poem is about sharper sounds penetrating more liquid ones. In lyric poetry of this nature, the experience of reading the poem is to a large degree its significance. To sense the sudden disruptions, the reader has to feel the calm placidity of the scene that precedes it and in doing so appreciate the connections among the sounds that compose the poem. Thus, the alliterative pattern is part of the work's "meaning."

A few persistent alliterations in *Harmonium* have more forthright implications. For example, Stevens often speaks of traditional religion with alliterating *h*'s. Thus, there is "*h*eaven and *h*eavenly script" in "The Ordinary Women"; the "*h*oly *h*ush" in "Sunday Morning"; a "*h*aunted *h*eaven" and a "*h*ankering for *h*ymns" in "A High-Toned Old Christian Woman." *H* is a very odd letter to alliterate, as the letter tends to be swallowed up in speech and some speakers of English do not pronounce it. At times, the *Beowulf* poet alliterates *h* with vowels. To sound the alliteration, you really have to work at it, maybe will it, force it—just as a skeptical poet might think something willful and forced about conventional religious belief. This seems a case of semantic alliteration. Certainly, not all poets use *h* in this way. It is a meaning Stevens built into his early verse, a formal allegory.

Of course, any consideration of Stevens's alliteration must examine "The Comedian as the Letter C," a poem with a title that hints of an interest in letters and their sounds. Stevens said more than once that the sounds of the letter *c* accompanied Crispin in his travels like bells around the ankles of St. Francis, and surely this does occur.[4] But what has escaped notice is that there is another player in the comedy, the letter *p*. Especially early in his career, Stevens observed a remarkably consistent semantic use of these two sounds.

In general, Stevens's *c*'s attend vital reality, while *p*'s attend statements of perception—sometimes poetical conceptions, sometimes rhetoric. Examples of this sort of thing can found all over *Harmonium*. In "Earthy Anecdote," the "bu*ck*s" go "*c*lattering" (until controlled) (3); in "Le Monocle de Mon Oncle" there is "the firefly's qui*ck,* ele*c*tri*c* stro*k*e" and the speaker goes on to notice "how the *c*rickets *c*ame" (with their "*k*in") (15); "The Jack-Rabbit" "*c*arolled in *c*ara*c*oles" (50); I have quoted the *c*'s in "Indian River." Stevens seems to have found the *c* a clattering sound, one that might be vital but threatens to be merely dull noise.

On the *p* side, there are the "*p*om*p*s" which seem "*p*rofound" in "On the Manner of Addressing the Clouds" (55); when the speaker of "Floral Decorations for Bananas" grows affected, he speaks of "women of *p*rimrose and *p*url" (54); in "A High-Toned Old Christian Woman" the speaker proposes to "*p*roject a masque / Beyond the *p*lanets" (59); "The Death of a Soldier" satirizes a view that would find a fallen soldier "a three-days *p*ersonage / Im*p*osing his se*p*aration / Calling for *p*om*p*" (97). Here, and everywhere, Stevens's "pomp" is a pejorative for rhetoric. Stevens seems to have found *p* a ripe, almost self-mocking, sound.

Now, Crispin has both a *c* and a *p* in him, and the descriptions of him pick up both letters. Thus he is "the So*c*rates / Of snails, musi*c*ian of *p*ears, *p*rin*c*i*p*ium / And le*x*". When Crispin goes to sea, his eye falls not on "a*p*ri*c*ots" (both *p* and *c*) but "*p*or*p*oises" (27), which to him are fantastic. He seeks to explain it all in "*c*li*ck*ering syllables" but the "*p*oly*p*hony" (28) is beyond his ability to describe it: that is to say, his descriptions are too mundane to capture the unbounded imaginative conceptions suggested by the sea.

The valet "Deje*c*ted his manner" (29) to his new reality, wiping away his previous imaginative assumptions, trying to understand a world where

> the sun
> Was not the sun because it never shone
> With bland complaisance on pale parasols (29)

That is, a world much more *c* than the bland *p* he is used to. By the time he arrives in Yucatan, he is "intri*c*ate in moody ru*ck*s" to such an extent that he is "as other freemen are, / Sonorous eggshells rattling inwardly," a sort of empty clicking.[5] However, his southern surroundings soon excite his imagination, so that "The fabulous and its intrinsi*c* verse / *C*ame like two s*p*irits *p*arleying" (31) and the *c* and the *p* are again conjoined.[6]

Tracing *c* and *p* throughout the whole poem is a very lengthy process, but suffice it to say the two letters chase the valet throughout. One more example should seal my argument: when he has children, they inherit both *c* and *p* genes. The first is an "inhabitant . . . of a *c*ountry of the *cap*uchins," the second is the first's "*c*ounter*p*art," the third is a "*c*ree*p*er," and the fourth is "*pink*" (44). Of course, Crispin learns he cannot ignore *c* or *p* and eventually acquiesces to a compromise between the two.

If this kind of consistent use of sound to point to specific ideas seems unusual and perhaps mechanical, it should be remembered that Stevens's poetry as a whole is unusual because of its remarkably stable systems of symbols, colors, and geography. New readers of Stevens must learn that blue (and the moon) mean "imagination," that the South is the ideal place for the imagination and the North for reality, that birds always represent the spirit, and a host of other correspondences. Stevens's letters and essays reveal that he frequently interpreted his poems as allegories of reality and the imagination, and critics have not been slow to expand upon these approaches. The patterns of alliteration I have outlined are, in fact, consistent with Stevens's other poetical practices.

The question remains whether Stevens is using alliteration in an innovative or traditional manner. A thumbnail history of alliteration is useful here. Alliteration is the main structural feature of Old English poetry and poems in the Alliterative revival—a device of expectation instead of surprise, because a competent Anglo-Saxon or medieval reader expects alliteration in certain places in the same way that a competent reader of Pope expects a rhyme at the end of every line. By the Renaissance, when the English line became accentual and syllabic, alliteration became a device of surprise, an ornament. Percy G. Adams's entry on alliteration in *The New Princeton Encyclopedia of Poetry and Poetics* says that by 1660–1780, poets used alliteration "to tie adjectives to nouns, to balance nouns or verbs or adjectives, to stress the caesura and end rhyme, to join sound to sense, and to decorate their lines." He adds that later poets used it "less" (37). Since I am arguing that Stevens's use of the technique is sometimes semantic, this would seem to be another step in the evolution of alliteration. *The New Princeton Encyclopedia*'s history is necessarily brief and general, but it is about all we have; there is no comprehensive history of alliteration.[7] It seems likely that other poets have used sound programmatically. What is likely unusual, however, is, the self-consciousness of the device in "The Comedian." Hopkins was self-conscious as well in a poem such as "The Wreck of the Deutschland," but he was subscribing to alliterative poetics like that used in *Piers Plowman.*[8] Swinburne, who used a lot of alliteration, self-consciously parodied himself in "Nephilidia." But all those *c*'s in "The Comedian," though comic, do not seem to me parodic (if they are, whom is he parodying?). The preponderance of *c*'s (and *p*'s) puts them in a category somewhere in between the structural expectancy and ornamental surprise, as the reader anticipates the *c*'s but cannot predict where they will appear.

The fact that Stevens should undertake such a poem under the mechanic rule that *c*'s and *p*'s be used whenever possible suggests that he was rethinking alliteration, a device other poets tend to use whenever convenient. The recondite diction of "Comedian" helps indicate that Stevens was willing to work very hard to get as many similar sounds as possible into the poem. The only kinds of poem like it that I can think of are the "aureate" poems of Dunbar, such as "Ane Ballat of Our Lady," which also exemplifies a desire to use as many similar sounds as possible, even if it means using awkward or abstruse vocabulary.

Stevens's use of alliteration illustrates the fact that his poetic was partly traditional and partly innovative; in this respect, he was not a "free-verse fanatic." His theories of poetry likewise show he adhered to a partly traditional, partly Modern, poetic. I have shown that Eliot subscribed to a mixed poetic which supposed that poems interspersed organic ("free") and inorganic ("metrical") elements, and that he differed from the Romantics in that he did not presume the inorganic parts assimilated by the whole. Stevens held a somewhat similar view.

Stevens's prose is replete with statements implying organic theory. *The Necessary Angel* many times quotes Coleridge and I. A. Richards and other times makes statements about the constructive powers of the imagination that recall Coleridge's distinction between Fancy and Imagination. Further, Stevens's prose shows that he agreed with Horace that *poeta nascitur non fit.* He frequently explained that he wrote "instinctively" (*Letters* 206); he argued Marianne Moore did as well (*Opus* 217), as did, presumably, every poet because "Poets continue to be born and not made" (*Opus* 224). Add to this Stevens's dictum that poetry is the reaction of the imagination to the pressures of reality, and what you have is a poetic insisting on the *sui generis* approach; each poem is a unique reaction to a particular reality, filtered through a particular sensibility. One of Stevens's many letters to Ronald Lane Latimer[9] provides an appropriate, if unsavory, metaphor:

> Whether beauty is roused by passion or whether passion is roused by beauty is pretty much the same thing as the question whether a poem about a natural

> object is roused by the natural object or whether the natural object is clothed with its poetic characteristics by the poet. While I brush that sort of thing aside, it is not because I am not interested. But I feel very much like the boy whose mother told him to stop sneezing; he replied, "I am not sneezing; it's sneezing me." (*Letters* 302)

Object, poet, poem: it all comes together as inevitably as a sneeze, and we do not, I think, look in our used tissues for genre and influence.

These statements, however, must be balanced against others that suggest a much different poetic. Although Stevens was at times, like Pope, willing to believe that when he was born he was dipped in ink, also like Pope he at other times stresses what he terms "the laborious element" (*Necessary* 165) of art. While making poems sometimes seems to him a sneeze, he also told Latimer that writing poetry "is a conscious activity. While poems may very well occur, they had very much better be caused" (*Letters* 274). Indeed, Stevens typically tempers his organicism with something more contrived. Sure, he says, "the personality of the poet" is what "keeps poetry a living thing, the modernizing and ever-modern influence" (*Necessary* 45), but it is an "indirect egotism," the mind of the poet that "describes itself" which requires in part "the power of [the poet's] reason" (*Necessary* 46).

Stevens's description here does not differ much from Wordsworth's famous preface, but it avoids the rhetoric of a free-verse fanatic like Lawrence. In this respect, Stevens's comment for William Rose Benét's *Fifty Poets: An American Auto-Anthology* is revealing. The poem he chose as his "favorite" (*Letters* 263) was one that "represented what was in my mind at the moment, with the least possible manipulation" (*Letters* 264). Stevens chose "The Emperor of Ice Cream," a poem whose formal properties are such that it is one of the few poems in Stevens's canon that has been treated to extensive prosodic analysis. Gabriella Bedetti has established that the "least possible manipulation" includes careful arrangement of alliteration, rhyme, rhythm, and grammar.

Still, Stevens tended to resist suggestions that he was very much influenced by form as much as he resisted the notion that contemporaries influenced him.[10] After expressing the concern that his Italian audience may regard poems "indifferent" to "familiar forms" as "lacking something," he told his Italian translator, "Yet I have never felt that a form matters enough to allow myself to be controlled by it" (*Letters* 817). "Form," as Stevens uses it here, means traditional stanzaic form.

In fact, early in his career, Stevens tended to classify himself as a free-verse poet. In 1916, he wrote a letter to his wife which consisted mostly of a mock newspaper article with the headline "Eminent Vers Libriste / Arrives in Town" (*Letters* 196),[11] and in 1920 he wrote Ferdinand Reyher, as I noted in the introduction to this book, that he was not "exclusively for free verse," but he was "for it." The rest of his comments on the matter to Reyher are of interest here. Stevens disclaimed being "exclusively" for free verse, partially because "there are miles of it that do not come off." Further, "People don't understand the emotional purpose of rhythm any more than they understood the emotional purpose of measure" ("Letters" 390).[12] George Lensing's comment on this letter is both acute and illustrative of what is wrong with much free-verse criticism:

> Stevens' reference to the emotional purpose of rhythm and measure hints, I think, at the theory that meter should be liberated from the form that insisted on numbering syllables and stresses by some predetermined metronome. The musical cadences should be emotional, that is, spontaneous, impulsive, and shrewdly self-effacing. The ideal mode for Stevens was not, finally, free verse, in which even the emotional purpose of rhythm was subverted. (*Wallace Stevens* 102)

Lensing rightly recognizes the organic impulse, but would seem to endorse tacitly an overly rigid view of traditional meter that Stevens actually argues against, and ascribes to Stevens a brand of organicism more appropriate to Monroe and Lawrence. In addition, the "theory" that Lensing mentions (it is unclear whether he agrees with it) conflates all of free verse so that the poetry of Stevens (and Eliot) no longer qualifies as free verse. The comment further asserts that music is the basis for poetic rhythm (as opposed to, say, speech), an ontology which may not be particularly condign for Stevens, especially for the meditative voice typical of Stevens's longer poems. What Stevens is more precisely saying is that *some* free-verse rhythm subverts an "emotional purpose." I take Lensing to task here not because his comment is particularly dull but because he is otherwise acute. In general Lensing's work on Stevens seeks to contextualize the poetry, but when he considers prosody he almost turns into a New Critic. Again, it is clear that prosodic criticism needs to be put in the context of the aesthetic debate of the day to be fully understood.

Stevens's comment to Reyher is carefully stated, and, like the comments from Eliot and Williams in chapter 1, it separates its speaker from both poles of the free-verse debate. A similar strategy is evident in a letter written in 1937:

> I am rather inclined to disregard form so long as I am free and can express myself freely. I don't know of anything, respecting form, that makes much difference.

> The essential thing in form is to be free in whatever form is used. A free form does not assure freedom. As a form, it is just one more form. So that it comes to this, I suppose, that I believe in freedom regardless of form. (*Letters* 323)

Again, Stevens acknowledges that he is part of the looser tradition. He refuses to say either that free verse is uniquely suitable for true expression (with the corollary that traditional verse is stiflingly restrictive), or that free verse is no verse at all. This letter was written shortly after Stevens completed "The Man with the Blue Guitar," a poem which establishes the decorum of proceeding in couplets then grows extremely free with that decorum. Though Stevens was "for" free verse, then, he was no "fanatic."

As the years went by, Stevens grew increasingly impatient with the kind of Modernity that insisted on a clean break from the past. The prevailing attitude, he wrote in 1947, was that

> All art that is not modern is antique; and all modern art (not, say, this or that picture, or the work of Matisse, Klee, Braque, but all of it without distinction) enjoys the completest possible prestige because it is modern. If I go into a gallery containing the work of a dunce, I am certain to find him protected; and if I tear my hair at his ineffectiveness, the dealer recognizes me as illiterate and insensitive. Free thought, free art, free poetry, have all produced this sort of tyranny. (*Letters* 574)

Such presumptive "protection" was not in Stevens's view being free with form, but dogmatic insistence on the fashionable. As a "tyranny," this approach is the opposite of freedom. The dealer defends the artist in a manner consistent with the strategy I have shown that many free-verse propagandists use.

"In painting, as in poetry," Stevens complained to Thomas McGreevy in 1949, "things that are revelation today are obsolete tomorrow, like things on one's plate at dinner." After an hour at the Museum of Modern Art, "you say the hell with it. Is all this hard thinking, really high feeling or is it a bunch of nobodies running after a few somebodies?" (*Letters* 647). I note in passing the vestige of connection between sublimity and irregularity here—Stevens assumes a work in an unusual form is supposed to be especially inspired. Later the same year, Stevens told Delmore Schwartz, "It is neither possible nor desirable to cut loose from the past to the extent to which the swarm has been cutting loose recently" (*Letters* 651). Thus, Stevens endorsed a poetic practice free with, not free from, traditional form, one that takes liberties but does not forget. In other words, one haunted by a traditional ghost. Again, I use the haunting metaphor because of its currency, not to suggest that Stevens could not, for some eerie or psychological reason, avoid traditional poetics.

To say that Stevens participated in traditional poetics is not to say that they controlled him. Stevens tended to avoid stanzaic forms, for example. Stevens's most formal poems occur at the beginning of his career, and while he wrote blank verse and couplets, there are no poems as rigidly organized as a villanelle, and no complex forms like Spenserian stanzas or ottava rima. Perhaps because he wrote so many in college, Stevens was particularly averse to the sonnet. In "From the Journal of Crispin" (an early version of "The Comedian as the Letter C"), Stevens describes a sonnet as "fourteen laboring mules" with "gorgeous leathers, gurgling bells." After wondering if they can "Convey his being," he concludes he needs "A more condign / Contraption" (*Opus* 51). In a similar vein, Stevens wrote Reyher in 1921 that he wanted to dissuade his friend Pitts Sanborn from writing sonnets:

> I have stored a case of brandy in his cellar, hoping that the idea will invigorate him and get him away from sonnets on Phryne, and so on. Why anybody should write sonnets on Phryne when he can disguise himself as a laundryman and take in Mary Garden's wash I haven't any idea. ("Letters" 388)

The wonderfully named Mary Garden was a leading diva of the day, a famous beauty who attracted the kind of ardor that beautiful divas often attract. Obviously the archaic subject of the sonnets has something to do with his distaste, but Stevens clearly associates the sonnet with the dead and artificial, preferring inspiration and activity in the present to the forms of the past. "Sonnets have their place," he wrote in his journal, "but they can be found to be tremendously out of place: in real life, where things are quick, unaccountable, responsive" (*Souvenirs* 80). Real life requires the free growth of metrical laws.

In light of this, I find it hard to agree with Taylor's assertion that he finds sonnets embedded in Stevens's poems, such as in the final fourteen lines of "Man on the Dump." Stevens's attitude toward the sonnet suggests that the form would only be available to him for satire, not for the serious statement the poem concludes with. Besides, the resemblance to a sonnet is rather slight: the only formal resemblances the ending of "Dump" has to a sonnet is that it is fourteen lines long and has a rhyme (that is, one) in it.[13]

The same might be said for the notion that there is terza rima in Stevens's poetry. Terza rima is not just three-line stanzas; the rhymes must interlock ABA BCB CDC, and so on. Stevens's stanzas almost never interlock. Occasionally a few of his three-line stanzas rhyme, but the strong cohesion, the most salient part of terza rima, is simply missing. The stanzas are better described as long couplets, as they conform to couplet decorum better than Dantean ones. More precisely, they are three-line, occasionally rhyming stanzas in Stevens's typical later line. It may be true that the disembodied spirit of Dante's prosody lingers in Stevens's three-line stanzas; if so, I am not sure what to make of it. Unlike many other Moderns, Stevens never made a special study of Dante, and I find no specific influence. Perhaps a good dictum would be, "three-line stanzas do not a terza rima make."

While Stevens did not follow the traditions of stanzaic form, he was haunted by rhyme. His use of the device is distinctly Modern. A historical overview is useful. Although Eliot used rhyme significantly, it is hard to make the case that all rhyme achieves this much meaning. When Milton complained about "the jingling of like endings" in the preface to *Paradise Lost,* he critiqued the practice of using rhyme merely as an ornament. Although he ignored rhyme's semantic function, the preface mostly criticizes rhyme in "longer" poems and poets who use rhyme simply because they think they must. Thus when we find that Keats's "Epistle to John Hamilton Reynolds" rhymes, we should think nothing of it. The poet merely followed convention. However, for Modern poets continuing the loose tradition, rhyming or writing in meter was no longer *de rigueur.* Far from functioning as an automatic cohesive device, rhyme and meter for Stevens are always semantic, nearly always a device of surprise, and undergo the same kind of resensitizing in Stevens's poetry that capitalization underwent in Cummings's.

Like Cummings, Stevens created special prominence for the device by not using it automatically. Stevens's prose reveals that he subscribed to the theory of rhyme articulated by Wimsatt. In a 1909 letter to his then-fiancée, Stevens castigates himself for rhyming "breeze" with "trees," a rhyme specifically censured by Pope in *An Essay on Criticism*[14]:

> It is a correct rhyme, of course,—but unpardonably "expected." Indeed, none of my rhymes are (most likely) "true instruments of music." The words to be rhymed should not only sound alike, but they should enrich and deepen and enlarge each other, like two harmonious notes. (*Letters* 157)

Stevens expands upon the equation between rhyme and linked ideas in the essay "The Noble Rider and the Sound of Words":

> I do not know of anything that will appear to have suffered more from the passage of time than the music of poetry and that has suffered less. The deepening need for words to express our thoughts and feelings which, we are sure, are all the truth that we shall ever experience, having no illusions, makes us listen to words when we hear them, loving them and feeling them, makes us search the sound of them, for a finality, a perfection, an unalterable vibration, which is only within the power of the acutest poet to give them. (*Necessary* 32)

The "perfection" unavailable elsewhere is available partly in the sound of rhyme. Mervyn Nicholson calls attention to the tactile sensation, the "vibration," of the passage, movement that can be registered and is part of the "experience" of reading poetry. Nicholson points out that Stevens's essay "The Irrational Element of Poetry" begins with a description of the sound of a cat running in the snow which Stevens says is one of the "pretexts for poetry" (*Opus* 224). Nicholson adds that Stevens always had faith that the mind would interpret sounds and make a "correspondence" with the world or the self (62), which, he argues, precludes Stevens from endorsing proto-deconstruction. That is, sounds do not merely link words together in a closed system, but instead they touch (even tactilely) something in the reader.

"Suffered more . . . and suffered less," Stevens said. For example, "We no longer like Poe's tintinnabulations. You are free to tintinnabulate if you like. But others are equally free to put their hands over their ears" (*Opus* 230–31). On the other hand, Eliot's "Rhapsody on a Windy Night" is a "specimen of what is meant by music today," unlike the music of "yesterday," which was "metrical poetry and regular rhyme schemes" (*Necessary* 125). Today's music

> is like the change from Haydn to a voice intoning. It is like the voice of an actor reciting . . . who speaks with a measured voice which is often disturbed by his feeling for what he says. There is no accompaniment. If occasionally the poet touches the triangle or one of the cymbals, he does it only because he feels like doing it. Instead of a musician we have an orator whose speech sometimes resembles music. (*Necessary* 125–26)

In these words lurks the vestige of sublime theory, with passages of special import surrounded by less inspired ones. However, the paradigm is flipped. For Cowley, irregular metrics and rhyme interrupt what Stevens here calls a "musical" flow, whereas in Stevens it is often the reverse. The basis for the poetic line is speech, not music.

This theory accounts for the sporadic appearance of rhyme in *Harmonium*. "Invective against Swans," for example, has a rhyme scheme AB AC DC EF GH II,[15] thus beginning in rhyme, moving away from it in the middle, and returning to it at the end. The lines focusing on direct observation have no rhyme:

> Behold, already on the long parades
> The crows anoint the statues with their dirt.

Those focusing on transcendence do rhyme:

> And the soul, O ganders, being lonely, flies
> Beyond your chilly chariots, to the skies (4)

Consider the complexity of rhyme in the first stanza of "Le Monocle de Mon Oncle," which ends with its speaker thinking over what he has just sworn:

> And so I mocked her in magnificent measure.
> Or was it that I mocked myself alone?
> I wish that I might be a thinking stone.
> The sea of spuming thought foists up again
> The radiant bubble that she was. And then
> A deep up-pouring from some saltier well
> Within me, bursts its watery syllable. (13)

The introduction of the couplets—alone/stone, again/then—makes me want to pronounce the last word "sil-a-BELL," but the point seems to be that the rhyme is not perfect. It is an accordance not conforming to conventional notions. Something real has disrupted the speaker's ruminations. When the speaker addresses earthly vitality, there is alliteration aplenty and loose pentameter, but no rhyme:

> The measure of the intensity of love
> Is measure, also, of the verve of earth.
> For me, the firefly's quick, electric stroke
> Ticks tediously the time of one more year. (14–15)

The conclusion, however, rhymes ABBACBDEFEG:

A blue pigeon it is, that circles the blue sky,
On sidelong wing, around and round and round.
A white pigeon it is, that flutters to the ground,
Grown tired of flight. Like a dark rabbi, I
Observed, when young, the nature of mankind,
In lordly study. Every day, I found
Man proved a gobbet in my mincing world.
Like a rose rabbi, later, I pursued,
And still pursue, the origin and the course
Of love, but until now I never knew
That fluttering things made so distinct a shade. (17–18)

Thus, there is an aural link between the pigeon's circling (there is just one pigeon, "blue" when engaged in imaginative flights, "white" when exhausted) and the young Wordsworthian poet. But he is Wordsworth in reverse, because he arrives at his grand conclusions while young and becomes interested in particularities when he is older. To underscore the last line's sudden incursion into newness, the poem ends on an unexpected note, an unrhymed line that is doubly surprising because the "shade" with its long *a* is not at all anticipated by the poem. That is, "world" and "course" do not rhyme, but share an *or* sound, and the stanza has much alliteration and a few internal rhymes. But "shade"—in rhymed position, on an end-stopped line, and with all the special prominence of the last word of a poem in which the previous prosody has led the reader to expect a concluding rhyme—is unprecedented. If the last two lines instead were to read, for example,

but until now I never knew
That fluttering things were so distinctly blue.

the reader would have felt that a contract was kept. But Stevens means to depict a situation in which observation disrupts *a priori* poetical conceptions, and he uses prosody to enact, allegorically, just that.

One more example, from the end of "The Weeping Burgher":

Permit that if as ghost I come
Among the people burning in me still,
I come as belle design
Of foppish line.

> And I, then, tortured for old speech,
> A white of wildly woven rings;
> I, weeping in a calcined heart,
> My hands such sharp, imagined things. (61)

When the speaker talks of sorrows, the lines do not rhyme. When the speaker is foppish, he rhymes facilely. I cannot but read the final rhyme, which seems to describe a more "realistic" imaginative conception, as more satisfying than the affected rhyme of the previous stanza. Consistently, then, Stevens uses rhyme to indicate the action of the imagination when it puts things together, draws conclusions, makes judgments, or in some other way seeks closure. The first stanza of "The Emperor of Ice Cream," only rhymes in its last two lines when it interprets the import of its erotic deathliness. Doing this sort of thing is not Modern at all; *only* using rhyme in this way is.

Stevens employs meter in a similar, though not identical, manner. As is typical of his remarks about form, Stevens's comment on the line is diffident. "Now I have never worried about the line," Stevens told Edwin Honig. "I've always been interested in the whole thing, the whole poem" (qtd. in Lensing, *Wallace Stevens* 104). This is good organic theory, but a false dichotomy. A poet can be interested both in his line and in "the whole thing." Stevens's comment does, however, suggest a relation between the line and the larger poem, and points to a procedure for modal lineation that persists throughout his poetry. In the *Harmonium* period, Stevens's typical line is an iambic pentameter that avoids syntactical inversion and frequently substitutes trisyllables. However, he was sensitive enough to the effects of regularity to notice it in others. After reading a book of poems by Samuel French Morse, Stevens wrote to the younger poet praising "the insistent use of iambics" that "must be deliberate, as a contribution to the New England effect, and certainly as part of the tone" (*Letters* 437). Since Stevens's New England is a cold place of worldly rather than imaginative concerns, his comment hints that he found regular, "insistent" meter austere and narrow though still evocative.[16]

Thus, when regular meter combines with regular rhyme, there should be a special insistence on things being brought together in a narrow compass. And this is exactly the case of "The Bird with the Coppery, Keen Claws." The bird lives apart from reality, "Above the forest of parakeets" (it is an ideal bird, "the parakeet of parakeets"), and is blind and unmoving. It is unaffected by the distinctive shades that consoled Stevens's monocled uncle. The poem ends,

But though the turbulent tinges undulate
As his pure intellect applies its laws,
He moves not on his coppery, keen claws.

He munches a dry shell while he exerts
His will, yet never ceases, perfect cock,
To flare, in the sun-pallor of his rock. (82)

The "tinges" are the bird's tail feathers. The bird is unresponsive and removed, perfect though motionless. He may not be the supreme fiction Stevens tended to advocate, but this bird does have tail feathers that "deploy . . . green-vented forms," and thus is potent. The sense is that the bird writes the poem, or rather that the regular meter and rhyme (the poem rhymes ABB CDD and so on) reflects the bird's similar unyielding perfection. Thus the lineal form allegorizes the constricting, though powerful and in its way satisfying, idea of order. The unrhymed line in each stanza does not match up, but then of course the bird is uninterested in accounting for everything.

For Stevens and poets like him, unvarying rhyme and meter accompany conceptions of the world more narrow than the poet likely endorses. This formal allegory is evident in "The Man Whose Pharynx Was Bad." Both food and air pass through the pharynx, so the title implies the man has trouble getting sustenance and, perhaps, pleasure:

The time of year has grown indifferent.
Mildew of summer and the deepening snow
Are both alike in the routine I know.
I am too dumbly in my being pent.

The wind attendant on the solstices
Blows on the shutters of the metropoles,
Stirring no poet in his sleep, and tolls,
The grand ideas of the villages. (96)

Line four calls to mind Keats's sonnet "To One Who Has Been Long in City Pent" (a double echo because Keats was rewriting Milton's *Paradise Lost* IX 445ff.).[17] Yet the man is caught in himself and not London. The regular rhymes and fairly regular meter attend the unbreakable "routine."[18] "Solstices" and "villages" come close to satisfying my ear, but surprises my eye. All the accordances feel just a bit off.

When the speaker imagines breaking through the commonplace, the lock-step progression of the seasons, the rhyme breaks too:

> The malady of the quotidian . . .
> Perhaps, if winter could penetrate
> Through all its purples to the final slate,
> Persisting bleakly in an icy haze (orig. ellipses)

That is, the abstract, imaginative conception rhymes, but the new vision of reality does not. When the speaker gives up this notion, the rhymes and iambs come striding:

> One might in turn become less diffident,
> Out of such mildew plucking neater mould
> And spouting new orations of the cold.
> One might. One might. But time will not relent.

The last line could hardly be more "insistent" and "deliberate." Though the poem has many iambic lines, in the last, word boundaries coincide with foot boundaries. Compare

> per-SIS ting-BLEAK ly-IN an-I cy-HAZE

with

> one-MIGHT one-MIGHT but-TIME will-NOT re-LENT

Both lines are regular, but only the second is really "insistent."

The keen bird and the man with pharyngitis illustrate the sensitivity to form common to the Moderns. Stevens cannot write an ABBA quatrain without worrying that such regularity might involve some falsification or unwarranted narrowness. Ford Madox Ford thought writing in iambic pentameter necessarily involved periphrasis; Stevens was not quite the enemy of rhetoric and conventional poeticism that Ford was, but he likewise considered strict form imposing too much. Rhyme and meter for Stevens indicate the handiwork of the artist. When a poem refers to tradition too regularly, the reader is supposed to feel the hand of the artist especially forcefully. *Harmonium*'s poems about the natural world, such as "Earthy Anecdote," "In the Carolinas," "The Jack Rabbit," "Life Is Motion," and "Thirteen Ways of Looking at a Blackbird," are the volume's "freest," the poems with the least relation to a metrical tradition, loose or otherwise. Thus, the second section of "Peter Quince at the Clavier," which describes Susanna's sensual encounter with nature, is in free verse with short lines,[19] while the conclusion, which celebrates the immortality of the idea of beauty, does so in relatively metrical lines largely divided between iambic pentameter and lines stressed U / U / U / U / U. The section has an ABBCDDEFFGGGHIJJI rhyme scheme with a majority of the rhymes feminine. By nineteenth-century standards, the versification is free, but by twentieth-century standards, it is traditional—though still, I think, meant to be satisfying.

Since rhyme and meter bring the artist to the reader's attention, Stevens's couplets take on particular import. The concision needed to bring off a neat couplet suggested to Stevens a narrow rightness of viewpoint. Thus, the epigrams of "New England Verses" appear in pairs, as if to acknowledge that the single viewpoints expressed are not all-inclusive. Hence *"Boston with a Note-book"* says the scholar can labor without much interaction with the phenomenal world:

> Lean encyclopædists, inscribe an Iliad.
> There's a weltanschauung of the penny pad.

That is, the pad he writes on is its own *welt* and has an *anschauung* to go with it. *"Boston without a Note-book,"* however, is more Emersonian:

> Let us erect in the Basin a lofty fountain.
> Suckled on ponds, the spirit craves a watery mountain.

It argues that the scholar's real text is the world, that there is an earthly vitality not within the penny pad's ken. The two perspectives are not really contradictory; each displays an attitude, and the meter and rhyme hint that there is something pat, perhaps contrived, about what is being said. It is a fiction, with all the satisfactions and potential falsity of Peter Quince's music.

These paradigms continue through all of Stevens's poems. For example, *"The Mechanical Optimist"* (section I of "A Thought Revolved") describes a "lady dying of diabetes" listening to the radio,

Catching the lesser dithyrambs.
So heaven collects its bleating lambs. (184)

The couplet is a good example of Popean satiric antithesis: whatever "dithyramb" should pair up with, it should not be "lambs." Likewise, the suggestively named poem, "Anything Is Beautiful If You Say It Is," enacts the prosodic drama common in *Harmonium*. The poem begins with deliberately affected rhymes:

Under the eglantine
The fretful concubine
Said, "Phooey! Phoo!"
She whispered, "Pfui!" (211)

It ends with a closer examination of reality *sans* rhyme:

And the window's lemon light,
The very will of the nerves,
The crack across the pane,
The dirt along the sill.

In "The News and the Weather," meter and rhyme march along satirically as Mr. United States, deliberately ignoring "picket lines," goes on parade, and rhymes and iambs march along with him:

His red cockade topped off a parade.
His manner took what it could find,

In the greenish greens he flung behind
And the sound of pianos in his mind. (264)

Green is usually a propitious color in Stevens, the color of spring and potentiality, but Mr. U.S. is interested only in "manner" and discards refreshment and music. Part II of the poem, about the "deep breath" that "fetches another year of life," (265), is noticeably free of rhyme and regular meter.

There is one more aspect of rhythm to attend to. Consider poem XII of "Like Decorations in a Nigger Cemetery":

> The comedy of hollow sounds derives
> From truth and not from satire on our lives.
> Clog, therefore, purple Jack and crimson Jill. (154)

Such poems prevent the interpretation that all of Stevens's metrical rhythms are parodic. The formality helps foreground the subjectivity of the speaker (one that, by the way, believes in "truth"). This reconstituted (perhaps sexualized) nursery rhyme is a peculiar mode in Stevens that is not satiric. Compare, for example, the first two stanzas of "Continual Conversation with a Silent Man," which begin in the manner of Mother Goose before moving to Stevens's more customary contemplative mode:

> The old brown hen and the old blue sky,
> Between the two we live and die—
> The broken cartwheel on the hill.
>
> As if, in the presence of the sea,
> We dried our nets and mended sail
> And talked of never-ending things (359)

The title indicates that the poem is a meditation. It mediates between the decay of age (Stevens was sixty-six when he wrote the poem) and the eternity of the earth. When the speaker and his companions speak of things that never end, they are implicitly comparing their mortality with timeless natural processes. The repaired sails, emblems of human frailty, will not be as strong as new ones and will inevitably fail, while the sea will continue unchanged. Humans do their best despite knowing that they will degenerate and die. It seems the "Silent Man" is the world, whose voice is not human speech but Heraclitean aimlessness. But the poem does not really depict the struggle of will versus the wind; instead, it implies the inevitable triumph of the wind.

Nursery rhymes are sometimes thought to refer to archetypes. Whether Stevens believed they did, these types of rhythms suggest an ever-renewing vitality that energizes the young but enervates the old, reminding the latter that each successive manifestation dies even as the archetype prevails. That which freshens, kills. It is all related, as is the jauntiness that the poem begins with and the somber conclusion with its intimations of personal danger. In Stevens's prosody, the irregular rhythm testifies to the truth of the relation.

Stevens's later line is typically long. He told Katherine Frazer of the Cummington Press, "My line is a pentameter line, but it runs over and under now and then" (*Letters* 407). Harvey Gross counted syllables in the first section of "Notes to a Supreme Fiction" and found that Stevens goes over more than half the time and under not at all:

90 lines	10 syllables
83 lines	11 syllables
28 lines	12 syllables
7 lines	13 syllables
2 lines	14 syllables (324)

As Justice points out, "[T]he foot itself is loosened in almost exclusively one direction: the anapest takes the place of the basic iamb" (67). But when unstressed feet start cropping up, foot boundaries become blurred. Lensing describes the same phenomenon as "extending the heroic line toward accentual verse and perhaps free verse" ("Stevens'" 407). The difference between the two judgments is a matter of terminology. It likens to George Saintsbury's claim that Coleridge's "Christabel" is "really" just loose tetrameter: when a poet writing an accentual-syllabic poem stops counting syllables precisely, the verse approaches (and sometimes amounts to) accentualism.

Stevens uses his extra syllables so that he can avoid meter-keeping poeticisms like excising or eliding articles, syntactical inversion, and contraction. It is easy to link this to keeping his language Modern, and further indicates that when Stevens does invert (such as when he writes "I am too dumbly in my being pent") the reader is supposed to recognize the speaker is being self-consciously "poetic." Most have found between four and six stresses in Stevens's later line, but again it is difficult to scan because in a strictly regular scheme often words like "of" are stressed; when the pattern is less predictable, the rule that the middle of three successive unstressed syllables takes stress may or may not apply, and so determining minor stress is largely a matter of taste. However, Stevens never called his later line loose hexameter or loose tetrameter.

Despite the fact that Stevens in general expressed great disdain for poems in which "the exploitation of form involves nothing more than the use of small capitals, eccentric word-endings, too little or too much punctuation, and similar aberrations" (*Necessary* 168),[20] he was interested in the way his poems looked. After he became financially secure, he had copies of his later books printed with fine bindings, high-quality paper, and marbleized endpapers. When writing out a poem by hand, if he saw a line that looked too short, he would space words out so that the line would look longer. This led to a book of poems in which the printer repeated this spacing. Stevens wrote to his publisher to complain (see *Letters* 325–26). Even after the printing error, he continued the practice, though he was careful to warn the publisher of a subsequent book that he did not "believe in queer punctuation"; he just wanted to make the "page of poetry look decent" (*Letters* 387). Stevens seems to have wanted the publisher to use subtle, unnoticeable manipulations in typography to make the lines look longer. This visual prosody was important enough for Stevens that he offered to rewrite a line to avoid a "tag end" (*Letters* 407) if the line could not be made to fit on a single line by small changes in type.

Stevens's "decent," then, means, "looking like iambic pentameter." His later pentameter tends to be generic rather than formal. The repetitions and general meditative nature characteristic of Stevens's later poetry suggest it is a Wordsworthian line generically—but not formally, as the Romantic poet enjambs much more than Stevens did. However, just because Stevens used space to organize his poetry does not mean he did not hear it. Stevens used two kinds of loose prosody (i.e., loose pentameter and a visual prosody) to replace traditional, "tighter" prosody.

I have shown that Stevens's rhymes are sites of special testing grounds for the artist's ability to construct imaginatively satisfactory relations. Rhyme and meter highlight the fictive nature of the construct. In particular, rhyme, a site of resolution for traditional poets, in Stevens is often a site of crisis, not asserting so much as asking whether the artist's composition satisfies. Nowhere is this clearer than in Stevens's extended meditation on rhyme, "The Man with the Blue Guitar." The poem begins with the guitarist bending over his instrument, and "They," society, complaining,

> "You have a blue guitar,
> You do not play things as they are."

The artist replies,

> "Things as they are
> Are changed upon the blue guitar."

Society wants a song about reality; the artist rejoins that art necessarily transforms reality. "They" will have none of what they apparently see as self-indulgent aestheticism. They instruct the guitarist to play

> A tune beyond us, yet ourselves
>
> A tune upon the blue guitar
> Of things exactly as they are

Society wants to have its cake and eat it too: it wants fidelity to fact and abstraction, idealism and realism. Society cannot stand airy abstraction or unrelenting realism—oh, and it wants it all in a song. This is a tall order for a social philosopher and a taller one for an artist interested in his own aesthetic explorations. That society's demand on the artist oversimplifies, in that it seems to feel it can just shout out requests that the artist will somehow find a way to satisfy, is signaled by the repeating "guitar / are" rhyme and the regular meter.

The first section also sets up a pattern of statement and variation that occurs many times in the poem. One of the reasons Stevens puts his man on a guitar ("blue" because it is imaginative) is that Stevens's guitar is a particularly rhythmic instrument. Stevens himself owned a guitar and could play a little. I suspect he knew a few chords and played them over and over. This seems to be suggested when he wrote to Jose Rodriguez Feo, "Are you visiting some new scene? A young man in a new scene, a new man in a young scene, a young man in a young scene—excuse my guitar" (*Letters* 767). The thought is turned and turned and turned in a manner reminiscent of Gertrude Stein. "Blue Guitar" likewise turns its thought again and again, attempting to mediate between "guitar" (the artist and his art) and "are" (reality and social concerns).

Readers looking to enjoy "Blue Guitar" had better learn to love the "are / guitar" rhyme, because it recurs many times throughout the poem, especially in the first seven sections. After that it occurs in its full form only three times, but the poem often seems to refer to the rhyme, putting "blue guitar" in seven sections at a rhyme position (i.e., at the end of a line) and "are" at two others. That is to say, the ghost of the rhyme haunts the poem. Thus, section XX ends,

> Believe would be a brother full
> Of love, believe would be a friend,

Friendlier than my only friend,
Good air. Poor pale, poor pale guitar . . . (175–76)

"Oh where are you, my beloved 'are'?" the last line seems to cry. Significantly, the lines lamenting the lack of belief assert the guitar but miss the "are." Faith presumes a reality that cannot be objectively verified. The only reality section XX affirms is that of air, which, however "good," is insubstantial and by definition empty (bad air is air with something in it).

As might be expected in a long poem about rhyme, early sections in the sequence depict unsatisfactory accordances. Section II explains that heroic portrayals of humanity do not capture their subject adequately:

I cannot bring the world quite round,
Although I patch it as I can.

I sing a hero's head, large eye
And bearded bronze, but not a man,

Although I patch him as I can
And reach through him almost to man.

If to serenade almost to man
Is to miss, by that, things as they are,

Say that it is the serenade
Of a man that plays a blue guitar. (165–66)

The easy rhymes and strict meter of many of these lines help indicate that the artist is particularly at work here, conforming reality to fit his conceptions. His song is a "serenade," a love song, and as such tells more of its singer's ardor than of his subject. Sonnet sequences are notorious for providing a full portrait of their speakers and a cardboard cutout of their beloveds.

The rumination on the dangers of appreciation more beholden to prior conceptions than to the flux of reality continues in sections III and IV. In section III, the artist turns brain surgeon, anatomizing human thought; the speaker calls the process

To strike his living hi and ho,
To tick it, tock it, turn it true,

To bang it from a savage blue,
Jangling the metal of the strings . . . (166)

toTICK itTOCK itTURN itTRUE: for once the metronome metaphor seems appropriate. "True" here is used as a carpenter uses the term, "make it level, square, balanced or concentric: bring it or restore it to a desired mechanical accuracy or form" (as *Webster's Third* puts it). The metal strings testify to the unyielding aspect of the instrument, and however gleeful the artist's song, there is something savage about it.

"Metal" strings, because though nylon strings are easier to fret, they do not provide the dynamics that metal strings do. Stevens must have known that if you do not press down hard enough on the strings, your chords will buzz. Thus, the buzzing in section IV:

So that's life then: things as they are?
It picks its way on the blue guitar.

A million people on one string?
And all their manner in the thing,

And all their manner, right and wrong,
And all their manner, weak and strong?

The feelings crazily, craftily call,
Like a buzzing of flies in autumn air,

And that's life, then: things as they are,
This buzzing of the blue guitar. (166–67)

The section proceeds in lock-step meter until the feelings enter into it, then suddenly the rhyme breaks and there is trisyllabic substitution. The serenade is disrupted, and the reader is encouraged to regard the dissonance—the untrueness in section III's terms—as more natural (since it mimics the flies' buzz), more according with "are" than the preceding neat couplets.

The same dialectic appears in section VIII, which pits "feelings" against the artist's "reason." The "cold chords" of "feeling" in the storm are

> Crying among the clouds, enraged
> By gold antagonist in air—
>
> I know my lazy, leaden twang
> Is like the reason in a storm;
>
> And yet it brings the storm to bear.
> I twang it out and leave it there. (169)

Eight low words creep in each of the last two lines, with word boundaries obeying foot boundaries, much unlike the lines describing the storm. The language of reason seems reductivist in relation to the storm, and one wonders why the artist should bring the storm "to bear" at all.

After the first fourteen sections, a significant transformation occurs in "Blue Guitar." From section XV to section XXIV there are no rhymes aside from words which rhyme with themselves. When rhyme does reenter, it does so in a big way:

> He held the world upon his nose
> And this-a-way he gave a fling.
>
> His robes and symbols, ai-yi-yi—
> And that-a-away he twirled the thing.
>
> Sombre as fir-trees, liquid cats
> Moved in the grass without a sound.
>
> They did not know the grass went round.
> The cats had cats and the grass turned gray
>
> And the world had worlds, ai, this-a-way:
> The grass turned green and the grass turned gray.
>
> The nose is eternal, that-a-way.
> Things as they were, things as they are,

Things as they will be by and by . . .
A fat thumb beats out ai-yi-yi. (178)

The rhyme scheme, AB CB DE ED GG DF CC, is fully interlocking, and, with the return of the C rhyme, a certain circularity is attained. As in "Continual Conversation," the rocking rhythms accompany descriptions of the periodicity of the earth, and this time the speaker sings without recognition of his own mortality. Like section III, joviality is attained at the expense of overlooking human pain.

If section XXV is a riot of rhyme, section XXX is the reverse:

From this I shall evolve a man.
This is his essence: the old fantoche

Hanging his shawl upon the wind,
Like something on the stage, puffed out,

His strutting studied through centuries.
At last, in spite of his manner, his eye

A-cock at the cross-piece on a pole
Supporting heavy cables, slung

Through Oxidia, banal suburb,
One-half of all its installments paid.

Dew-dapper clapper-traps, blazing
From crusty stacks above machines.

Ecce, Oxidia is the seed
Dropped out of this amber-ember pod,

Oxidia is the soot of fire,
Oxidia is Olympia. (181–82)

The section replays section II, this time constructing a comic figure instead of a tragic one. The successive transformations are startling—the human is described as a puppet, whose eye follows the strings which control him to the "cross-piece," looking upward for the puppeteer, an image of humans looking for God, with the eye settling on, significantly, a cross; this is suddenly transformed to telephone poles in a rusty old suburb (Stevens said the name was "from Oxide" [*Letters* 790]), to the smokestacks which made it rusty, finally to Olympia, the abode of the gods. The subject of the section transforms as well, turning from "man" to his place. The pararhymes (e.g., "pod" and "paid"), repeating words, and other repeating sounds help the section cohere, but in "Blue Guitar" excessive rhyming generally accompanies repetition, the same idea going round. Thus in a section about transformation, rhymes do not occur.

From what I have argued, a satisfying conclusion should rhyme but not too much, and it should refer to meter but avoid perfect regularity. The conclusion offers "bread of time to come," something sustaining, but only sporadically:

> we shall sleep by night.
> We shall forget by day, except
>
> The moments when we chose to play
> The imagined pine, the imagined jay. (184)

Note especially the scansion of the last couplet: U / U / U / U / // U U / U / U U / U /. The extra unstressed syllables prevent a singsong conclusion, and the poem offers an entirely new rhyme (one might have expected a final encore of "are" / "guitar") for its end. The pronoun, too, announces a conjunction. No longer "they" and "I," it is now "we," and we are cooperating, not making demands on one another. As section XXV transforms its subject from humans to their place (and Stevens was willing to write in "Theory," "I am what is around me" [86]), the attention of the larger poem shifts from the artist creating alone in a garret to a cooperative effort to make a better society, or, put more accurately, to perceive in such a way as to make life bearable. To put it another way, the artist helps society see that Oxidia is at least potentially Olympia.

If "Blue Guitar" is Stevens's most rhyming poem, it is his most repeating one as well. Repetition is a kind of patterning in Stevens's verse that distinguishes his freer poems in shorter lines in *Harmonium* from the meditative voice in the later poetry. Mary Doyle Springer links Stevens's repeating strategy to the repetitions of Gertrude Stein, quoting Stein's theory that "there is no such thing as repetition. And really how can there be." Springer adds, "No two occurrences are alike—what sounds like repetition is actually what Stein calls beginning again and again, 'with new insistence, with the freshness of children, and not what might and might have been'" (193). Springer goes on to distinguish among "recollection" (which "merely re-collects what has happened"), unceasing pointless change, and "willed repetition" (in which a poet chooses "not the spanking new, but the fresh rediscovery as a basis for renewal") (198). She argues that Stevens's repetitions are of the third sort. I find Springer's argument convincing for some of Stevens's poetry but not for his verse in shorter lines. Consider the first poem in *The Collected Poems,* where "the bucks" go clattering over Oklahoma,

> Until they swerved
> In a swift, circular line
> To the right,
> Because of the firecat.

The next stanza exactly replicates these lines, adding only an initial "or" and substituting "left" for "right." Springer argues that the poem "allows us to rest in the suggestive assurance that tomorrow morning the firecat will begin again—and again," but that this is not repetition, because now "we know" about the bucks, and besides they do not just clatter, they swerve in two directions. This reading seems overly sanguine. Springer seems to have lost sight of what the word repetition means. Of course we "know"; knowing does not preclude repetition, it is a necessary precondition of it. Personally, I derive little excitement from the variation, left to right. The point of the variation seems to be that variation does not make much difference. Left, right, it is all the same, the clattering bucks are now swerving in swift arcs.

Since Springer does not recognize that Stevens uses differing verse forms to signal differing modalities, she does not consider that, like the keen-clawed bird, "Earthy Anecdote" offers a conception of the world that is beautiful within its own narrow compass. Eliot's repetition in "Prufrock" seems to offer something like Stevens's meaningless repetition. When the women come and go talking about Michelangelo the second time, the words are repeated exactly, giving the impression that the same thing is happening exactly, a periodicity refreshing for the seasons but stultifying for discussions of art.

Thus Stevens's and Eliot's bald repetitions seem to have the feeling of senselessness. "Domination of Black" helps show that Stevens's repetition insists as well. Anca Rosu writes of the latter poem, "The sense of these repetitions seems to be that everything is reminiscent of everything else" (185)—everything, that is, in the restricted world of the poem, which is limited to fire, leaves, wind, hemlocks, and peacocks, all of which are related to what Rosu characterizes as "a suggestion of death." This sort of repetition does repeat: it means to depict perfect systems of order that do not incorporate, or are unconcerned with, the human.

However, Springer's comments on repetition do a good job describing a poem from the middle part of Stevens's career like "Martial Cadenza." The musical term in the title suggests that the reader should anticipate a solo variation upon a larger theme (as well as bringing to mind "cadenced verse," a synonym for free verse in the teens and twenties). The poem's occasion is its speaker trying to interpret the meaning of "it," the evening star (traditionally associated with love) in a time of war. The poem ends,

> Yet it is this that shall maintain—Itself
> Is time, apart from the past, apart
> From any future, the ever-living and being,
> The ever-breathing and moving, the constant fire,
>
> The present close, the present realized,
> Not the symbol but that for which the symbol stands,
> The vivid thing in the air that never changes,
> Though the air change. Only this evening I saw it again,
> At the beginning of winter, and I walked and talked
> Again, and lived and was again, and breathed again
> And moved again and flashed again, time flashed again. (238)

This is the ever-freshening new Springer described, and the repeating phrases do not exactly repeat, but undergo constant variation. Take the word "again." The poem moves from "Talked / again" to "was again" to "breathed again" to "moved again" to "flashed again" (referring to the speaker) to "flashed again" (referring to time). The varying verbs stress the successive reimaginings of the speaker, while the repeating complement, "again," stresses the continuity of the star.

This same procedure occurs in section XXV of "Blue Guitar," and at other times when Stevens dramatizes the imagination trying to get a hold of something. In "Martial Cadenza," it is "Not the symbol but that for which the symbol stands." It should not be surprising, then, that something of this sort goes on in the last poem in *The Collected Poems,* "Not Ideas about the Thing But the Thing Itself," in which the speaker hears "a scrawny cry" which "Seemed like a sound within his mind." The speaker dismisses the notion that the cry is a "vast ventriloquism" (with God, presumably, the ventriloquist). The final six lines begin by repeating the occasion of the poem:

> That scrawny cry—it was
> A chorister whose c preceded the choir.
> It was part of the colossal sun,
>
> Surrounded by its choral rings,
> Still far away. It was like
> A new knowledge of reality. (534)

The *c* puns off the musical chord, but it is still the *c* of "Comedian." "Chorister" / "choir" / "choral" varies the same idea, but the scrawny cry, like the evening star, remains unchanged. It is the speaker's knowledge that changes. Here as everywhere in Stevens, reality doggedly repeats itself; that which is distinctly human moves toward meaning. Since Stevens's rhymes are rarely predictable, his repetitions perform the same aural function as his rhymes. When the repetitions vary, again the reader is encouraged to read this as a particularly crisis-prone act of the mind. Semantically, however, there is a significant difference, as rhyme brings together two things, while varied repetition tends to pursue just one.

In the way that "Prufrock" demonstrates the continuity of genre, Stevens's canon shows the continuity of mode. In a sense, the decorum Stevens followed in "Ode," which is the same decorum Wordsworth observed, split into two differing systems of poems: short-line "freer" poems, which I will discuss in the next chapter, and "haunted poems," which eventually sought to invoke the manner of iambic pentameter while not following the rules very closely. For Stevens, an apt metaphor might be that of a mechanic creating a new car mostly from the parts of an old one. The old car will not really take you where you want to go, but the new car is built along the lines of the old one, and uses old parts not for new purposes, just a bit differently than before.

The Modern poetry of Eliot and Stevens extend the loose tradition of verse, endorsing the loose tradition's claims of greater transport and closer ties to reality and inspiration. Modern poetry of this nature does not turn its back on tradition, but extrapolates upon a tendency already over two hundred and fifty years old. The Modern period continued the trend of putting structures into the unexpectable category, while making those already in that category even more unstable. Finally, with such an unstable framework, it should not be surprising that Stevens and Eliot turned to repetition to supply some of the coherence poetry loses as it moves away from meter and rhyme. Repetition has one advantage over rhyme and alliteration—it repeats the same word as well as repeating the same sound. As Stevens and Eliot proceeded to the poetry of statement in their later periods, it makes sense that they should worry a little less about tintinnabulating and a little more about the continuity of ideas.

CHAPTER FOUR

Straight Talk, Straight as the Greeks

A certain heterogeneity, juxtaposing traditional and more contemporary (i.e., "free") modes, is central to the ghost-of-meter paradigm. In contrast, the short-line poetry that flowered in Imagism offers a kind of homogeneity that follows its own set of decorums, tending to exclude other modes. The many traditional elements in haunted free verse have led some to conclude that it is not free verse at all,[1] but nearly everyone regards the short-line verse of Williams and H.D. as free. Because it does not follow traditional prosody's decorums, this mode of poetry is commonly considered to be peculiar to the twentieth century. However, the short line associated with Imagism, the starting point of much twentieth-century free verse, also grew out of traditional poetics. After showing the importance of translation theory for H.D.'s poetic, especially her grammatical line decorum, I will spend some time establishing the tradition of classical imitation that influenced H.D. before returning to the prosody of her early poetry.

During her lifetime, H.D. was often acknowledged to be the Imagist *par excellance:* Pound's first manifesto on Imagism was accompanied by an H.D. poem as an exemplar; Lowell set out to prove to Dr. Patterson that free verse had a rhythm different from prose by reading rhythmically H.D.'s "Oread"; in 1924, Louis Untermeyer entitled his appraisal of her poetry, "The Perfect Imagist." Though in the past twenty years attention has shifted to her later works and her prose, her stature as a founder of Imagism has, if anything, grown. Those paying close attention to dates, like Cyrena Pondrom, have pointed out that H.D. wrote Imagist poems before the movement existed. "Many writers and literary historians," adds Susan Stanford Friedman, "have speculated that Pound created the Imagist movement to describe the poems H.D. was writing" ("H.D." 122). Given the impact of Imagism on twentieth-century lyric verse, describing

H.D.'s early verse is tantamount to describing one of the century's most prevalent approaches to poetry.

Friedman suggests Pound's association with T. E. Hulme in 1908 was an important influence on Pound, and, through him, the Imagism of H.D. Still, Hulme's own poetry was generally not very Modern. The epigraph to his poem, "Mana Aboda," for example—"Beauty is the marking-time, the stationary vibration, the feigned ecstasy of an arrested impulse unable to reach its natural"—is much more adventurous than the actual poem:

> Mana Aboda, whose bent form
> The sky in archèd circle is,
> Seems ever for an unknown grief to mourn.
> Yet on a day I heard a cry:
> "I weary of the roses and the singing poets—
> Josephs all, not tall enough to try." (266)

With its inverted syntax and grave accent to signal an uncolloquial voicing of a syllable, the second line especially shows traditional versification's strong influence on Hulme. Whatever Hulme's influence on Pound and H.D., he does not seem to have provided many prosodic ideas.

H.D.'s own account of how she became an Imagist is probably the best evidence of whether Pound was her teacher or student. She explains in her memoir, *End to Torment,* that she showed a poem to Pound, who exclaimed, "But Dryad . . . this is poetry":

> He slashed with a pencil. "Cut this out, shorten this here. 'Hermes of the Ways' is a good title. I'll send it to Harriet Monroe of *Poetry.* Have you a copy? Yes? Then we can send this, or I'll type it when I get back. Will this do?" And he scrawled "H.D., Imagiste" at the bottom of the page. (18)

Though the anecdote demonstrates that Pound made some lines more concise, he no more wrote the poem than he wrote *The Waste Land.* H.D. evidently learned from her association from Pound, but for the most part she developed her short line apart from him.

Of course, the sources of Imagism are various. Most agree that the movement revolted against the didactic, moralizing poetry of the nineteenth century by creating a lyric poetry focused on the image. The Imagists themselves and subsequent scholars have cited precedents in the lyric verse of Japan, ancient

Greece, Provence, and nineteenth-century France, as well as Ernest Fenollosa's theories about the Chinese written character.

So where did H.D.'s line come from? The obvious answer would seem to be from ancient Greece, since her poems have often struck readers as classically derived.[2] Pound characterized her early verse as "straight talk, straight as the Greeks" (II.80). Thomas Burnett Swann points out that thirty-five of the eighty-nine poems in *Collected Poems* (1925) have classical titles, and most of the rest of the poems employ classical subject or allude to classical literature (3). The appendix to Eileen Gregory's *H.D. and Hellenism* lists even more classical allusions, though it includes more "broad" and "speculative" references (233). Barbara Guest quotes from C. M. Bowra's *Ancient Greek Literature,* which describes the Greek spirit as "simplicity" gained by omitting anything "unessential" and emphasizing "what seems structurally or emotionally important," thus avoiding "the sentimental and merely decorative." Guest comments, "H.D. set out to achieve this distinction Bowra attributes to the Greeks" (44).

Nevertheless, H.D. did not get her poetic "straight" from the Greek, at least not in 1913. When Swann wrote to H.D. about the influence of Greek literature on her works, he asked if her early works were perhaps more influenced by translations than by the originals. H.D. replied, "Yes, I read very little Greek, and what possible translations there were—Gilbert Murray's prose rather than his poetry" (10). Further, Glenn Hughes cites a letter in which H.D. remarks that near the time she was creating her first Imagist poems she had enjoyed reading Latin poetry of the Renaissance, partly because it was "easy to read" (11). Swann remarks that H.D. could not read "difficult works" until she was in her late twenties. Since H.D. was born in 1886, this means that when she was composing *Sea Garden* (1916), she had just begun serious study of the translation of classical languages. This would seem to explain why, as I shall show, the procedures and tasks of the translator are intimately connected to her poetic.

Gregory notes that H.D.'s formal training in classical languages consisted of learning Latin in high school and studying Greek independently, adding that H.D. "never had, nor aspired to, any but an amateur knowledge of" classical languages (55). However, Gregory also points out that while H.D.'s knowledge of Greek and Latin was not "profound," neither was the knowledge of such Modern classicists as Pound and Aldington. Pound's idiosyncratic, loose, and mis-translations are well known and yet often understood as part of a new approach to translation. H.D.'s lack of easy fluency in classical languages,

Gregory maintains, does not mean "she did not have considerable knowledge of primary and secondary sources" (55).

Gregory argues at length that H.D.'s reaction to Murray and the late nineteenth- and early twentieth-century brand of classicism he helped create and propagate was one of her constant preoccupations. More importantly for this study, H.D.'s preference for Murray's prose over his poetry indicates something of her Modern temperament. If she had been more enthralled with Murray's poetry, she would have never become an Imagist. Here is Murray's translation from lines 1407–12 from Aeschylus's *Agamemnon*—a play that Gregory remarks was particularly resonant in the Modern era[3]—a strophe rather late in the play in which the chorus just realizes that Clytemnestra has killed her husband:

> Woman, what evil tree,
> What poison grown of the ground,
> Or draught of the drifting sea,
> Way to thy lips hath found,
> Making thee clothe thy heart
> In rage, yea, in curses burning
> When thine own people pray?
> Thou has hewn, thou has cut away;
> And a thing cast away thou art,
> A thing of hate and spurning! (133)

Like other verse translations, this one (line four in particular) struggles mightily between the Scylla of the difficulty of the Greek source and the Charybdis of traditional English lineal form. Such a translation, accurate, perhaps even musical to some ears, nevertheless seems strained and ornamental, much different from the austere simplicity associated with Greek art.

When Murray puts Greek poetry into prose, however, the results are more poetic to a Modern ear. Compare the directness of his prose translation from *Prometheus Bound*[4]:

> There is a cry in the waves as they fall together, a groaning in the deep; a wail comes up from the cavern realms of Death, and the springs of holy waters sob with the anguish of Pity. (*History* 220)

It seems just to observe that H.D.'s preference for Murray's prose over his poetry was at least as much a matter of good taste as it was instruction from Pound. The connection between such prose translations and H.D.'s Imagist verse is even more striking when Murray's prose is broken into lines as H.D. might have broken them. Take, for example, a lineated version of Murray's prose translation of an orphic hymn with a title similar to the poem Pound slashed:

I call Hecate of the Ways,
of the cross-ways,
of the Heaven and the Earth,
and the sea;
saffron-clad goddess
of the grave
exulting amid
the spirits of the dead

Perseia,
lover of loneliness,
Queen who holdest
the Keys of the World,
be present,
at our pure service
with the fullness
of joy
in their hearts (*History* 66)

Compare to this these lines from "Hermes of the Ways":

I know him
of the triple path-ways,
Hermes,
who awaits.
Dubious,
facing three ways,
welcoming wayfarers,
he whom the sea-orchard
shelters from the west,
from the east
weathers sea-wind;
fronts the great dunes. (37–38)

The two poems exemplify three features characteristic of H.D.: relatively short lines, an absence of traditional rhyme and meter, and the decorum that each line presents a discrete grammatical unit. This is not to say that H.D.'s poetry, and thus Imagism and much of twentieth-century free verse, is just warmed-over Gilbert Murray. Though Murray's prose translations exemplify the direct approach typical of H.D., the prosody I gave "Hecate of the Ways" is H.D.'s.

The question remains—from where did H.D. get her linear decorum? William Pratt argues that H.D.'s "distinctly musical cadence" was "derived from her discipline in the classical Greek lyric" (17), by which he means the musicality and not the actual prosody, what Pound called "the feel of the thing" and not the literal disposition of lines. At no time did H.D. seek to reproduce classical meters. For instance, her translations of Sappho are not in Sapphics. Though a number of critics have pointed out that H.D. does not employ classical prosody, the prosody that she does use remains unexplored. Many have echoed Hughes's comment that "H.D.'s cadences are her own" (27) and left it at that.[5]

My argument can be summarized in this way: though everyone finds a Greek influence in H.D.'s work, the poet herself conceded that she was not fluent in Greek when she developed her line. The various attempts to trace H.D.'s classicism in specific relation to her line have never examined the tradition of classical translation that H.D. did acknowledge. The following pages examine the Greek tradition *in English*. In the end, I will show that her debt to the classics goes further than the direct approach and the use of myth. In many respects, her approach is akin to translating, an activity she was earnestly engaged in at the time when she was inventing the Imagist line.

The notion that a poet treats her subject as a translator treats her source is by no means original to H.D. It was a prevalent trope in the nineteenth century, one that has implications for the line. Emerson's representative poet, for example, participates in the same life as his compatriots, but differs from them because he can translate the "Beauty" that created the universe:

> We hear those primal warblings, and attempt to write them down, but we lose ever and anon a word, or a verse, and substitute something of our own, and thus miswrite the poem. The men of more delicate ear write down these cadences more faithfully, and these transcripts, though imperfect, become the songs of nations. (207)

He goes on to say the poet is the "interpreter" (209) who listens to nature and "endeavors to write down the notes, without diluting or depraving them" (217). Concern for faithfulness to the source was widespread in the century, as I shall show.

Like Emerson, Whitman often describes the poet as a translator, insisting on accuracy and fidelity to the poem's subject. *Leaves of Grass* constantly advocates precise observation and study, an eye seeing everything, and capable, unbowdlerized translation. It also articulates an increasingly important attitude toward traditional prosody. "The greatest poet," Whitman remarks in his 1855 preface, "has less a marked style" than the poet writing in rhyme and meter,

> and is more the channel of thoughts and things without increase or diminution, and is the free channel of himself. He swears to his art, I will not be meddlesome, I will not have in my writing any elegance or effect or originality to hang in the way between me and the rest like curtains . . . What I experience or portray shall go from my composition without a shred of my composition. You shall stand by my side and look in the mirror with me. (456–57)

Whitman finds traditional lineal form "curtains" between thing and poet, and between translation and audience. Readers are to open up one of Whitman's poems and read the translated world—not poetry, not style, and not Whitman himself, though the mirror figure he uses indicates that he will be reflected in the verse. This may sound like strange talk from the author of *Song of Myself,* but it is important to bear in mind that Whitman subscribed to an enthusiastic philosophy that did not always acknowledge an insuperable barrier between what Emerson called the Me and the Not-me. In his poems and prose, Whitman generally considers himself coextensive with the universe. Like Emerson's Poet, Whitman believed it was the poet's job to find relations between himself, the world, and humanity.

Obviously, poets as well as translators face the difficulties of form and accuracy. Yet H.D.'s poetry, and the short-line verse her poetry did so much to engender, does not look much like typical nineteenth-century translations. Here are two more very different versions of *Agamemnon* 1407–12. The first is by Robert Potter and was published in 1809:

> What poison hath the baleful-teeming earth,
> Or the chaf'd billows of the foamy sea

Given thee for food, or mingled in thy cup,
To work thee to this frenzy? Thy curs'd hand
Hath struck, hath slain, for this thy country's wrath
Shall in just vengeance burst upon thy head,
And with abhorrence drive thee from this city (237)

In 1900, George C. Warr published a version that rendered the same text thus:

> Woman, what poison from earth's veins has thou eaten or bane of sea-brine hast drunk, that thou layest the people's curse as incense of wrath upon thy head? For thy hewing and thy hacking a hue of the burgher's hate will cast thee out. (41)

Conscious of the commentary of past editors, these two translations fill lacunae. In addition, they are laden with archaic diction and inverted syntax, techniques thought by translators to endow translations with an aura of poetic antiquity. In the "Muse in Tatters" chapter of *The Pound Era,* Hugh Kenner argues that the approach to translation exemplified by these two translations is the very sort of thing Pound and his era seeked to revolutionize, and helps explain such Modern techniques as the use of fragmentation and contemporary diction. Thus, in H.D.'s novel, *Bid Me to Live,* Julia voices an opinion surely held by her author indicating that H.D. shared Pound's dissatisfaction with most translations:

> Anyone can translate the meaning of the word. She wanted the shape, the feel of it, the character of it, as if it had been freshly minted. She felt that the old manner of approach was as toward hoarded treasures, but that treasure had passed through too many hands, too carefully assessed by grammarians. She wanted to coin new words. (163)

The "old manner of approach" led to dull and archaic-sounding renderings. Julia argues for a translation that would make the text seem as contemporary to her twentieth-century audience as it seemed to the ancient Greeks. Closer attention to the more profound underlying characteristics of the source (not to the surface "meaning") creates the new translation.[6] H.D. and the Imagists constructed an original poetry similarly interested in seeming "freshly minted," yet they did so by recovering the ideals of the very translation theory Julia, H.D., and Kenner find wanting. H.D.'s genius was not merely using a reconstituted theory of translation for translations, but also by using that theory for original poetry as well.

Although Kenner is surely right in saying that Pound, H.D., and the Moderns resisted the old manner of approach, the new approach shared many ideals with the old manner. A convenient touchstone for the Modern theory is Pound's concept of the translatability of his "three 'kinds of poetry'" ("How to Read" 25), *melopoeia, phanopoeia,* and *logopoeia*. As I will show, Pound more harmonizes nineteenth-century views than revolts against them. The translations by Potter and Warr illustrate the two strands of nineteenth-century translation theory that influenced Pound and H.D. My narrative here concentrates on the way that the theories' higher ideals influenced prosodic practice.

One side always insisted that poetry should be translated into verse. Coleridge, for example, said he did not "admit prose translations," especially in "so capable a language as" English (qtd. in Selver 13). However, those in agreement with Coleridge usually did not think it possible to employ classical meters in English translations.[7] R. D. Blackmore's comment about his own translation of Virgil's *Georgics* is typical:

> As to metre . . . it is easy to assert that the heroic couplet does not suit the subject; but unless a better can be found, we must put up with it, or have none at all. The heavy Spenserian stanza, the splay-footed English hexameter, the cork-legged trochaic, and all the acephalous, anapestic, dactylic, or other awkward squad of naturalized or native rhythm, have suggested themselves and been declined. (qtd. in Ryan 241)

Potter similarly assumes that English verse cannot be written according to quantitative rules, so that translations should be in "naturalized or native" lineal form. Even Arnold, who argued for a hexameter translation of Homer, expected the line to be in the traditional accentual-syllabic prosody. He did not call for quantitative dactyls.[8] Pound followed this line of thinking when he explains in "How to Read" that essentially musical poetry (the *melopoeia*) "is practically impossible to transfer or translated . . . from one language to another" (25).

Thus it is that, from the Renaissance onward, verse translations of classical texts have almost always been cast in native meters. This is not to say that translation theory did not change. In his survey of translations from the Greek, Finley Foster remarks that, much different from the "embellished" translations of the Elizabethans (xxv), nineteenth-century translators "insisted upon a certain amount of literalness in the translations. It was to be the endeavor of the translator to present his author to the public without change or adaptation on his part in bridging the gap between" the source and the target language (xviii). This desire for accuracy led to a rise in the number of prose translations. Theodore Alois Buckley's introduction to his prose translation of Aeschylus (for the Bohn Classical Library, the standard until the Loeb Classical Library superseded it) is revealing:

> The following translation was undertaken with the view of presenting the classical student with a close and literal translation of Aeschylus, and of furnishing the general reader with a faithful copy of the Author's thoughts and words, although the graces of poetic expression must be sacrificed in a literal prose version. (iii)

Buckley's sentiments seem tame enough until their implications are explored. He is saying that lineal matters—rhythm, alliteration, lineation, and so forth—are merely ornamental, not essential to the poet's "thoughts" at all. The exigencies of translation leave the translator with two choices: a "faithful copy" in prose without the frills, furbelows, and decorations of verse, or a decorative but inaccurate verse translation. Like Whitman, Buckley finds traditional prosody a curtain between source and target.

The example of Ossian complicates this translatorly poetic. James Macpherson's prose poems are not much read today because they are considered hoaxes—that is, original compositions based on oral traditions (instead of translations of ancient texts, as Macpherson claimed). In *The Origins of Free Verse,* H. T. Kirby-Smith several times states the importance of Ossian to proto-free verse, but does not consider the influence of Ossianic poetics, which is my interest here. In 1765, Hugh Blair offered an extensive defense of Ossian in his "A Critical Dissertation on the Poems of Ossian." Howard Gaskell points out that "all subsequent (authorized) editions of *Ossian* published in Macpherson's lifetime, and most nineteenth-century ones, contain the dissertation" (542). For most readers of Ossian, then, the dissertation provided a guide for reading.

Important for this discussion is Blair's concluding comments on Macpherson's translation. "To transfuse such spirited and fervid ideas from one language into another; to translate literally, and yet with such a glow of poetry," Blair informs his readers, "is one of the most difficult works of genius, and proves the translator to have been animated with no small portion of Ossian's spirit." Thus, he believes the poetic quality has been translated, even if the original versification was not. Blair continues in a way that anticipates free-verse theory:

> The measured prose which [Macpherson] has employed, possesses considerable advantages above any sort of versification he could have chosen. Whilst it pleases and fills the ear with a variety of harmonious cadences, being, at the same time, freer from constraint in the choice and arrangement of words, it allows the spirit of the original to be exhibited with more justness, force, and simplicity. (Gaskill 399)

Freed from the constraints of rhyme and meter (which Blair implies leads the poet to unnatural locutions and syntax) Macpherson's prose poems still achieve a various and natural harmony. Though such a translation puts the "original to a severe test," since the reader loses all the "charm of versification," the work still has the ability "to command, transport, to melt the heart." In eighteenth-century terms, Macpherson translated the sublimity and had to leave a little of the beauty behind.

This sense of a translatable *logos* independent of lineal form is prevalent in the nineteenth century. Even Goethe, who might be expected to scorn prose translation, endorsed this view. "I honor both rhyme and rhythm," the poet wrote, "but what is really deeply and thoroughly operative, what really shapes and improves, is what is left of a poem when it has been translated into prose" (qtd. in Lefevre 38). The ramifications of this sort of thinking are potentially devastating to traditional ideas of prosody. Blair, Goethe, and Buckley share the conviction that the translator can bridge the temporal and cultural gap between source and target, that lexical and grammatical equivalents can be found. But to do all this and put the words into rhythm and rhyme—well, that's the straw that breaks the camel's back. The idea of a translatable poetic essence independent of form is consistent with sublime theory and the nineteenth-century notion, detailed in chapter 1, that traditional prosody was unimportant to true poetry.

By 1925, the association of prose with accuracy and verse with ornament was so strong that John Middleton Murry asserted,

> Poetry ought to be rendered into prose. Since the aim of the translator should be to present the original as exactly as possible, no fetters of rhyme or rhythm or metre should be imposed to hamper this difficult labour. Indeed, they make it impossible. (14)

In the "original" the thing said is separate from the manner of saying it. Traditional prosody acts only as "fetters." Pound sums up this strain of translation theory in his designation of the other two types of poetry, the *phanopoeia* (a poetry of images) and *logopoeia* (a poetry of verbal play). Like Goethe, he finds images translatable, but not the specific "verbal manifestation." Still, he does hold out the possibility that the more general "original author's state of mind" may be translated (25), which seems to be what Goethe and Blair had in mind.

The sense of the poet as translator, freed from the chains of traditional versification while seeking to recover the essence of her subject, runs very deeply in H.D.'s poetic. She thought that the poet ought to approach experience in the way that Julia approached words—she ought to recover its "treasure." For her, full and honest appreciation of the world awakened the classical spirit, making the poet simultaneously a perceiver and a translator. Though the project of recovery might seem at odds with the Modern valorization of the New, H.D.'s poetic insists that it is not. Friedman argues, "The imagery of [H.D.'s] early poems . . . was not Greek at all, but rather drawn from her memories of the North Atlantic shores in New Jersey, Rhode Island, and Maine" ("Exile" 31), citing a letter H.D. wrote to Norman Holmes Pearson as evidence. In it, H.D. tells Pearson that the phone has just rung and the caller informed her that her "islands were on the air" at Radio City Music Hall:

> I should like to hear my "islands on the air" here in this island [i.e., Manhattan], to have made that link with those other islands, Calypso's Island or Catalpa Island as some have called it, vanished Atlantis in a river in Pennsylvania, sea-islands of the coast of Maine, Aegean islands . . . and [one near] Cornwall. ("Letter" 74)

The letter suggests, as Friedman argues, that H.D. did base her imagery on her memories. Important for this discussion, H.D. does not assign priority—her islands are *both* classical and contemporary. She also mentions her "nostalgia for a lost land. I call it Hellas. I might psychologically just as well have listed the Casco Bay of the coast of Maine, but I called my Islands Rhodes, Samos, and Cos" ("Letter" 72). That is, the mind experiences the pastness of classical literature in the same way as it does the pastness of personal experience. For H.D., islands off the coast of Maine have the same spirit as those in the Aegean. As Betty Vanderwiden argues, H.D. encourages her readers to "experience" the "Greek world and the contemporary world in a single flow of time" (74).[9] "The echo of island within island," Gregory explains, "all lost, all anterior, yet all remaining, recoverable in memory and affection, is continuous with H.D.'s conception of the islands throughout her life" (36–37).

This might be called H.D.'s "mythic method." Unlike Eliot's *Waste Land,* where the centuries are often felt as the weight of chains, H.D. and short-line poets in general found this conflation of classical and contemporary a way of reaching a timeless, lyric now. Paradoxically, whatever "nostalgia" H.D. says the islands aroused in her, the poem's feeling is of emotional presentness. Hence, the poet is a translator of a contemporary world in which the classical world is inscribed. In a sense, she translates both at once.

When H.D. began to publish poetry in 1913, the avant-garde circle she frequented tended to exalt the idea of poetry while denigrating traditional meter as lethal to scrupulous attention to the subject. Her poetry demonstrates the logical conclusion of such premises: the best and most poetic poetry should be cast into verse that eschews the debilitating demands of rhyme and meter—that is to say, into free verse. Her peers were willing to consider unmetered verse poetry. In fact, as Murry's comment helps indicate, the shunning of traditional prosody was taken as a token of the poem's fidelity to its subject. This is the basic philosophical background for H.D.'s theory.

Like her poetic theory, H.D.'s practice is indebted to nineteenth-century translations. The lineal form H.D. chose was already associated with especially close connection to a poem's source. Most of the rest of this chapter will focus on the tradition that informed H.D.'s Imagist line; at the end, I will return to how H.D. adapted that tradition in her early poetry.

Even though her contemporaries sometimes used H.D.'s poetry as model for the New Poetry, its prosody has a long history. Just as H.D.'s theory of poetry grew out of translation theory, so her lineal decorum also derives from the way past writers have dealt with classical texts. I begin this history of the formal tradition H.D. participated in with another translation of *Agamemnon,* this one by Robert Browning. Yopie Prins points out that in many ways the translation and the introduction to it are an "extension of" Browning's "own poetics" (157). I have chosen this translation because Browning was particularly influential on the Moderns, especially those in proximity to Pound. More centrally, Browning's view of translation in many ways mirrors H.D.'s, and his prosody likewise anticipates hers.

Browning's preface to his translation reflects both his age's concern for accuracy and its dissatisfaction with iambic pentameter translations. "I should require" a translator, Browning remarks, "to be literal at every cost save that of absolute violence to our language" (293). He insists that the important part of translation is the transmission of the "thing." This thing is not the "reputed magniloquence and sonority of the Greek," which is "impossible" to translate, but instead the thought of the author: "there is abundant musicality elsewhere, but nowhere else than in his poem the ideas of the poet." Like Goethe, Browning believed that the "really important thing" could be translated. Browning finds music and "ideas" so separate he is willing to set the libretto to a new score based, presumably, on an underlying music intrinsic to the ideas. It is easy to see in these words a precursor to Pound's distinction between the musical quality of a work and its other aspects.

What, according to Browning, does the music of Greek ideas sound like? Here is his version of that chorus from *Agamemnon:*

> What evil, oh woman, food or drink, earth-bred
> Or sent from the flowing sea,
> Of such having fee
> Didst thou set on thee
> This sacrifice
> And popular cries
> Of a curse on thy head?
> Off thou has thrown him, off hast cut
> The man from the city: but
> Off from the city thyself shalt be
> Cut—to the citizens
> A hate immense! (353)

Though no one, I believe, feels this is his greatest achievement (Prins notes that most contemporary readers thought the work "unreadable" [151]), this translation does differ from other Victorian translations in that Browning does not render the lines into a single meter. The form of his choruses tends to correspond to the irregular ode outlined in chapter 2. The specific lineal construction concerns me now. Obviously, Browning is writing to rhyme and perhaps in loose iambics. However irregular the meter and line length, the grammatical disposition of the lines is orderly. Line one contains the subject, lines two and three modifiers, line four a verbal phrase, line five object of the verb, line six another object of the verb, and line seven two prepositional phrases to modify the objects.

Subject-verb-object, with modifying clauses lined up vertically, spatially separated: this systematic progression is remarkably similar to the activity of the English translator, who must search for subject, object, and verb, and then identify which phrases modify which parts of speech. The translator then fits the pieces together, placing modifiers where appropriate. Grammatically, Browning's translation reads like a translator's nearly final draft (before smoothing things out, making the translation more idiomatic, and so forth).

If Browning followed Aeschylus's lineation, the world will never know it. Like many classical texts, *Agamemnon* survives only in copies of differing authority, and it is generally recognized that an absolutely authoritative version of what Aeschylus wrote is unrecoverable. For this reason, Martin L. West's definitive edition of the play is a composite text collating some forty manuscripts. Thomas G. Rosenmeyer points out that the lineation of the choruses, the part I am concerned with, is particularly problematic:

> The iambic passages of speech and dialogue, corresponding roughly to the blank verse of Elizabethan drama, were always arranged as lines of verse. But the lyric portions . . . representing primarily the contributions of the chorus as singers and dancers, were in the first copies written out as if they were prose, without regard for the structure of the verse. It was probably only in the second century B.C. that an Alexandrian scholar, Aristophanes of Byzantium, introduced the fashion of writing the text of the lyrics as they are printed today. (19–20)

Rosenmeyer's analysis of choral form is similar to Jannaris's of accent marks and prosody, in that both argue that the received lineal form was imposed by later scholars and therefore without sure authorial sanction. There is no way of knowing how Aeschylus conceived his choruses. Perhaps he did not consider them poetry at all, or perhaps he thought of them as some kind of unlineated poetry. In this regard, the very early texts of Aeschylus resemble the unique manuscript of *Beowulf,* which is also copied as prose and lineated today according to our understanding of its rhythm. Maybe the Anglo-Saxon copyists of *Beowulf*[10] wanted to preserve sheepskin and so ignored lineation, or maybe they thought that that sort of poetry did not properly fall into lines. Perhaps they considered *Beowulf* rhythmic prose.

Editors trying to decide upon the correct way to lineate the choruses of *Agamemnon* face a problem that *Beowulf's* editors do not have to face. The rhythm of most of Aeschylus's play is relatively easy to understand. The choruses, Rosenmeyer points out, are another story. Unlike the clearly alliterative pattern of Old English poetry, for Aeschylus's choruses it is "very difficult to determine" just "where a poetic line ends and another begins. Without a recognition of these termini, no true assessment of the nature of the verse and of the relation of the lines from one to the other is possible" (30), and these termini were only provided long after the playwright's death—long after, in fact, the language of plays was current.[11] Thus it is that the lineation of the choruses of *Agamemnon* and indeed many ancient lyric texts is influenced by the grammatical identification necessary for translation. Simply put, the grammar had a strong influence on, indeed seems to have been the determining factor in, lineation.

In any case, Browning did not follow the received lineation. The received text has six lines, and Browning uses twelve. He did not just halve the lines. Consider line 1410:

> απεδιχεζ απεταμεζ, α<πο>πολιζ δ'εσηι (West 72)[12]

which Rosenmeyer translates

> Cast off, cut off? They'll cut you out (35)

The received lineation rather balances the ideas on the same line. Browning clips this so that the word "cut" is near line breaks; thus, there is both "thou has cut / the man" and "thou shalt be / cut"—the first separates a transitive verb from its object, and the second time divides a verbal phrase. That is, he likes the mimetic line break (the line is "cut" unnaturally, just as Clytemnestra has cut down her husband) so much, he does it twice. It seems that one way that Browning expresses the music of Aeschylus's ideas is through imitative enjambment.

In this way, Browning's Englished Aeschylus observes the decorum that each line shall constitute one phrasal unit, and any breaking of that shall be for expressive, perhaps mimetic, reasons. Oddly, Alexander Pope believed the same thing. This couplet from *An Essay on Criticism* brings together two independent clauses:

> A *little Learning* is a dang'rous Thing,
> Drink deep, or taste not the *Pierian* spring (ll. 215–16)

This is Pope's favored mode, especially when delivering *dicta*. Pope is not above mimetic enjambment, however. At a crucial juncture in *The Rape of the Lock,* the interaction of grammar and lineation enacts the snipping described. The "Points" in the following lines are the tips of scissors:

> The meeting Points the Sacred Hair dissever
> From the fair head, for ever and for ever! (ll. 153–54)

The line break dissevers the "Sacred Hair" from the "fair head." From even this brief example, it is clear that poets of every genre have used grammar as well as rhythm to determine lineation. However, there is a significant difference between traditional and free verse. Whereas Pope uses an iambic rhythm to determine the line and fits grammar within that rhythm, long- and short-line poets use grammar to determine the line and find a rhythm within it. While long-line poets use the longer line to support an oracular voice, in doing so they lost the localized expressive line breaks that are so important to short-line free verse.

Browning's short and irregular lines have a classical, not traditional, patina. I have shown that Cowley and irregular odists in general found sanction in the versification of Pindar. The decorums for H.D. and Browning have a similar history. Again, it is a tradition of imitation, and it is manifest in the work of one of English literature's great classicists, John Milton.

Although Modern poets, especially in the teens and twenties, tended to consider Milton an example of all that was wrong with traditional verse (usually on the grounds that he was didactic), Milton's extremely varied prosody exerted a strong influence on the poets who influenced the Moderns. *Samson Agonistes* falls within the purview of this discussion. The prosody of that poem has long occupied those interested in lineal form. Williams includes the choruses from *Samson* in his discussion of free verse for *The Princeton Encyclopedia of Poetry and Poetics.* Such Modern precursors as Coleridge and Hopkins scanned the poem extensively.[13] Indeed, the poem has often been a target for those committed to the smooth tradition. Dr. Johnson found the choruses "harsh and dissonant" (380); in 1788, Richard Cumberland said that in "some places" there was "no measure at all, or such as at least the ear will not patiently endure" (110), presumably because the "the ear" is so accustomed to regularity. Correspondingly, Hopkins, who favored irregularity, loved the choruses. He told Robert Bridges that they were really "sprung" though they keep up "a fiction of counterpointing"; it is a "real poetical rhythm, having its own laws and recurrences, but further embarrassed by having to count" (*Bridges* 46). When Hopkins says "sprung," he means something like "accentual with accentual-syllabic feet" and when he says, "counterpointing rhythms" he means, say, an iambic line succeeding a trochaic one.[14] He thus argues that Milton (probably for convention's sake) makes a gesture toward providing an iambic norm (and thus counting all his syllables), but actually writes very freely, only counting stresses. Since the poem is so rarely iambic, Hopkins argued, the "standard rhythm" in *Samson* "does not really exist" (46).[15]

Similarly, *A Milton Handbook* finds "the variation from the iambic pattern is so great that one is inclined to abandon the attempt to recognize a theoretical conformity to English pattern and consider [the choruses] frankly as reproduction of Greek and Roman rhythms" (270). Of course, by converting quantity to stress, a poet can imitate classical rhythm and still conform to English patterns. Saintsbury argues that though the choruses are irregular, "they all lend themselves to the strictest foot-scansion" (II.252). Although I will show that Saintsbury's assertion has much truth in it, his phrasing suggests an unrealistic agency on the part of the lines, and Saintsbury finds very little that does not similarly lend itself to traditional foot scansion. He felt "Christabel" likewise lent itself to traditional scansion.

Samson's choruses are a particularly difficult part of the overall problem of Milton's prosody. The variety evident in Milton's verse is such that there are two book-length studies of his prosody, and indeed probably more comment on Milton's versification than on all of free verse.[16] Milton's blank verse is so varied that, Richard Bradford has pointed out, some consider it syllabic (instead of accentual-syllabic). Bradford himself includes the epic within his "sliding scale" of visual prosody—i.e., though *Paradise Lost* looks like iambic pentameter, it often does not fulfill that contract. The irregular parts of *Samson* do not even *look* metrical. Nonetheless, P. T. Prince remarks that, though "Everyone feels that the choruses in *Samson* disport themselves by law," few if any "have been able to detect, or at least formulate, the code which governs them" (165).

Milton's account of his prosody in *Samson* does not explain it well. He attributes his inspiration to the "Greek manner" one that was "still in use among the Italians."[17] He continues,

> The measure of Verse us'd in the Chorus is of all sorts, call'd by the Greeks *Monostrophic,* or rather *Apolelymenon,* without regard had to *Strophe, Antistrophe,* or *Epod,* which were a kind of Stanza's fram'd only for the Music, then us'd with the Chorus that sung; not essential to the Poem, and therefore not material; or, being divided into Stanza's or Pauses, they may be called *Allœostropha.* (332)

Milton paraphrases the meaning of his Greek terms, which only indicate that the poem does not follow the typical strophe-antistrophe-epode stanzaic pattern of Greek choruses.[18] As Frank Kermode says, the terms "could be quite correctly applied to the Pindaric of Cowley." They tell "us nothing whatsoever about the system of his choral verse except that it is not divided as the Greek tragedians divided theirs" (103). Milton might as well have used the word *cadence*.

The variety of meter in *Samson Agonistes* presents a problem for traditional scansion. As I have argued in chapter 1, only the overall, abstract pattern of any poem can usually be determined with any assurance. Scanning short lines is especially difficult. For one thing, scansion is always contextual. Although some syllables always take stresses, others are stressed by position. For example, in this line from *An Essay on Criticism,* "which" is stressed:

> *Are nameless* Graces which no Methods teach (l. 144)

However, later in the same poem,

> Which lives as long as *Fools* are pleas'd to *Laugh* (l. 451)

it is not. The rule for iambic verse is that the middle of three unstressed syllables is counted as a stress. Trisyllabic words that stress the first syllable are another example of contextual prosody. Take

> Know well each ANCIENT's proper character (l. 119)

A reader might read the last word on the line as a dactyl, but Pope's scheme insists that it is the second half of an iambic foot and all of another (/ U /). Though competent readers may not read it this way, these types of rules allow Pope to keep the meter, even if they do not always exactly describe English pronunciation.[19]

Short lines, of course, have fewer feet and so provide less context from which to determine a norm. Consider this line from *Samson:*

> Life in captivity (l. 108)

Is it / U U / U U, / U U / U / , or even U / U / U / ? Decontextualized, it is impossible to determine.

Further, by ignoring the prosody's contextual rules, clearly iambic lines may appear to be "really" accentual. If Franz Klaeber (the editor of the received *Beowulf*) had found an unlineated text of *An Essay on Criticism,* he may have found something akin to Anglo-Saxon measure:

     /   /   /   /
Know well each Ancient's   Proper character
      /   /   /   /
Its fable, subject   Scope on ev'ry Page
   /   /   /   /
Religion, country   Genius of his Age
 /   /   /   /
Without all these   at once before your eyes
  /   /   /   /
Cavil you may   but never criticize (ll. 119–23)

Further, consider this relineation:

A little learning
Is a dang'rous thing
Drink deep or taste not
The Pierian spring

Not only are the first two lines now in dimeter (thus losing the stress on "Is"), but does the third line have two stresses or four?

I have chosen Pope for this exercise because he is such a touchstone for smoothness. The relineations help indicate that the line suggests meter by controlling prosodic context, and that much of Pope's smoothness occurs because the reader knows to look for it and hence knows where to read a stressed preposition or relative pronoun. Even at his smoothest, Milton is comparatively rough, and those who complain about the lack of consistent meter in *Samson* should put their estimations of meter in the context of Milton's typically varied line.

If this is kept in mind, Saintsbury's appraisal seems just. The nonchoral parts of *Samson,* certainly, can be quite regular. The tragedy begins in fairly smooth iambics—

/ / / / /
A Little onward lend thy guiding hand
/ / / / /
To these dark steps, a little further on;
/ / / / /
For yonder bank hath choice of Sun or shade (ll. 1–3)

Scanning the first four syllables of the second line U U / / does not seriously endanger the iambic pentameter progression. Other sections, though, are more irregular. Take

He would not else who never wanted means,
Nor in respect of the enemy just cause
To set his people free,
Have prompted his heroic *Nazarite,*
Against his vow of strictest purity
To seek in marriage that fallacious Bride,
Unclean, unchaste. (ll. 315–21)

When looking for the meter, a good rule of thumb is to begin in places where it seems unmistakable. Line 321, it seems to me, must be read as iambic; and line 316 seems fairly unmistakable as well. This gives sanction to find a stressed "that" in line 320, and concluding cretics (/ U /) on lines 317 and 318. In this context, the irregularity of line 315 looks tamer—even mostly iambic (i.e., U / U / U U / U / U /, though without this context U / U / U U / U U / / seems equally likely). Perhaps some of my readers will argue that my scansion does not precisely represent typical English speech, but, again, no scansion ever does. Overall, the pattern of *Samson* may not be the "strictest" foot scansion that Saintsbury claims it to be, but it is recognizable. The abstract pattern, the meter, is iambic.

Samson's early lament over his blindness demonstrates important decorums of twentieth-century free verse:

O, first created Beam, and thou great Word,
Let there be light, and light was over all;
Why am I thus bereav'd thy prime decree?
The Sun to me is dark
And silent as the Moon

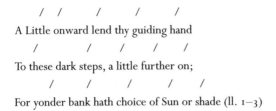

When she deserts the night
Hid in her vacant interlunar cave. (ll. 83–89)

Though the lines move from pentameter to trimeter, they evince much orderliness. The lines are all recognizably iambic—Milton's desire for iambics was strong enough to lead him to paraphrase Genesis 1:3—and in neat grammatical units, so much so that Milton could have placed a period after any line from 86 to 89, excised the rest, and had a perfectly grammatical text. Compare, in this respect, the Chorus's opening words:

This, this is he; softly a while,
Let us not break in upon him;
O change beyond report, thought, or belief!
See how he lies at random, carelessly diffus'd,
With languish't head unpropt,
As one past hope, abandon'd,
And by himself given over;
In slavish habit, ill-fitted weeds
O'er-worn and soild;
Or do my eyes misrepresent? Can this be hee,
That Heroic, that Renown'd,
Irresistible *Samson?* whom unarm'd
No strength of man, of fiercest wild beast, could withstand (ll. 115–27)

I scan most of these lines as iambic; however, my focus now is on the play of grammar across the line. When the chorus describes what it sees, there is an orderly grammatical progression, with line endings corresponding to phrase endings. Like Samson's lament above, many lines could be excised without damage to the grammar (especially lines 119, 120, 124). But when the chorus begins to speculate and feel uncertain, suddenly line breaks do not follow the sentence, and the enjambment following the question marks feels all the more marked because of the grammatical decorum preceding it.

Similarly, when the chorus later counsels Samson rather sententiously not to blame God for his betrayal by Delilah, it does so in blank verse:

Tax not divine disposal, Wisest men
Have err'd, and by bad Women been deceived;
And shall again, pretend they ne'er so wise. (ll. 210–12)

However, when the chorus takes up the subject of women later in the play, its uncertainty is mirrored prosodically:

> It is not vertue, wisdom, valor, wit,
> Strength, comeliness of shape, or amplest merit
> That womans love can win, or long inherit;
> But what it is, hard is to say,
> Harder to hit,
> (Which way soever men refer it).
> Much like thy riddle, *Samson,* in one day
> Or seven, though one should musing sit. (ll. 1010–17)

Not only are there irregular line lengths and even rougher iambics, but Milton's use of rhyme here seems gauged to keep the reader off balance. Line 1010 seems to want to rhyme with line 1011, though the *it* in "merit" is unstressed (and thus finds true rhymes with "inherit" and at least an eye rhyme with "refer it") while a true rhyme for "wit" only occurs four lines later. Perhaps the masculine and feminine rhymes uncertainly rhyming with each other is meant to mirror the difficulty the chorus has in naming the unnamable—perhaps this is even a prosodic pun with the masculine and feminine rhymes enacting the incompatibility between sexes the line describes. While such cleverness may seem unMiltonic, at other places in the poem Milton seems to pun on "foot" and "stride."[20] It can be said with more certainty that *Samson* observes the same decorum of line length and enjambment that Browning's *Agamemnon* does—though of course the influence must go the other way.

However undescriptive his nomenclature, Milton used shorter lines to imitate (not copy) Greek choral meter and the emotional attachments associated with the form. Rosenmeyer's description of the "dochmiac" meter (which he likens to sprung rhythm) in many ways describes the irregular patches in *Samson*. The dochmiac,

> a violently syncopated rhythm which in the end only distantly recalls the flow of iambs [that characterizes the other parts of the play], comes to be the favorite pattern for the expression of horror and acute pain in song. Dochmiac is singular in a number of respects. It is just about the only dramatic verse form of which we can predicate a distinct ethos—excitement, pain, revulsion; never joy, never elegiac grief, never sermonizing; it is unique to Attic tragedy and may well be an innovation of Aeschylus.' (34)

Milton's irregular choruses express "Elegiac grief," but it is "acute" grief. Rosenmeyer's greater point is that this is a lyric meter. Milton's irregularly lengthed iambics, unrhymed or rhyming irregularly, are the English imitation of choral, lyric meters such as the dochmiac.

Nineteenth-century imitations of Greek tragedy often observed Milton's lineal decorums. Though the action of Shelley's *Prometheus Unbound* occurs in blank verse, the various speeches of spirits typically occur in lines of three or fewer feet. Particularly interesting is the "Song of Spirits" from Act II scene iii. It begins

> To the Deep, to the Deep
>   Down, down!
> Through the shade of Sleep,
> Through the cloudy strife
> Of Death and of Life;
> Through the veil and the bar
> Of things which seem and are,
> Even to the steps of the remotest Throne,
>   Down, down! (*Complete II* II.iii. ll. 54–61)

The meter here is particularly difficult to reckon—I find a lot of anapests and iambs, though certainly a case could be made for trochaic lines with an iambic one mixed in. Maybe it is best to consider the section as accentual dimeter. However you hear the rhythm, the grammatical evenness and regularity differ greatly from the tumbling blank verse of the narrative sections, such as

> Disdain! Ah no! I pity thee.—What Ruin
> Will hunt thee undefended thro' the wide Heaven!
> How will thy soul, cloven to its depth with terror,
> Gape like a Hell within! I speak in grief,
> Not exultation, for I hate no more,
> As then, ere misery made me wise.—The curse (*Complete II* I.i. ll. 53–58)

The poem goes on from there. Of course, one reason why this speech by Prometheus runs over is that in those passages Shelley is counting syllables and allowing the line to break after he has reached ten.[21] His desire for grammatical correctness in the spirit's song, however, is so great that he allows for lines of differing numbers of syllables so long as the grammatical decorum is maintained. Shelley was an accomplished poet, and the regularity that the blank verse speeches enjamb strongly—and the short-line songs do not—surely indicates an intentional decorum. The classical subject of the poem, coupled with the fact that Shelley's procedure regarding short lines is very similar to Milton's, suggests that this disposition of lines according to grammatical phrases is part of a tradition of classical imitation.

Matthew Arnold's *Empedocles on Etna* further illustrates this tradition. Like *Prometheus Unbound,* it deals with a classical subject, and also like Shelley's drama, it is prosodically diverse. The line of Empedocles's speech in Act II offers no consistency of syllable count or accent, but similarity of grammar:

> I am weary of thee.
> I am weary of the solitude
> Where he who bears thee must abide—
> Of the rocks of Parnassus,
> Of the gorge of Delphi,
> Of the moonlit peaks, and the caves.
> Thou guardest them, Apollo! (*Poems* ll. 198–204)

When the lines become short, it becomes even more difficult to read them as iambic. Note the grammatical evenness of the catalogue that anticipates Whitman:

> The smallest thing that could give us pleasure then—
> The sports of the country-people,
> A flute-note from the woods,
> Sunset over the sea;
> Seed-time and harvest,
> The reapers in the corn,
> The vinedresser in his vineyard,
> The village-girl at her wheel. (*Poems* ll. 250–57)

There is a similarly neat disposition of grammar and line endings in the following:

> To the elements it came from
> Everything will return—

Our bodies to earth,
Our blood to water,
Heat to fire,
Breath to air.
They were well born, they will be well entomb'd—
But mind?... (*Poems* ll. 331–38)

As with Shelley, Arnold's desire for lining up grammatically equal elements—modifying clauses, appositives, and so forth—overrides a concern for metrical regularity.

Something similar occurs in "Philomela," a poem that, again, treats a classical subject. Consider these two sentences:

And can this fragrant lawn,
With its cool trees, and night,
And the sweet, tranquil Thames,
And moonshine, and the dew
To thy rack'd heart and brain
Afford no balm?
Dost thou to-night behold,
Here, through the moonlight on this English grass,
The unfriendly palace on the Thracian wild? (*Poems* ll. 10–18)

The rhythm seems to be vaguely iambic, an appraisal made mostly on the evidence of the rest of the poem (with a U U / / U / pattern on lines eleven, twelve, and fourteen), but in truth the poem is irregular. Grammatically, however, it is another story. Lines ten through fifteen, progress subject, modifier, modifier, modifier, indirect object, verb and object; lines sixteen through eighteen, subject and verb, modifier, object. The rest of the poem is similarly orderly. As in Whitman and Hebrew poetry, it is as if the grammatical order is meant to compensate for metrical irregularity. Again, phrases of equal grammatical rank are stacked up. Any or all of lines eleven through fourteen could be excised without leaving the remainder ungrammatical.

It seems, then, that poets who took the received classical prosody as a sanction for unequal lines often used grammatical decorums to determine their lines in lieu of counting (that these lines are sometimes iambic does not imply any line length). Decontextualizing these lines often makes them prosodically identical to twentieth-century free verse. Arnold's "Philomela" is unusual in this respect, inasmuch as it does not occur, as *Samson*'s choruses do, in the context of traditional meter, though perhaps readers are expected to place the poem in the greater context of the classical spirit. Be that as it may, it is a short step from writing these free though grammatically decorous poems on classical subjects to writing the same type of poem on a contemporary subject.

Something of this sort occurred in the domestication of the irregular ode detailed in chapter 1. Indeed, the decorums I have outlined above also hold for most of the short lines of Sidney Lanier's irregular odes. Like the irregular ode, these poems attempt to imitate classical meters without mimicking them outright. This led to the freer aesthetic that led to free verse. Most of the poems discussed above are not usually considered free verse because a greater, recognizable prosody subsumes the irregular parts. This tradition of imitation differs from that of the irregular ode because it carried no particular name and had a greater propensity to ignore rhyme, and, correspondingly, greater freedom.

William Ernest Henley's *In Hospital* took the short step from free poems using classical subjects to free poems using contemporary ones. Henley's sanction for looser rhythms again centers on the issue of translation. In the introduction to his 1898 edition of *Poems,* Henley describes the sequence as "those unrhyming rhythms in which I had tried to quintessentialize, as (I believe) one scarce can do in rhyme, my impressions of the Old Edinburgh Infirmary" (viii). Henley might have added that occasionally he found meter an obstacle as well. Still, ten of the twenty-nine poems are sonnets—and only five are in free verse.[22] Though quintessentialization involves distillation, it also presumes fidelity. Henley is saying, such was his experience, and such his desire to be faithful to it, that it could not be described in the usual manner. The free verse of *In Hospital* is in effect forgiven because the poems describe scenes not usually considered poetic. Because the experience of being in the hospital was so unsettling (several poems address the feeling of being drugged, for example), some of the poems avoid convention and the comfortable feeling conventions are supposed to elicit.[23]

Two of the five free poems are pastoral and observe the line-length decorums I have shown typical of the late-century carefree pastoral ode. Thus "Pastoral" begins with a short line:

It's the Spring.
Earth has conceived, and her bosom,
Teeming with summer, is glad. (33)

as does "Discharged":

> Carry me out
> Into the wind and the sunshine,
> Into the beautiful world. (42)

More interesting, perhaps, are "Clinical" and "Vigil." The former begins with a short line:

> Hist? . . .
> Through the corridor's echoes
> Louder and nearer
> Comes a great shuffling of feet.
> Quick, every one of you
> Straight your quilts and be decent!
> Here's the Professor. (16)

Assigning meter is difficult. Is the fourth line / U / / U U / , / U U / U U / , or U U / / U U / ? The poem really never makes a decisive gesture in any direction. Likewise, "Vigil" does not seem to demand any particular meter. It begins

> Lived on one's back,
> In the long hours of repose,
> Life is a practical nightmare—
> Hideous asleep or awake. (10)

Note the light enjambment. Similarly,

> All the old time
> Surges malignant before me;
> Old voices, old kisses, old songs
> Blossom derisive about me;
> While the new days
> Pass me in endless procession:
> A pageant of shadows
> Silently, leeringly wending
> On . . . and still on . . . still on!

The ellipses are reminiscent of the line "Asleep . . . tired . . . or it malingers" in "Prufrock."

Grammatically, the lines alternate subject / verb-object / subject / verb-object. The ensuing lines break this decorum somewhat,

Far in the stillness a cat
Languishes loudly. A cinder
Falls, and the shadows
Lurch at the leap of the flame. The next

Now, the procession is subject/verb-new subject/verb. A striking aspect of Henley's free verse is the large number of lines beginning with a verb—six of the thirteen lines above do, for example. Significantly, the relatively "harder" enjambment occurs when there is direct observation, whereas recollection and statement do not use such enjambment. Thus, the poem observes the lineal decorum of *Samson*.

The title of the final free poem in the sequence, "Ave, Caesar," probably means to imply a celebratory (though here ironically so) ode. The poem has a more metrical feel than the other free poems:

From the winter's grey despair,
From the summer's golden languor,
Death, the lover of Life,
Frees us for ever.

The lines seem vaguely trochaic, though some may prefer the first two lines anapestic/iambic. Still, the poem places all but one of its present-tense verbs at the beginning of a line, and the exception is a sentence in which the verb in question is not the main verb of the sentence.

Not taking freer form are character studies and poems where the speaker expresses resolve. With the exception of "Ave, Caesar," the free poems seem to satisfy only the first half of Wordsworth's dictum. That is, they read like spontaneous overflows of emotion (or random observation) not yet recollected in tranquillity. Formally, grammatical regularity seems to have replaced metrical regularity. The fiction of composition for these poems is that they are direct impressions unmediated through a poeticizing consciousness. Consequently, the lack of the traditional lineal form seems to signal faithful translation, and implies, as noted in Henley's preface, that the reality portrayed differs essentially from the reality traditional poetry describes.

Such an approach to poetry approximates a poetic usually thought more

Modern than Victorian. If the prosodic innovations of the Moderns were really so unprecedented, it would be expected that the conservative contemporary critics of Henley would have vilified him as much as Pound was vilified. Such was not the case. To be sure, some reviewers expressed the wish that some of the poems had not been so free, but the Victorians were much more concerned with subject matter than scandalized by form. For example, the *Critic* implied that it found Henley in alliance with Whitman by saying the poem emulated a "'barbaric yawp,'" but its major critique was that the sequence was "not without effectiveness," that is, "if the reader's sense of recoil from . . . the life represented be taken as proof of power" (5). The *New Princeton Review* admired the poems to a degree, but could not help wishing that Henley would restrict his efforts to "more cheerful" subjects (qtd. in Jerome Buckley 91). The *Nation* found the poems "extraordinary" and "unique in literature," but only because of the unusual albeit "repellent" subject matter (522). The review does not mention form. These views are typical.[24]

One contemporary who did attend to form was Oscar Wilde, whose review probably constitutes the fullest and most sensitive of contemporary reactions.[25] Wilde admits that he prefers "the beautiful thing," but goes on to argue that Henley had a "real passion for what is horrible, ugly, or grotesque" (90). Wilde finds that "it is impossible to deny" *In Hospital*'s "power" (91). Still, Wilde contends that the free poems were "preludes, experiments, inspired jottings in a notebook," indeed "like everything and anything, except perfected poems" (91). For example, Wilde says that "Clinical," is "dainty . . . from a typographical point of view," but was really just "ingeniously printed prose" (92). The charge that this sort of free verse is really just chopped-up prose is one I have shown to be prevalent and repeated by Francis Thompson twenty years later, when he claimed *In Hospital*'s "Novelty . . . lay in assimilating poetry to prose—and that blessed day of the Lord when poetry shall be prose is a consummation for which the great heart of the British public ever yearns" (188). However, if the free poems of *In Hospital* really are just ingeniously printed prose, it is a very strange prose indeed. Take this sentence from "Discharged":

As of old,
Ambulant, undulant drapery,
Vaguely and strangely provocative,
Flutters and beckons. (42)

This reads like unremarkable free verse. Here are the same lines set as prose: "As of old, ambulant, undulant drapery, vaguely and strangely provocative, flutters and beckons." I find myself getting lost in the modifying phrases and commas. A similar relineation from "Pastoral" reads, "Vistas of change and adventure, thro' the green land the grey roads go beckoning and winding, peopled with wains, and melodious with harness-bells jangling: jangling and twangling rough rhythms to the slow march of the stately, grey horse whistled and shouted along" (33). Set as prose, the grammar seems eccentric and the passage affected. When the words are set as poetry, its reader will likely accept the echoic sounds and rhythms as something a poem is "supposed to" (or allowed to) do.

This experiment again underscores the fact that early free verse used lineation to clarify grammar, create rhythm, and signal to the reader that the words were to be taken as poetry and thus appreciated in the rather nonnarrative way poetry is often appreciated. Wilde and Thompson found *In Hospital* prosy because a few of its poems did not have rhyme and meter and sometimes eschew meter-keeping conventions such as syntactical inversion and elision (though, as the relineated passages above demonstrate, not all the time). The poems also seem like prose because of the sense of narrative that pervades the sequence, and, indeed, as I have shown, its contemporary audience often did read the poem as it would a novel, with special attention to the story and to the "reality" depicted, not to the form and to "ideas" or ideals.

Wilde classifies the free poems as "sketches" because he supposes a procedure in which the poet thinks up an idea (or has a sensation), sketches it out in prose, then works it into a poem. *In Hospital,* then, seems like the intermediate step of the translator. By not "finishing" the poem, Henley made a significant choice (which Wilde acknowledges later in the review when he says that the poems' "faults" are "deliberate and the result of much study" [96]). In Henley's fiction of composition, he chooses the immediate and the "literal" over the polished and the "poetical." If it is raw, so goes the fiction, then it is also faithful and closer to the source. It is supposed to be the world free of the poet's ornament.

The preface makes it clear that in *In Hospital,* such ornament, so often idealizing, seemed to Henley inappropriate. Of course, this approach greatly oversimplifies traditional prosody. Certainly, such poets as Chaucer, Crabbe, and Frost found they could record everyday or unpleasant realities faithfully (indeed, more acutely than Henley) in rhyme and meter. I will take up this issue at greater length in the conclusion to this book, but my point here is that

Henley's poetic almost exactly states the most prevalent twentieth-century justification for free verse.

Henley's free verse adapts a mode of poetry already available in the English tradition, and this explains why his contemporaries were not particularly shocked by the poems' form. This is further evidence that the real objection to free verse was a general feeling that Pound and company were attacking a whole way of life and that free verse was somehow connected with that. Henley, however, had no such agenda. He was simply describing what he saw and felt in the form that he thought appropriate. Without the propaganda, his contemporaries did not feel particularly threatened by his free-verse poems, and most found something at least to praise.

Many readers coming across Henley for the first time in 1888 assumed, as the *Critic* put it, "Gallic influence." But the practice of Laforgue and the French *vers librists* could not have influenced Henley because the poems of *In Hospital* were first published in the *Cornhill* magazine between 1872 and 1875. *The Oxford Companion to French Literature* points out that although Rimbaud perhaps wrote a few free poems in the 1870s, the first French *vers libre* poems did not see print until 1881. My point is, again, that Henley, like Arnold, was participating in the same *zeitgeist* that Laforgue was, and the innovations of *In Hospital* are easily comprehensible within the English prosodic history of the nineteenth century.

Henley found the experience in the Old Edinburgh Infirmary so alien to the world of poetry that the forms of some of the poems, in order to be faithful, had to be alien as well. If a poet has the same sort of attitude toward the language and the task of the poet—that the language is difficult and traditional form unyielding and that the poet must above all translate accurately—while finding the everyday world as strange and variable as Henley found the hospital, then the only recourse is free verse. And elevation of the ordinary is a hallmark of the sort of Modern poets that this chapter addresses. While the Moderns were not the first to notice the everyday world, they tended to claim that they were.

Nowhere is this clearer than in the poetry of Williams, who was often unsubtle in his insistence that ordinary reality was the proper subject of the poem. Thus, "Pastoral" describes sparrows and old men "Gathering dog-lime," then concludes, "These things / Astonish me beyond words" (I.43); another "Pastoral" ends "no one / will believe this / of vast import to the nation" (I.65) though the speaker clearly does; "To Be Written on a Small Piece of Paper which Folded into a Tight Lozenge Will Fit Any Girl's Locket"—a title implying that "any girl" ought to carry the poem around with her, reads in its entirety:

> Lo the leaves
> Upon the new autumn grass—
> Look at them well . . . ! (I.123)

And of course the famous wheelbarrow poem begins with the unexplained assertion, "So much / depends."

If Williams made these sorts of assertion the most often, most Modern writers did occasionally. Even Stevens wrote

> Vines that take
> The various obscurities of the moon,
> Approaching rain
> And leaves that would be loose upon the wind,
> Pears on pointed trees,
> The dresses of women,
> Oxen . . .
> I never tire
> To think of this. (24)

Carl Sandburg, in *Chicago Poems,* describes working people, then says,

> Find for your pencils
> A way to mark your memory
> Of tired empty faces. (11)

In the teens, Eunice Tietjens caused a stir when she wrote a longish poem about a steam shovel, and Amy Lowell wrote a poem about a lunch counter. This sort of thing was more than just literary slumming. It was part of a more general attempt to establish the modern world as the proper subject for poetry. I don't mean to argue that such an attitude is particularly Modern. Nearly every poetic (and more generally literary) movement attempts to do the same thing, and, like the Moderns, tends to assert that previous movements were false in some way.

For H.D., as I have argued, part of the elevation of the ordinary was her assumption that it was connected to the classic spirit. Looking at the islands off the coast of Maine, she believed she had recovered the emotion Sappho felt when beholding Lesbos. For her, the appropriate verse was presentational and lyric. A full accounting of it, however, attends not only to (as A. D. Moody puts it) the poetry's "spareness and hardness" but also "how charged it is with desire" (80); likewise, Louis L. Martz comments on how the austerities of Imagism "provided H.D. with a discipline that enabled her to control the surges that arose from the depths of her violently responsive nature" (xiii) into a "dynamic and unified complex" (xiv). The poems often depict very strong emotions, the very sort Rosenmeyer explains as typical of dochmiac choruses. It is thus fitting that H.D. used the form imitating these choruses when writing her own poems.

H.D. is more subtle than Williams, but nevertheless a sense of elevation pervades *Sea Garden,* often literalized as a lifting by the waves. For example, it occurs in the third stanza of "Sea Rose," the poem which opens the collection and in many ways stands as an emblem for all of H.D.'s early poems:

> Stunted, with small leaf
> You are flung on the sand,
> You are lifted
> in the crisp sand
> that drives in the wind. (5)

Martz points out that H.D. often writes poems about vulnerable objects living "at the seething junction of opposing forces" (xi); in *Sea Garden,* this is usually in the area where the ocean and the land meet. The beauty and fragility depicted is mirrored by the austere slightness of the line. Just as the sea rose is lifted by the waves and wind, so the image and its simple description is lifted into the status of a poem by *Sea Garden.*

"Pursuit," similarly, while surely calling to mind Greek mythology—identified by Gregory as Dante Gabriel Rossetti's translation of a Sapphic fragment (234)—also suggests the impassioned pursuit of the beautiful. The poem describes a lover following the trail of the object of her desire:

> A patch of flowering grass,
> low trailing—
> you brushed this:

> the green stems show yellow-green
> where you are lifted—turned the earth-side
> to the light (11)

Not only does the poem exemplify the portrayal of "unnamed daimonic presences compelling responses at once fearful and erotic" that Gregory says characterizes many of the poems of *Sea Garden,* but these lines seem to provide a good description of Imagism: the passionate earthiness of things lifted to the light.

At the heart of H.D's poetic is a presentational strategy in which the poem identifies something and then describes it. Compare the similar rhythm and organizations of the first stanza of "Sea Rose"

> Rose, harsh rose,
> marred with stint of petals,
> meagre flower, thin,
> sparse of leaf (5)

with the first stanza of "Sea Iris":

> Weed, moss-weed,
> root tangled in the sand,
> sea-iris, brittle flower,
> one petal like a shell
> is broken,
> and you print a shadow
> like a thin twig. (36)

with the first stanza of "Cliff Temple":

> Great, bright portal,
> shelf of rock,
> rocks fitted in long ledges,
> rocks fitted to dark, to silver granite,
> to lighter rock—
> clean cut, white against white. (26)[26]

In two of the above stanzas, there is no verb, just successive description with past participles acting as adjectives—verbs made into modifiers which indicate that the thing's present state is a result of past action—and in the other the verb is delayed so that these modifying phrases interpose. The movement—name, followed by description—is similar to the epithets typical of oral poetry and poetries influenced by oral poetry. It happens twice in my lineated version of Gilbert Murray's translation and often in Homer and *Beowulf.*

H.D.'s short-line poetry is usually paratactic or in coordinate, rather than subordinate, clauses. This effect is sometimes highlighted by anaphora, as in "The Helmsmen":

> We forgot—we worshipped
> we parted green from green,
> we sought further thickets,
> we dipped our ankles
> through leaf-mould and earth,
> and wood and wood-bank enchanted us—
>
> and the feel of the clefts in the bark,
> and the slope between tree and tree—
> and a slender path strung field to field
> and wood to wood
> and hill to hill
> and the forest after it. (6)

This is not quite a catalogue, but the reader can instantly recognize that clauses of identical grammatical structure are stacked up. As in the free sections of poems from the seventeenth and nineteenth century, almost any line could be excised without rendering the passage ungrammatical. Thus, there is a sense of lineal integrity, a self-sufficiency that endows the poem with a kind of clarity, cleanness, and peculiarly a sense of direct impression. The fiction such poems enact is that complex subordination and enjambment are the messy result of a speaker's thinking things over too much (or, conversely, of her being unsure of what she has seen). In the stripped-down world of perception and emotion, there is only sequence.

Poems of this sort mean to imitate classical poetry to the extent that a sense of the translator pervades the very lineation of the poem. Moody, attending mainly to her terse imagery, calls H.D. an "elemental" poet. Yet, as in the passage above, it is often clear that H.D. could easily cut out words from her poem—her ultimate poetic is not to use the least amount of words possible.[27] While H.D. does frequently describe elements such as the sea and the wind, Wallace Stevens does so as well, yet few call him "elemental." Part of the elementalism of the poetry's feel stems from its grammatical decorum. Subject, verb, object: readers are likely to feel that they are being handed the very building blocks of language.

The line as grammatical phrase was fairly common amongst the Imagists. Thus, from *Des Imagistes,* Richard Aldington's "The River":

> I drifted along the river
> Until I moved my boat
> By these crossed trunks. (16)

"I" by F. S. Flint:

> London, my beautiful,
> I will climb
> into the branches
> to the moonlit tree-tops,
> that my blood may be cooled
> by the wind (31)

and from *Some Imagist Poets,* John Gould Fletcher's "Blue Symphony":

> The vast dark trees
> Flow like blue veils
> Of tears
> Into the water (35)

Amy Lowell's "Venus Transiens":

> Tell me,
> Was Venus more beautiful
> Than you are,
> When she topped

> The crinkled waves,
> Drifting shoreward,
> On her plaited shell. (81)

These examples could easily be multiplied many times. The Imagist substitution of the grammatical phrase for a set number of syllables was widespread enough to be noticed by contemporaries. In 1921, Ruth Mary Weeks described the Imagist line as "phrasal prosody" governed by "emphasis" rather than stress (12). In 1922, Robert Bridges's "Paper on Free Verse" elaborated on the idea: one characteristic of free verse, Bridges argues, is that each line is to consist of a "grammatical unit or unity" (651); this led to one of the "adverse conditions" of free verse, "sameness of line structure" (655). Though many of his contemporaries professed to find free verse a jumbled chaos, Bridges considered it over-uniform—an opinion likely shaded by his revision of *Milton's Prosody* a year earlier. Bridges tentatively put forth the notion that the lack of lineal variety was peculiar to free verse.[28]

More recent readers have concurred with Bridges. J. V. Cunningham, for example, writes that "Early free verse,"

> and much still written, has a discernible principle. I call it grammatical meter: a line may end at any terminal juncture, any completed grammatical unit. If the line is short, as in much Imagistic verse, the sentence is, in effect, diagrammed. I call it parsing meter. (259)

Donald Justice, examining this sort of lineal organization in Wallace Stevens's *Harmonium,* concludes, "that the line was prevalent in the Imagist period, and if ever vaguely Oriental poems, modest in scope, with a relaxed air and a certain wit, should come into fashion, this is the line in which they shall be written" (63). Justice finds the line "relaxed" because it is not strongly enjambed and "Oriental" because Stevens wrote haiku-like poems using the line. However, a sense of being relaxed does not characterize H.D.'s verse in the same form, and the line is certainly not "Oriental." Ming Xie, comparing Ezra Pound's translations of Chinese poetry with their originals, points out that while Pound may have had a sensitive appreciation of Chinese imagery, he ignored the rigid structure of Chinese verse—which included counting syllables and rhyme—in his free-verse translations. Guiyou Huang likewise argues that though Pound's use of Chinese poetry is "creative" (95) and exemplary in some ways, the Modern poet's renditions are often inaccurate. Moreover, Hirosake Sato shows that though Western imitations of haiku and tanka reproduce Japanese syllable counts, most of the Japanese poets imitated had no notion of lineation. The idea to break each group of syllables into separate lines only came about in Japanese poetry in the nineteenth century—and then, ironically enough, from influence from the West and especially Western translations.

Thus, the line seems Oriental because Stevens used it, just as it seems Greek when H.D. used it, and American when Williams used it. Because the line is short, it is associated with unrhetorical, presentational poetry. Since it avoids the polished urbanity of Pope, presumably never having to "fill out a line" or otherwise conform to traditional prosody, it often strikes readers as unfinished. Cunningham unwittingly echoes Wilde's estimation of Henley when he says that free verse in short lines has the force of "notations that might have been journal entries" (260). Similarly, George Oppen's short lines strike Rachel Blau DuPlessis as "ur-syntactic" (143). The feeling many readers get is of something prior to poetry, of a translation without the translator's later machinations. Of course these poems are highly wrought; however, they are done so in a style often associated with closeness to the source. Short-line poetry, then, implicitly proffers another ontology of poetry: the essence of poetry is the author's perception of the thing described.

This grammatical decorum, however, does not preclude hearable rhythm, as these lines from "Mid-day" show:

> A slight wind shakes the seed-pods—
> my thoughts are spent
> as the black seeds.
> My thoughts tear me,
> I dread their fever.
> I am scattered in its whirl.
> I am scattered like
> the hot shriveled seeds.
>
> The shrivelled seeds
> are split on the path—
> the grass bends with dust,
> the grape slips
> under its crackled leaf:
> yet far beyond the spent seed-pods,

and the blackened stalks of mint,
the poplar is bright on the hill,
the poplar spreads out,
deep-rooted among the trees. (19)

Seven significant words[29] repeat in the eighteen lines, and there are many repeating sounds, notably *s* and *p,* which rather whirl about each other like the black seeds: "*s*eed-*p*od*s*," "*sp*ent," "*sp*lit," "*s*li*ps*," "*sp*read*s*." Most of the lines repeat a word from the previous line, or cohere as strongly as "*gra*pe" and "*gra*ss" do. The passage is insistent in its repetitions, though not consistent. As in the poetry of Stevens, in this verse repeating words imitate a concept as well as sounds. The poem presents a world in which the same things appear again and again. The speaker identifies the natural world with her own thoughts, and thus the circling, black seeds on a sere landscape come to represent her own arid thoughts which will not change or revitalize, and threaten dissolution and perhaps death. She searches for stability and finds it in a poplar tree. The description of the tree is noticeably not enjambed, though the parts of the poem describing more disturbed thoughts are only lightly so. For all the poem's images of turning, there seems to be a sense of stasis, further emphasized by the past participles acting as adjectives. I experience the stasis as an intimation of timelessness.

The lines also demonstrate the way free-verse poems establish rhythm. Another way H.D. does this is by juxtaposing long and short lines; thus

where you are lifted—turned the earth-side
to the light;
this and a dead leaf-spine
split across (11)

and

The boughs of trees
are thistles
by many bafflings;
twisted are
the small-leaved boughs (38)

But these poems never repeat these patterns throughout. Stanzas are not of uniform length, and short-line/longer-line progressions are broken up soon after they are established.

Free verse of this nature reprioritizes traditional decorums of grammar and rhythm. In traditional versification, the rhythm establishes the line,and the poet manipulates grammar for expressive purposes. In this sort of free verse, grammar establishes the line, and the rhythm varies against that. But the grammatical decorum is rarely so uniform as the pattern of regular iambic pentameter. It is the grammatical equivalent of the disposition of lines in an irregular ode: the lines usually follow a pattern but often vary it, in the way that Cowley's lines are usually iambic. It is no use arguing that in these poems rhythm is preeminent. The grammatical progression is clear and unmistakable, while the rhythm is, by design, variable. No one has ever identified the controlling rhythm, the meter, of this sort of free verse because there is only local rhythm and grammatical control.

Part of the stripped-down, elemental feel of short-line poetry, then, is that the poem is stripped down to separate grammatical elements. After Imagism lost its steam, some poets continued their pursuit of ever-more-elemental lines. The phrase is not the smallest unit of the sentence, of course. Three poets committed to the techniques and implications of Imagism—H.D., Williams, and Louis Zukofsky—continued their pursuit of the naked poem for years afterward. Yet after a while the poets reached an impasse. This is dramatized in H.D.'s "Saturn":

> let prayer
> be fires:
>
> admire
> re-light
> relate
> regain:
>
> champion: (471)

It is also in these lines from Williams's "Christmas 1950":

The stores
guarded
by the lynx-eyed
dragon

money
humbly
offer their
flowers. (II.234)

This is all of Zukofsky's "THE":

The
desire
of
towing (*All* 87)

Once you reach one-word lines, the only thing left is the typographical pyrotechnics of Cummings:

l

l(a

le
af
fa

ll

s)
one
l

iness (673)

Most poets avoided this sort of thing. Clearly, the words fall down the page like leaves, but it is equally clear that Cummings finds puns that have nothing to do with the nature of language. That is to say, he finds a(n) "l" (indistinguishable in typescript from the number) and a "one" in "loneliness," which Cummings in effect makes lonely by isolating them on a line. He thus takes accidental qualities—and visual qualities, not aural or etymological ones—and renders them meaningful in the context of the poem. This is much different from

red wheel
barrow

which separates a word according to its semantic composition. Williams's split wheelbarrow might be said to replicate the processes of language, with enjambment making evident the compounded nature of the word *wheelbarrow.* The one's in "loneliness" are connections only made by the artist.

The one-word lines of H.D., Williams, and Zukofsky represent a crisis in short-line prosody. They thinned the line as far as they could without breaking the language apart. In the process of giving each word the prominence of the line, larger units of grammatical organization went by the wayside. There was only the bare word. Where to go next? All three poets promptly moved in the opposite direction. H.D. began to write the longer lines that characterize *Trilogy,* and Zukofsky finally settled on the five-word line that makes up *Fifty Flowers* and the concluding books of '*A*.' As for Williams—well, that story is much more complicated, and my next chapter will tell it.

My argument differs from previous comment on H.D. in several important respects. I have argued that the genius of the Imagists and the free verse indebted to Imagism was not, as is often asserted or implied, the invention of a new line. Instead, the genius of the Imagists was using the prosody of the free sections of classical imitations for entire poems. The Moderns promoted this poetic from a specialized prosody to that of a major aesthetic. Instead of the exception, it became the rule, requiring no special occasion or explanation.

There is historical precedent for this sort of change. The development of short-line free verse mirrors that of the sonnet. Tracing the sonnet from Dante to Petrarch to Renaissance England and beyond, it is fairly easy to see a general tendency. In *La Vita Nuova,* Dante intersperses prose narratives between lyric poems. Part of Petrarch's innovation was to tell a similar story through implication in lyric poems, dispensing with the prose narrative. This is also evident in Spenser's *Amoretti* and Sidney's *Astrophil and Stella.* But pretty soon many sequences did not have the same strong sense of narrative. Shakespeare's sonnets only sometimes seem to be telling a story, and Drayton's *Idea* has even less of a clear narrative. By the eighteenth century, it was possible to open up a magazine and read a single sonnet all by itself. Through its history, then, the sonnet has maintained its reputation for lyrical statement, but the sense of narrative, so strong in early sonnets, is often now missing.

Similarly, short-line free verse started only in the presence of iambic pentameter narrative before gradually losing its sense of connection with a story. Like the sonnet, short-line free verse has retained its position as a site of lyrical expression, often with the aura of classical austerity. It further retains the association of existing as a kind of fragment, vitally connected with the emotional perception often taken as the source of the poem. The fact that it does not avail itself of traditional rhyme and meter marks the poetic as avoiding the "old manner of approach." The poem, then, seems "new," or at least seemed so in 1916.

Hence, my argument adds a new dimension to the way I believe H.D. ought to be appreciated. It is not enough to say that she caught the spirit of Greece. She did so within the customs of traditional English poetry. Swann argues that H.D.'s classicism includes not only Greek texts but also the contributions of archaeologists, anthropologists, and psychologists. To this complex should be added the English tradition of classical imitation, a tradition which shares with H.D. the desire to create new works that partake of the aesthetic spirit of the ancient world. My account explains why poems that are not fragmentary strike many readers as fragments and casts into doubt the notion that H.D. created her poetry simply out of her intense reaction to classical texts and her contemporary world. It places a poet associated with the avant-garde within a recognizable tradition of English poetry.

CHAPTER FIVE

The Parsing Meter and Beyond

This chapter explores the poetics of another poet included in *Des Imagistes* (1914), William Carlos Williams. By and large, contemporaries did not consider Williams, as they did H.D., the standard-bearer of Imagism. As Bruce Bawer puts it, "[D]uring the heyday of the Modern movement, Williams was widely regarded as, at best, a second-tier figure" (14), yet "out of his work grew" such movements as Confessional, Beat, and Black Mountain poetry (25). Though Bawer finds much of Williams's influence pernicious, the fact remains that Williams's corpus presents the most consistent exploration of short-line poetics in Modern poetry.

Free-verse poets are indebted to both Williams's practice and his theory. Williams demonstrated that grammatical and visual prosodies could create a poetry that evinced at least as much compression as verse written in rhyme and meter. His organicism posits the rhythms of natural speech as the true basis of poetic rhythm, finding other rhythmic principles necessarily false and ornamental. These ideas have served as a frequent justification of free verse. Chapter 1 of this book established that free-verse proponents often assert an undefined, perhaps indefinable, rhythmic principle. I will explain why this is so. I conclude with an extended discussion of Williams's "variable foot," not with the intention of rehabilitating Williams's nomenclature, but instead because Williams's theory considers, or attempts to consider, the theoretical and practical difficulties of hearing verse composed according to the rhythms of speech. Williams in fact created a mythical foot; using it as a basis for reading or writing only creates new prosodic problems while intensifying the old ones.

Williams deserves special consideration in any discussion of twentieth-century lineal form because, as Carroll Terrell notes, his "lifelong ambition was to change the poetic line"—change it from, that is, the iambic pentameter norm and more generally from what Williams would term the metronome of traditional metrics. Though there were short-line poems aplenty, no poet so consistently wrote in the line, experimented with it, and proselytized for it. More than any other poet, Williams pursued a revolution in the line that, as Terrell points out, he was convinced would "change civilization" (29). My method will be to summarize those elements of Williams's prosodic philosophy that seem to make sense—putting aside, for instance, Williams's contention that his "variable foot" had something to do with Einstein's theory of relativity,[1] and then examine the extent to which his poetry realized his ideals. Further, I will focus on the assumptions about poetry that Williams held throughout his career. This approach is especially fruitful for Williams, because unlike Stevens, who could be reserved while discussing lineal form, Williams frequently asserted that the line was one of his central concerns.

Williams's prosodic criticism is notoriously vague, contradictory, and confusing. Hollander comments that Williams's writings reveal the poet as "a cranky autodidact who has never had anyone serious to talk to" (*Vision* 235). Kenner's assessment is similarly condescending. The "problem was inherited terminology": Williams "simply" used "nouns he could hear learned men uttering in the general vicinity of what he meant" ("Rhythms" 37). Since Hollander and Kenner find much in Williams's poetry to praise, they fall into the first of Stephen Cushman's two categories of Williams's admirers. On the one hand, there are those who lead "double lives, admiring [Williams's] poems while apologizing for his theory"; on the other are those "determined not to apologize, [who] have found themselves hypnotized by Williams' logic and terminology, until soon they are repeating his slogans and formulations" (*Meanings* 1). Cushman concludes, "Williams' theory of measure does matter," not because it describes his poetry very well, but because it reveals "the mind behind the verse" (*Meanings* 2). Although I will show that Williams's statements on verse form are more coherent than is generally recognized, I too am after the "mind"—more specifically, the myths and formal allegories that underlie poetic practice.

Hollander was right that Williams was self-taught and could be "cranky," even to the point of mimicking in his correspondence Pound's penchant for putting points he especially insists upon in all capital letters. Nevertheless, Williams had many "serious people" to talk to. He carried on lengthy discussions with Pound, H.D., Stevens, Marianne Moore, George Oppen, Louis Zukofsky, Theodore Roethke, Charles Olson, Robert Creeley, Allen Ginsberg,

Denise Levertov, and many others. He tried to talk about the line to Eliot and Auden, neither of whom responded to his invitations. Certainly these poets, included in most anthologies of twentieth-century poetry, should be considered "serious."

Further, the inconsistencies of Williams's prosodic writings are often overstated. As I have pointed out before, imprecise and inconsistent terminology generally accompanies prosodic criticism. Williams's appropriation (or misapplication) of prosodic and linguistic terminology is symptomatic of a time when prosodists simply ignored the twentieth-century poetry that did not conform to traditional models. Present-day theorists still struggle to establish terms and reading procedures for the types of poetry Williams frequently addressed.

Still, Williams's prose stretches over a period of fifty years, and all the while he was tinkering with his line. Moreover, he rarely if ever wrote in an academic context, subject to review and revision. For the first thirty years or so of his career, he usually paid to have his own books published and sometimes published articles in magazines he edited. By the time others were paying him, he had attained such stature that what he said was significant just because he said it. Thus, although the editors of *The Princeton Encyclopedia of Poetry and Poetics* (1974) slightly expanded his definition of free verse, they allowed Williams's patently false assertion, that the "variable foot" was widely accepted, to stand.

I have argued that different kinds of free verse endorse differing brands of organicism. Short-line verse is no exception.

The notion that Williams's poetic is organicist flies in the face of the inorganic metaphors that Williams frequently used to describe poems. Though at times he finds the poem like a tree or the waves, it is also an "object" invented by (*Autobiography* 265), or a "house" (*Autobiography* 334) constructed by, the artist. It is a "machine made of words" (II.54). Anne Janowitz, noting that "Williams returned again and again to a mechanical, manufacturing metaphor for the 'creation' of a poem," finds many such images to support her thesis that Williams is an "'indigenous tinker,' or inventor" (301–2). Likewise, Eleanor Berry remarks, "For Williams, the verbal composition largely preceded the mechanical manipulation, rather than being, as in [Marianne] Moore's case, partly carried along with it" ("Marine" 54). Thus, the poet thinks something up and then manipulates it, "mechanically," into a machine made of words. This seems to be the narrative implied in "Fine Work with Pitch and Copper," a poem, Williams said, "really telling about my struggle with verse" (*I Wanted* 57).

That poem ends:

> The copper in eight
> foot strips has been
> beaten lengthwise
>
> down the center at right
> angles and lies ready
> to edge the coping
>
> One still chewing
> picks up a copper strip
> and runs his eye along it (I.405–6)

The poem likens the poet (the "One still chewing") to a craftsman beating his material to a usable shape. This does not seem very much like Coleridge's plant developing from an internal source of energy.

From this sort of evidence, Jonathan Mayhew argues that "two contradictory notions" governed Williams's poetics: the "nineteenth-century concept of organic form" that "demands that the intrinsic qualities of the world come into the poem without distortion," and the notion that "the artist must assert an order of his own through art, organize his materials actively and creatively. Williams called the imitation of the 'senseless / unarrangement of wild things' the 'stupidest rime of all.'"[2] However, even if the two notions are contradictory, it is not so much a contradiction in Williams's thought as it is in organicism itself. Simply put, Williams's poetic is one long testament to ardent organic faith.

Organicists do not believe that imitating the "intrinsic qualities of the world . . . without distortion" is inconsistent with the artist's creative making, because, as I have shown, it is an article of faith that the artist's creativity partakes of the Creation—it is the same force that divided light from dark, made the Word into Flesh, and every day manifests itself in animal and vegetable procreation. In his *Autobiography,* Williams assails the notion that the highest art was to copy nature. Instead, he says,

> the artist should imitate nature, which involves the verb to do. To copy is merely to reflect something already there, inertly; Shakespeare's mirror [held up to

> nature] is all that is needed for it. But by imitation we enlarge nature itself, we become nature or we discover in ourselves nature's active part. (341)

Coleridge and Whitman would endorse this opinion without reservation. Cushman points out that Williams echoes Coleridge's metaphor for the relation between God's creation and poetic creation—that the poet repeats God's I AM at Exodus 3:14[3]—in *The Desert Music*. The lines also contain a prosodic pun:

> I *am* a poet! I
> am. I am. I am a poet, I reaffirmed, ashamed (II.284)

The Desert Music is about, among other things, the music of poetry, which it portrays as the still, sad music of humanity (represented in the poem by a joyless stripper and reappearing beggars). This music is not composed by the traditional "law" (which "gives us nothing / but a corpse" [II.274]), and so the lines enact the idea that honest, accurate music involves breaking up the iamb as well. In order for the poet to declare himself, he must depart from traditional rhythm.

Telling, too, is this snippet from *The Williams-Siegel Documentary:*

> SIEGEL: What you're saying is that the poem is related to the original energy of the world which will not be denied.
> WILLIAMS: Good. That's fine, that's fine. In other words, you've got to believe it above all that, and you sometimes lose faith—well, not faith, you don't lose faith, you lose courage, that's all. (96)

Like most honest adherents to any system of belief, Williams acknowledges that though he does not always act according to his beliefs, his faith is nonetheless unwavering.

A corollary to this kind of organic faith is Coleridge's notion that natural creativity is continually adaptive. Williams's metaphor for the sonnet implies this opinion: "Forcing twentieth-century life into a sonnet," he told John W. Gerber, "is like putting a crab in a box. You've got to cut his legs off to make him fit. When you get through, you don't have a crab any more" (*Interviews* 30). Williams thinks the box should be made to fit the crab. In another context, he wrote that the pre-set form of the sonnet controlled the thought expressed:

> All sonnets mean the same thing because it is the configuration of words that is the major significance . . . it is not an invention but anchors beyond the will—

> does not liberate the intelligence but stultifies it—and by its cleverness apt use stultifies it making pleasurable that which should be removed. (*Embodiment* 17)

So stifling was the sonnet form that Williams once called it "fascistic" (*Selected Essays* 236). The exception to this appraisal proves the rule. Williams's reason for praising the one twentieth-century sonneteer he liked further confirms his organicist credentials. Merrill Moore's sonnets are works of art, he declared,

> because Moore has broken through the binding stupid formality of the thing and gone after the core of it, not of the sonnet, which is nothing, but the sonnet form, which is the gist of the whole matter. That's what is seldom understood. It's not a matter of destroying forms so much as it is a matter of observation, of resensing the problem, of seeing, of comprehending that of which the form consists as a form, of rescuing the essence and re-forming it. (*Something* 92)

The review reveals that underneath his materialism lies a surprisingly platonic theory of forms. The sonnet verse form has an "essence" that precedes its various manifestations. There is, presumably, an Ideal Sonnet, profound and capable, behind its earthly corruptions that Williams thought Moore discovered by considering the form anew. Hence, the ideal is expressed as an "essence," a "core," and a "gist." In short, the idea precedes and vitalizes the thing.

However, unlike Coleridge, Williams did not feel meter was assimilatable by a greater organicism. The "restraint" necessary for form, Williams said,

> lies in a fidelity to the object, the thought about it, and their passionate welding. It is the movement of this constrained passion limiting itself to the objective of its immediate purpose, which creates the meter as the obstructions in a river create the pattern of its flow. (*Something* 62)

Thus lineal form was to be "invention of perception" (*Something* 99). It is in this respect that many, Charles Doyle and Hartman, for example, cite Williams's poetic as organic.[4] "Poem" is often cited to illustrate this principle:

> As the cat
> climbed over
> the top of
>
> the jamcloset
> first the right
> forefoot

carefully
then the hind
stepped down

into the pit of
the empty
flowerpot (I.352)

Kenner's comment on this poem perhaps cannot be improved. He remarks, this "sinuous suspended sentence, feeling its way and never fumbling" enacts the action of the cat, so that "The cat is as much an emblem of the sentence as the sentence is of the cat" (*Pound* 399).

Though I have been offering the connection between form and content as organic, a skeptical reader may object that the notion that form should follow function is not original to Coleridge and Williams. A comparison of Williams's "Fine Work" with William Cowper's "The Flatting Mill" should make the distinction between organicism and functional form clear, while also clarifying how Williams could use inorganic metaphors to detail his organic faith. Cowper's poem is doubly useful for my argument, because Cowper employs imagery similar to Williams, and because the Romantics often singled out Cowper as a practitioner of the kind of mechanical poetry they wanted to revolutionize.[5] The differences in the theory and practice of the poems demonstrate the differences between organic and inorganic approaches to poetry.

"The Flatting Mill" begins by describing the process by which ingots of gold are "flatted and wrought into length" by "an engine of utmost mechanical might." It then laments the state of the poet "who dares undertake / To urge the reformation of national ill." The pressures on him are likened to the pressure exerted by the flatting mill. In the last two stanzas, however, Cowper flips the metaphor so that, as in Williams's "Fine Work," the poet is the artisan and the poem his craft:

If he wish to instruct, he must learn to delight;
Smooth, ductile, and even, his fancy must flow—
Must tinkle and glitter, like gold to the sight,
And catch in its progress a sensible glow.

After all he must beat it as thin and as fine
As the leaf that enfolds what an invalid swallows;

> For truth is unwelcome, however divine;
> And unless you adorn it, a nausea follows. (203)

To make the bitter pill of social criticism palatable, the poet ornaments it with a finely wrought gold veneer. Thus, there is a neat separation between the unpleasant but salutary matter and the delightful but merely ornamental form. It is strongly implied that if society knew what was good for it, it would not need the gold veneering at all. In "Fine Work," though, the hammered copper does not adorn something else. It is the end unto itself. In this way, Williams's organicism is highly aesthetic, assuming that a satisfying poem can consist solely of description and needs no social criticism to justify itself. The work talks about and allegorizes its own form.

Further, Williams's workman is "chewing." In the poem's narrative he is eating lunch, but Williams seems to have in mind a pun about rumination. The artisan is chewing over in his mind the form he thinks the copper ought to take. The metaphor links the gustatory with the intellectual and the artist's conception with his creation. He is figuratively digesting the form. For Cowper, the reader must swallow something, and so Cowper tries to make his matter as digestible as possible. Williams's workman is concerned with his own ideas; the reader is merely allowed to observe.

The forms of the poems mirror the poetic they imply. Cowper writes in anapestic tetrameter quatrains (with a little iambic substitution at the beginning of lines), a form his audience recognized as musical. Williams's visual form—three-line stanzas with each line visually about the same length—announces the work as a poem, but otherwise has little in the way of predictable lineal decorum. The nontraditional though rigid form allegorizes the notion that the artist needs both restraint and freedom from convention. Both poems thus allegorize their form, but proceed from very different assumptions about the role of the poet and the nature of poetry.

Williams's most profound organic faith has nothing to do with the sort of mimesis thus far discussed. A first tenet of Williams's greater belief is that, as he wrote to Frances Sterloff, "Impassioned language takes on, by physical law, a rhythmic flow." He doesn't say why this is a "law," but he repeated this idea many times in his prosodic writings. He goes on,

> The poet's task, in any age, is to listen to the language of his time, when it is impassioned and whenever it occurs, and to discover in it, from it, the essentials

of his form, his form, as of his own day. From these essentials he makes his patterns —embodying the characteristics of what he finds alive in his day. ("Letter" 24)

Poems are made of passionate rhythmic language, but the poet is not merely a reporter; instead, he must extract, analyze, and use only the essence of speech. In *I Wanted to Write a Poem,* he writes that the "rhythmic pace" of his poetry "was the pace of speech, an excited pace because I was excited when I wrote" (15). Again, the poetry is not, itself, a record of excited speech, only its rhythm is.

Traditional meter was, to Williams's mind, "arbitrary" and "wholly unrelated to our own language" (59); in *Spring and All,* he argues that meter was "designed to separate the work from 'reality'" (I.189). Kenner remarks, Williams was "right" that "the individuating rhythms that run sentence-long, utterance-long . . . aren't usefully described by the micro-units of meter, the iambs and the anapests" ("Rhythms" 38–39)—but then the original purpose of meter does not seem to have been to represent speech accurately. Jannaris argued that meter has to do with the Melic tradition in verse, and was adopted by poets who, not believing in the "law" of excited rhythm, wanted what they considered to be musical rhythms in their poetry.

Williams preferred to think that metrical poetry was composed by the metronome, that traditional prosody was a "meaningless metric" leading to "meaningless words put there for sound alone" (*Something* 61), a "da ding da ding da ding da ding" (*Interviews* 46). Like Ford and Pound, Williams thought that poets customarily filled out iambic pentameter lines with "slush." Since the line was a unit of perception, traditional poems have "primitive perception," whereas freer poems have "quicker perception" (*Interviews* 67–68). "When I came to the end of a rhythmic unit," Williams said, "I ended the line" (*I Wanted* 15), and for this reason each line should be a single unit of rhythm as well as a perception.

If Williams sometimes seems to say that he was creating rhythm and sometimes that he was organizing information, it is because he had the faith that the two were the same. The rhythm that he wanted was "under the language which we have been listening to all our lives, a more profound language," an "essence hidden in the very words that are going in our ears and from which we must recover underlying meaning" (*Autobiography* 362). He was no reformer, he told Gerber and Wallace, "I take what I find, I make a poem out of it" (*Interviews* 24).

"Under the language," a "profound language," an "essence": clearly Bollobás is right when he labels Williams an "immanentist" who believed that the "poet's task is not to impose rules upon the language but to interrogate it" ("Measured"

267). The rhythm of language, like Williams's Ideal Sonnet, must be discovered and not devised. It is no wonder Carl Rapp calls Williams's "pursuit of the new measure" the "high water mark of American transcendentalism" (114).

However, whether Williams succeeded is an open question. R. W. Butterfield's comment on "Portrait of a Woman in Bed" exemplifies the difficulties. First a sample from the poem:

> I won't work
> and I've got no cash.
> What are you going to do
> about it
> —and no jewelry
> (the crazy fools) (I.87)

Now Butterfield:

> What is remarkable about this is not simply the accurate recording of complex feeling, but also the manner in which the structure is controlled by the tones and habits of the woman's own speech. The questions, assertions, and disruptions are all signs of her disturbed and defiant emotional presence. (65)

Although Williams would no doubt have been pleased with Butterfield's remarks, the poet never claimed the poem was a "recording." He told John Thirwall it was merely his "idea of what happened" (I.487). Nonetheless, Butterfield's sentiments are often echoed. Paul Mariani, for example, calls the Phyllis and Corydon section of *Paterson* book IV "authentic speech" (615). In both cases, judging whether Williams has caught the rhythms of speech is an exercise in subjectivity. For every critic who claims Williams has caught the rhythms of speech, there is one who claims Williams has not done so. For instance, Kenner points out in *A Homemade World* that the red wheelbarrow lyric is an unlikely utterance. Even during the period which Williams most insisted that he was imitating speech, Marjorie Perloff contends, Williams's poems were "surely not the natural idiom" ("To Give" 160); in fact, Mayhew argues, Williams "distorts natural speech rhythms" (295). The debate is, as of this date, not resolvable. When I first started researching this book, I found many more books about prosody written by linguists trying to establish the rhythms of speech than there were by literary historians trying to find the rhythms of poetry. Since the rhythms of speech remain a subject of debate, the answer to the question of whether Williams has reproduced them must be deferred.

Still, Rapp points out that one theory Williams seemed to have had was that "poetry is to exhibit for purposes of contemplation the speech rhythms in the spontaneous utterances of both the poet himself and his neighbors" (81). While Rapp puts this as the justification for Williams's poems written in the fifties, "Portrait of a Woman in Bed" was written in 1917, and Williams's poetry throughout his career is sprinkled with a fair number of examples of heard speech, such as this one written in 1931:

> "Over Labor Day they'll
> be gone."
> "Jersey City, he's the
> engineer—" "Ya"
> "Being out on the Erie R. R.
> is quite convenient" (I.354)

But that poem ends with a re-entry of unspoken language:

> "No, I think they're—"
> "I think *she* is. I think—"
> "German-American"
> "Of course the Govern—"
> Very quiet
> Stillness. A distant door
> slammed. Amen.

In truth, at no time in his career did Williams write mostly heard speech. His "core" or "spirit" of the American idiom is just the twentieth-century version of Wordsworth's contention that his poems were natural speech purified. If you want to be Coleridge about it,[6] you are perfectly welcome to argue that the kind of investigation and artistic working Williams thought necessary to get to the *rhythmos* behind the rhythm actually "distorts" the rhythm.

But just as Wordsworth's diction and syntax were less "literary" than many of his contemporaries, so Williams's poems were more like speech than many written by others in the same years. Obviously, the poems copied out above sound a bit more like something overheard than, say, "The Love Song of

J. Alfred Prufrock" or "Le Monocle de Mon Oncle." Further, it is probably unwarranted to dismiss all of Williams's documented speech. Williams listened very closely for a long time, and Mariani notes instances in which Williams raced home from a house call to write down what he had just heard.[7] As I shall show at the end of this chapter, some of what Williams said about measure is consistent with what some present-day linguists are saying about language.

Williams's theory of concision also influenced his line. Two letters exemplify this theory. The first is from H.D. to Williams:

> I trust you will not hate me for wanting to delete from your poems all the flippancies . . . I think there is real beauty—and real beauty is a rare and sacred thing in this generation—in all the pyramid, Ashur-ban-i-bal bits and the Fiesole and the wind at the last. (I.493)[8]

The second is from Williams to Denise Levertov: "Cut and cut again whatever you write—while you leave by your art no trace of your cutting—and the final utterance will remain packed with what you have to say" (*Something* 17). The two letters articulate the philosophy of the slashing pencil Pound used on the early draft of H.D.'s "Hermes of the Ways." Though cutting out unnecessary verbiage is part of the design of almost all poetics, for short-line poets it is the very path to the spirit. The notion is that poetry purged of "slush" (in practice, this often means poetry largely without adjectives or adverbs) is a poetry in which each remaining word has undergone the rigors of examination and holds special potency. The fictional narrative of composition for short-line poetry is in effect that "this is what is left after you have excised the unpoetical from the poetic"—even though, as I argued last chapter, the line seems to have descended from a tradition of classical imitation that often sponsored expansion, not contraction.

In the context of Williams's poetic of concision, words like "naked" and "bare" take on a moral tinge. The alternative to nakedness is false adornment, padding. Thus Williams describes a novel as a striptease down to the underwear, but when "you get down to nothing more than the sheer (nylon) panties, or, shall we say, jock strap, slip a finger under the edge and snap it off—we have, hopefully, the poem" (*Autobiography* 368). A poem is speech pared to its essentials, stripped and made naked for display. Like the ultimate end of generative linguistics, what you have when all the surface is discarded is a model for the human mind, a demonstration of the way that people think—not, as in a stream of consciousness narrative, a record of the actual thoughts and utterances, but a laying bare of a deeper structure. This idea can be called transcendental because it assumes a veil of appearances must be penetrated in order for the deeper meaning to be brought forth. Though Williams does not often seem to think that there is an extrahuman spirit, his faith in deeper meanings and a kind of abstract, transcendent truth that directs physical manifestation is every bit as strong as that of his nineteenth-century forbears.

The importance of transcending appearances is evident in the opening prose section to *Spring and All*. The opening prose section asserts

> nearly all writing, up to the present, if not all art, has been especially designed to keep up the barrier between sense and the vaporous fringe which distracts the attention from its agonized approaches to the moment. It has been always a search for "the beautiful illusion." Very well. I am not in search of "the beautiful illusion." (I.178)

Thus Williams conceives of an epistemological lyric in which close examination provides lyricism. Traditional poetry's "barrier" between the senses and the "vaporous fringe" recalls Whitman's description of traditional prosody as a "curtain" that the poet should transcend. Of course, Williams would substitute the here and now for the vast spaces Whitman often explored.[9] Consequently, throughout the volume Williams's characteristic image for transcendence is neither the mountain climbing of the Romantics nor the lifted objects of *Sea Garden*. As in his comment on Merrill Moore, the metaphor repeated time and again is that of breaking asunder, a kind of destruction that leads to birth and greater revelation. *Spring and All* attempts to break down obstacles to the sight and see clearly what the first poem calls "the new world naked" (I.183).

"The rock has split, the egg has hatched, the prismatically plumed bird of life has escaped from its cage" (I.184), the prose declares, and the volume is replete with images of things breaking: "Burst it asunder" poem IV directs, "break through to the fifty words / necessary" (I.187) to connect the sense to the thing; the wind "breaks it" in poem V, while men are "splitting their heads open" at a boxing match (I.190); in poem VII, the edge of a rose petal "cuts without cutting" (I.195), and finally "penetrates / the Milky Way" (I.196); poem IX, after defining "unclean" as "not straight to the mark" (I.200), insists that

> Clean is he alone
> after whom stream

the broken pieces of the city—
flying apart at his approaches (I.201–2)

Implicitly, breaking is the only way to see clearly and not by the light of old illusions. Thus, poem XII juxtaposes the archaic "renaissance/twilight" with "triphammers // which pulverize/nitrogen" (211). Poem XV asserts, "destruction and creation / are simultaneous" (213) as it looks at the way that movie houses have replaced passion plays. Perhaps most strikingly, Elsie, one of the "pure products of America" (I.217) described in poem XXVII, expresses "with broken // brain the truth about us" (I.218). The line break mirrors the brokenness of her "brain." Because her brain is broken (not only what we might today call "learning disabled," but also not functioning within the self-conscious rules of social self-protection that most follow), she has no desire or apparent ability to adhere to the social rituals that mask earthiness and gloss over social inequality. In this broken-down nakedness "we" see the "truth"; indeed, *only* in these places of breakage, for

It is only in isolate flecks that
something
is given off (I.219)

Isolated and pure, only in those cut off from the mainstream plainly manifest the essence of America.

Things breaking, creation in destruction, revelation in clarity: these processes are not peculiar to *Spring and All,* for Williams used such paradigms throughout his career. For instance, Jessica Levine has shown that a dominant metaphor in *Paterson* is the flow of the Passaic (as the flow of the mind), where it is "Blocked" (*Paterson* 62) and where it breaks through. Yet for all this emphasis on breaking, much of Williams's free verse and most of his early poems follow the grammatical decorums of H.D. Thus, "Stillness" begins,

Heavy white rooves
of Rutherford
sloping west and east
under the fast darkening sky (I.52)

and "Metric Figure,"

There is a bird in the poplars!
It is the sun!
The leaves are little yellow fish
swimming in the river. (I.66)

and "Pastoral,"

The little sparrows
hop ingenuously
about the pavement
quarreling
with sharp voices
over those things
that interest them. (I.70)

There are many such poems scattered throughout Williams's corpus. The movement, as in H.D.'s poems, is coordinative, each line maintaining a phrasal integrity, with the result that many lines could be excised without rendering the poem ungrammatical. I experience this movement as not exactly slow, but measured rather than rapid. The studied integrity encourages, I think, a momentary degrammaticizing of the hierarchies of the sentence. Since the phrases are usually of similar length visually, and are given identical prominence by their isolation in the line, the reader is seemingly encouraged to appreciate each clause before continuing.

The isolating quality of short-line lineation creates a paradox in Williams's poetic. Though Williams wrote a number of poems like the cat in the jamcloset, a striking aspect of Williams's short-line poems is not their presentational nature but instead their abstractions which are foregrounded by the action of the parsing meter. Occasionally, a whole poem will be thingless, as "Descent":

From disorder (a chaos)
order grows
—grows fruitful.
The chaos feeds it. Chaos
feeds the tree. (II.238)

More frequently, readers come up to stanzas such as

for this is eternity
through its
dial we discover (I.210)

and

the aggregate
is untamed
encapsulating
irritants
but
of agonized spires
knits
peace (I.212)

and

a stateliness,
a sign of finality
and perfect ease.
Among the savage (I.239)

Despite the fact that these passages appear in poems full of things, the stanzas isolate the abstractions so that they stand apart from the things they describe. The reader is, in effect, given little idea poems within a material whole. This frequently happens when Williams talks about movement:

An edge of bubbles stirs
swiftness is molded
speed grows

the profuse body advances
over the stones unchanged (I.288)

The poem describes not the stream but the movement of the stream, activity and not water itself. In "The Crimson Cyclamen," Williams describes a painting by Charles Demuth:

where the under and the over
meet and disappear
and the air alone begins
to go from them (I.421)

Again, the thing described is movement. Such abstractions, Levertov argues, help indicate that "the irresistible impulsion towards metaphor" caused Williams to "betray" his dictum in *Paterson,* "No ideas but in things." She remarks, "There are commonly more 'ideas' in William Carlos Williams' 'things' than he is commonly credited with" ("Ideas" 141). Really, though, so long as a "thing" appears somewhere in the poem, Williams need not be said to betray himself, since most of the poems imply that the idea came from the thing. Williams did not say, "No ideas."

The presentation of these found abstractions, a procedure where abstractions are set apart on lines and often stanzas, is a major part of Williams's contribution to short-line verse. By the time he was becoming an Imagist, the short line was already the site of things and emotions. He found a dynamic way to describe abstract ideas. Though abstraction is a feature of Modern artists in a variety of media, it is particularly striking in the work of Williams, whose poems so often focus on the phenomenal, material world.

Part of the dynamism of his poetry stemmed from Williams's practice of putting his verbs in the present tense (instead of concentrating description in past participles as in H.D.) and writing poems about actions in progress. More radically, Williams is Modern poetry's foremost experimenter with enjambment, a device he used diversely and extensively, and one that has been so influential that one of the most important aspects of a new methodology for approaching free verse, Wesling's "grammetrics," is that it attempts to register degrees of enjambment. I have already quoted in chapter 1 Leithauser's contention that the prosody of free verse is limited to enjambment.

Williams's short-line poetry can be classed into two types according to their enjambment. The first is the parsing meter already described in the previous chapter. The second proceeds along lines of fracture. Though in short-line poetry enjambment is unavoidable, Williams soon started experimenting with ever-more-radical enjambment, so that, as Perloff points out, syntax "purposely goes against the line, blocking its integrity" ("To Give" 166). Thus, "Summer Song" detaches article from noun:

a detached
sleepily indifferent
smile, a
wanderer's smile (I.79)

"The Winds" in a similar manner severs articles from nouns, prepositions from the nouns they make genitive, and opens with a mimetic line break to boot:

flowing edge to edge
their clear edges meeting—
the winds of northern March—
blow the bark from the trees
the soil from the field
the hair from the heads of
girls, the shirts from the backs
of the men, roofs from the
houses, the cross from the
church, clouds from the sky
the fur from the faces of
wild animals, crusts
from scabby eyes, scales from
the mind, and husbands from wives (I.275)

The disorder brought by the wind is imitated by the grammar blown willy-nilly across the line. As in *Spring and All,* destruction brings clearer sight, divulging that which was once hidden, here to the disadvantage of the marriage bond. But Williams's true genius was to bring this tumbling verse to still things. Nowhere is this more apparent than in his many poems about flowers and paintings of flowers. "It Is a Small Plant," for example:

It is a small plant
delicately branched and
tapering conically
to a point, each branch
and the peak a wire for
green pods, blind lanterns
starting upward from

the stalk each way to
a pair of prickly edged blue
flowerets: it is her regard,
a finished thing guarding
its secret. Blue eyes— (I.125)

The poem goes on from there. Notice how many lines end with a preposition, conjunction, or some word that seems to demand another. J. Hillis Miller describes this as "each word reaching out with its strength to other words that are for the moment absent. Conjunctions, prepositions, adjectives, when they come at the end of the line, assume an expressive energy as arrows of force" (41). Arrows, Marie Borroff adds, pointing ever onward in the "downward pull" ("Questions" 106) of short-lined, strongly enjambed verse. Borroff prefers to read this procedure mimetically and quotes from "The Term" to show how the line breaks can imitate the thing described. A piece of paper with the

apparent bulk
of a man was
rolling with the

wind slowly over
and over in
the street as

a car drove down
upon it and
crushed it to

the ground. Unlike
a man it rose
again rolling

with the wind over
and over to be as
it was before. (I.452)

Likewise, Sharon Dolin finds mimesis in *Spring and All:*

Of death
the barber
the barber
talked to me

cutting my
life with
sleep to trim
my hair (I.212)

She might have added this from "The Poem":

          something
immediate, open

scissors (II.74)

These passages might call to mind the last line of Stevens's scissors, "The Comedian as the Letter C":

So may the relation of each man be clipped. (46)[10]

Though Dolin points out the prevalence of the mimetic line break in Modern poetry, I have shown it in Pope, and any number of poets have used it. But, Cushman asks, "How does enjambment enhance meaning in 'To a Poor Old Woman'?" (24):

munching a plum on
the street a paper bag
of them in her hand

They taste good to her
They taste good
to her. They taste
good to her (I.383)

Hollander compares this sort of thing to Noam Chomsky's sentence, "They don't know how good meat tastes." A speaker can manipulate the sentence's meaning by emphasizing different words (or, if you are a poet, manipulating different words to the end of the line).[11] However interesting the experiment, Cushman insists that the "pattern exists apart from the woman." The closest mimetic connection Cushman can find is by analogy, the speaker "has been savoring the possibility of English syntax as [the old woman] savors the plums" (24).

Cushman's point is just, but it strikes me that in "To a Poor Old Woman," the repeating phrases mimic the repeating but not exactly identical actions of eating, each bite of which brings a new sensation of pleasure (hence a repetition of the statement about how good they are), just as the enjambment of "The Term" enacts the repeating though not identically recurring tumbling motions of the piece of paper. The old woman's eating motion presents a natural rhythm that the grammatical form of the poem mimics. A better example of nonmimetic enjambment, I think, is a similar exercise that takes up the first section of "Calypsos":

> Well God is
> love
> so love me
>
> God
> is love so
> love me God
>
> is
> love so love
> me well (II.426)

There is no registerable natural motion, so it is hard to see what the line breaks could be imitating. This supports Hollander's and Cushman's contention that such verse experiments are often meant to interrogate language and not to copy the action described. Indeed, making the case that all of Williams's enjambment is mimetic is as tenable as asserting every line break in *Paradise Lost* is locally significant. Most enjambment in truth is a style in which poets use visual puns when they occur.

As Mayhew argues, when Williams enjambs strongly, he breaks the "unit of meaning" typical of H.D. (288). Berry takes this idea further:

> These radical enjambments throw emphasis on the function words put in line-terminal positions, by deferring fulfillment of syntactical expectation, on the

> predicated elements when they appear. They also produce syncopation in the movement of the verse. ("Williams'" 23)

The syncopation is between "completed units" and fractured ones, a point I will return to shortly. Berry is surely right when she says that this procedure "de-automatizes the process of reading" and emphasizes the poem as a construction, a "perceptible verbal object" (23). By aligning function words at the area of greatest prominence (at the end of the line), the enjambment emphasizes the relations between words and interstices between clauses. Berry further argues that enjambment also calls attention to language when it "induces" the reader to interpret a word as one part of speech and then another. Consider, for example, "10/14":

> the scraping of
> fallen leaves still leaves
> your loveliness
> unshaken (II.26–27)

Here, the reader is not instantly sure if the second "leaves" is noun or verb. Similarly, "War, the Destroyer" seems to offer "serious" as an adjective before revealing it as a noun:

> The deadly serious
> who would have us suppress (II.43)

"Close" in the first of "Three Sonnets" seems to be a verb until the next line suggests that it may be an adjective:

>   heavy slabs close
> packed with jagged rime-cupped (II.73)

But this sort of thing happens in H.D.'s relatively lightly enjambed verse. Is "Tear" a noun or a verb?

> Tear—
> tear us an altar (15)

The isolated word seems to tug both ways, functioning as a verb in the narration of the poem but punning on the noun to indicate the pain.

Short-line verse tends, in Mariani's phrase, to bring out the "multifoliate possibilities" of words (197). These types of experiments are what the speaker of A. R. Ammons's poem "Scribbles" refers to as finding "(if on purpose) by accidence" (23). Nonetheless, Williams's most radical enjambment, since it so often ends in function words which point to connections (hence Miller's "arrows"), typically does not render words ambiguous. Rather, like brush strokes on an Impressionist canvas, the odd line endings say, "the artist was here."

The two modes of the short line—that which proceeds in the parsing meter and that which breaks the grammatical phrase—are not necessarily discrete. Many times a poem will, as Berry puts it, go "out of phase" ("Williams'" 25) and back into it. Bollobás, following Wesling, argues that grammar as prosody was "Whitman's innovation," but "the refinement of grammatical rhythm toward continuity and discontinuity, predictability and unpredictability, was the prosodic achievement of Pound and Williams" (*Tradition* 268). That is to say, this prosody demands that its readers recognize which lines present full clauses and which that do not, and so understand that the poem's form enacts a drama of "doubt and certainty, the mind hesitant and determined" (37), as Edward Hirsch puts it.

Two assumptions are implicit in these comments. First, free verse of this sort operates under a grammatical, not metrical, contract. It uses the reader's expectation that line conclusions usually coincide with phrase conclusions. When line and phrase do not conclude simultaneously, readers feel rushed onward. Second, I have been assuming that the last word on a line of poetry takes on special prominence. Although I can imagine readers for whom these assumptions do not hold, the simple fact is that there is considerable evidence that most readers do read in this way. Such suppositions underpin the arguments of Kenner, Perloff, Borroff, Hirsch, Cushman, Hartman, and others quoted in this chapter. Rosemary Gates says that they are qualities of the language itself.

Whether or not these assumptions reflect truly intrinsic qualities of the English language, others confirm it as an accepted procedure of reading. Thore Pettersson, chopping up technical prose into enjambed lines, found that readers did indeed give greater prominence to words at the end of lines, finding temporary and perhaps lasting ambiguities in texts that, when printed as prose, readers considered unambiguous. James C. Stalker typed out poems as prose and asked groups of readers to lineate them. He found that most people lineated grammatically. He comments,

> Readers then do have at least one expectation about the structure of lines, that being, at the first level of approximation, that lines generally do end at major syntactic breaks. The data bear this out. The corollary rule seems to be, if the line is too long after cutting at the major syntactic break, choose the next lowest syntactic line juncture. (252)

Perhaps eighteenth-century readers would have counted syllables and broken the line at ten, and Anglo-Saxon readers would have counted stresses, but—whether taught by poets, institutionalized by English teachers, or inherent in written language—it seems safe to claim that readers expect a line to end with the conclusion of a sentence or a phrase.

These conventions for reading are especially important for short-line poetry. Since the lines have fewer words than those in, say, iambic pentameter, more words are placed in the position of greatest prominence. Because short-line poetry must enjamb to avoid a succession of very short sentences, grammatical relations are constantly highlighted. The structure of the line coupled with the greater percentage of prominent words bring syntactic relations to the reader's attention. The short line thus encourages readers to read each word more carefully. For this reason, short-line poetry sometimes sponsors the intense reading usually reserved for religious or constitutional texts—few poems can claim, as Williams's wheelbarrow poem can, that each word of the poem has been commented upon and weighed in relation to all the others. However, there is a cost: since they are associated with presentational, lyric poetry, short-line poems are not often read philosophically as, say, Wordsworth often is. Further, while a few short-line poems are read intensely, most are simply unread, or read and not discussed.

If Williams uses enjambment for stylistic or mimetic effect and is free to enjamb or enjamb lightly (or not at all), then we are still not any closer to finding what determines a line for Williams. Hollander asserts that the patterning is visual, often a "rough typographical width of somewhere around thirty ems" (*Vision* 111). That this is the case cannot be denied. H.D.'s grammatical decorum results in poems that look like this:

—
———
————
———
————
———
———
—
——————
—
—
—

whereas Williams's poems are more apt to appear

————   or   ———
—-   ————
————   ———

He has had to manipulate the words to fit the space. To claim that Williams organizes these poems by sound forces the conclusion that such poems just so happened to fall into perfectly symmetrical stanzas.

Henry Sayre, arguing for Williams's poetic as essentially visual, points to the Modern poet's comments about his revision of "The Nightingales," a poem originally consisting of a five-line stanza and a four-line stanza. Williams excised a line for purely visual reasons, exclaiming, "See how much better it conforms to the page, see how much better it looks" (*I Wanted* 166). Berry calls this type of structure a "sight stanza" and argues that it was Williams's new prosodic form. She remarks,

> To arrange a text in sight-stanzas is to lay a grid across it that cuts the flow of language arbitrarily into visually equal segments; the interruptions made by metrical divisions obtrude and have . . . the effect of defamiliarizing individual words and the manner of their syntactic relations. ("Williams'" 26)

Thus, the visual stanza replaces the poet's "numbers," and, in the same way that Milton overlays enjambment across decasyllables in *Paradise Lost,* so Williams uses a visual norm as the pattern on which to enact his interplay of phrasal coincidence and non-coincidence.

Just as traditional poets occasionally take great liberties to "fill out a line," manipulate a rhyming word to the end of a line, or create a consistent meter, so Williams occasionally makes extravagant gestures to squeeze his words into their predetermined shape. For example, from "The Unfrocked Priest,"

> his
> ego nourished by this,
> mount-
> ed to notable works (I.351)

and from "The Fight,"

> But you know—none
> of us had any dough we
> 're all on relief (II.28)

and from "Apres Le Bain,"

> (I'll buy
> you one) O.K.
> (I wish
>
> you'd wig-
> gle that way
> for me (II.190)

In these cases, Williams is willing to split words to maintain the visual pattern.[12]

The visual approach differs from traditional prosody in that it does not include a stable aural element. Hollander concludes that Williams's poems have no "rhetorical sound" and give the reader "a soundless picture of a soundless world" (*Vision* 287), a statement that surely must have Williams turning over in his grave. "Damn the bastards for saying you can't mix auditory and visual standards in poetry," Williams wrote James Laughlin. "Who the hell ever invented these two categories but themselves?" (47). Indeed, that a poem can be both visual and aural is quite evident in the visual poems by George Herbert that

Hollander quotes in the same chapter in which he claims Williams's poetry is soundless. Herbert's "The Altar" is not just in the shape of an altar; it is in rhyme and meter as well. For Herbert, the visual is just another organizational decorum to superimpose upon the ones already in place. Further, most visual poems take on the additional decorum that, while discussing its ideas, the poem should comment on its own shape. Thus, the center of Herbert's "Easter Wings"

> Thou didst so punish sinne,
> That I became
> Most thinne (43)

These additional rules make shaped poems harder to write. Most shaped poems are devotional (or amatory, which poets usually claim is the same thing) and allegorize the difficulty in fitting words into form as that of acquiescing to what seems to be, at times, arbitrary or inflexible rules. As Herbert puts it in "The Altar,"

> Wherefore each part
> Of my hard heart
> Meets in this frame
> To praise thy Name (26)

The final achieved form is thus a testament of sincere devotion, of willingness to bend the individual will to a greater ideal. These lines from Herbert overtly insist on the meaning of their visual attributes. They thus allegorize their prosody at least as overtly as the Pindaric Odes of Herbert's fellow seventeenth-century poet, Abraham Cowley.

However, while it is easy to make the case that Herbert attends to the ear as well as the eye because his poetry rhymes, the "NEW auditory quality" that, Williams told Laughlin, "determines and underlies the visual quality" (47) is hard to identify. Hollander argues that those finding rough accentualism may be discovering something not put there by the author:

> It may be that the poet's intention, for example, to use as a roughly governing principle of composition a line of about 24 typeface ems in width; the probability is that—unless his syntax is most distorted, his density of emphatic monosyllabic imperative and expletives unduly high, his latinate polysyllables likewise

> —most of his lines will have three or four stresses, if counted in accentual-syllabic terms. But it surely would be wrong to hold the stress-patterning to be the principle. (235)

Now, this is surely correct, but it does not warrant Hollander's later conclusion that Williams does not hear his lines. Like Herbert, Williams applies his metrical principles within his shapes and thus takes on two organizational systems simultaneously.

As I have shown, Williams constantly talked about his poems in terms of sound. Although sometimes he splits words to retain a visual shape, the poet himself explained word-splitting as a way of emphasizing "the primacy of sound" in a word (*Something* 166). Sound is certainly why Marianne Moore does it with her

> ac
> cident-lack (33)

and

> or reverted duck-
> head; kept in a buck (11)

Since Williams's poems rarely rhyme, it is difficult to prove he does split words for the sound. However, while splitting words sometimes seems necessary to preserve a visual pattern, some of Williams's split words do not. Take "Passer Domesticus":

> domestic you're drab.
> Peep peep!
> the nightingale
> 's your cousin but (II.237)

It seems the apostrophe-*s* could be attached to its noun without seriously disturbing the square look of the quatrain that prevails through the whole poem. Still, while word-splitting may indeed emphasize the sounds of words, it also calls attention to the poem's organization as arbitrary or in some way unnatural, a construction upon which words are pressed.

A poem fit into a visual pattern may also be fit into an aural and grammatical one. To see how Williams uses these three organizational strategies to shape his poems, it is useful to turn to the nastiest knot of all in Williams's prosody, the variable foot. Both Cushman and Steele note in passing that Williams found the term in Poe's "The Rationale of Verse," though neither develops the idea very much. It is valuable to look a bit closer at what Poe said because Williams used the term in a similar, though not identical, fashion.

"The Rationale of Verse" reveals that Poe was very much the same sort of cranky autodidact that Hollander said Williams was. Poe begins his explanation of the variable foot by quoting this line from Cranch's "My Thoughts," which Poe inexplicably finds especially beautiful:

> Many are the thoughts that come to me

Rather than accepting a commonsensical scansion,[13]

> MAny/ AREthe / THOUGHTSthat / COMEto / ME

Poe insists on quantitative rules, and divides thus:

> Many are the thoughts that come to me

The first foot, he explains, is paeonic, the next two are trochees, and the last—which he admits looks short—is actually "fully equal in time to each of the preceding" (50). Thus, poetic feet should be construed quantitatively, as measures of units of duration rather than stress. Like Campion before him and Lanier afterward, Poe tries to impress upon his reader the notion that this sort of versification is more melodious than traditional accentual-syllabics. For Poe, it is a "foot" because it measures the same duration and "variable" because the number of syllables varies. In theory, this differs from accentual prosody, which also does not count unstressed syllables, because a quantitative foot can consist entirely of short (corresponding to unstressed) syllables.

Williams's variable foot is composed in much the same way. The crucial document is a letter Williams wrote to Richard Eberhart. "Count each single beat to each numeral," Williams instructs:

<1> The smell of the heat is boxwood
<2> when rousing us
<3> a movement in the air
<4> stirs out thoughts
<5> that had no life in them
<6> to a life, a life in which
<or>
<1> Mother of God! Our Lady!
<2> the heart
<3> is an unruly master:
<4> forgive us our sins
<5> as we
<6> forgive (*Selected Letters* 326–27)

"You may not agree with my ear," he concedes, "but that is how I count the poem. Over the whole poem it gives a pattern to the meter that can be felt as a new measure" (327). Like the feet Poe found in Cranch's poem, Williams's feet constitute a single unit with a varying number of syllables. In an interview with Walter Sutton, Williams declared that adhering to iambics "is as stupid as saying every musical measure in 2/4 time must contain only two notes" (68), a very similar comment to Pound's (quoted in chapter 1 of this book) that writing in meter is like composing a symphony using only quarter notes. As do his nineteenth-century precursors, Williams appeals to music.

Unlike Poe, however, Williams does not apply the rules of Latin verse. While criticizing traditional prosody, he asked Sutton rhetorically, "[H]ow can syllables of no known length be taken three and three, five and five, et cetera, and made into a unit of rhythm?" (68)—but if syllables have no known length, how can he claim to organize them into "measure" at all? Williams's answer, "by breath, by inflection" is virtually the same as Pound's "feel of the thing." Williams here seems to refer to the fact that speakers of English do not say the same syllable the same way every time they say it; thus, part of the variability of the variable foot is the different contexts of the poem.

There is a deep-rooted problem here, and Williams's apparent solution to it explains why he spent so much time expounding on the American idiom and also why he insisted that he had been attending very closely to American speech. If he was not going to follow classical or traditional rules, but wanted measure, he was going to have to find some way of gauging duration. He needed a speaker to perform the utterance. In doing so, he based his prosodic system on individual performance and not abstract rules. He attempted to circumvent the problem of idiolect, the notion that each speaker utters words differently, by positing a deeper structure, a "core," of the American idiom; in a sense, he intuited, formulated, or supposed generative rules for duration that everyone followed and that a close listener could ascertain and a careful reader could reproduce.

The notion that each variable foot (read rightly) constitutes a similar unit of duration is often called the isochronous theory. Further evidence that Williams thought about his variable foot in this way comes from Levertov, who read Williams's poems to the older poet, self-consciously trying for isochrony, and reports that Williams told her she was reading it rightly. Thus, Levertov says, each variable foot "has the same duration," so that a reader "must either say words slowly" or "give full value to the spaces between words" to make the separate feet have the same duration. She goes on to explain it is not accentual prosody at all:

> the ultimate determinant of what goes into a line is the totality of the demands of expressiveness, comprising intellectually comprehensible syntax, sensuousness and expressive musicality (including variations of pace), and above all emotional charge—delicate or forceful and intense—of content. Each of these interpenetrates the others. The more fully wrought the poem, the less discrete the strands. ("On Williams'" 144)

Levertov here states in aesthetic terms what the more linguistically minded critic, Rosemary Gates, calls an "intonation/information unit" ("Forging" 503). More specifically, Berry defines the "norm" of the variable foot as a "single complete syntactic unit (word-group or clause) that lends itself to be realized as an intonational unit in a performance of the text in which one is reading 'for the sense'" ("Williams'" 28). A careful reader will have noticed that I have moved from duration to grammar, from sound to sense. For Williams, the attraction of the variable foot was precisely this connection. Recall that he found traditional prosody "arbitrary"; his own, if grammatical units do carry a consistent beat, would be based on the rhythms of speech. Williams assumed that people speak in phrasal units.

The question then becomes, do people talk in phrases of equal duration? The answer is no, if you carry around a stopwatch and time everything. However, Gates makes the same point many have made before and after her:

"Isochrony is a perceptual reality rather than a quantitative one" ("Forging" 508–9). On this basis, Hartman accepts Williams's measure as measured—not because it can be proven to be isochronous, but instead because a listener or reader, attending to sense, is likely to supply a consistent beat to accompany the grammatical flow. Attridge summarizes the findings of many linguists when he states that "languages are conditioned by rhythm—which is not simply a matter of the way they move through time" but also in the way that they are perceived, specifically the "constant interaction with the syntactic and lexical properties of language" ("Poetry Unbound?" 354).

I have thus far demonstrated that the variable foot has some theoretical claim to being possible, which is not the same thing as saying Williams succeeded. Many careful readers have simply not heard anything close to isochrony. Looking at Williams's letter to Eberhart, Perloff finds the only way to make the lines isochronous is to use "wholly unnatural speech pauses" ("To Give" 180), an opinion echoed by Mayhew. Cushman's attack on the isochronous theory is most elaborate and forceful. After quoting these lines from the variable foot poem, "The Descent,"

> a sort of renewal
>
> even
>
> an initiation, since the spaces it opens are new places (II.245)

he argues

> What can it possibly mean to say that the two lines "even / an initiation, since the spaces it opens are new places" occupy the same amount of time? . . . Suppose a thousand people read the line out loud a thousand times apiece. It is unlikely that one will be able to get seventeen syllables into the time it takes to say two, or draw two into the time of seventeen, without distorting the words into something bearing little resemblance to the American idiom. (82)

He concludes, sensibly enough, "an abstract scheme must include at least the possibility of being performed correctly." Cushman rather overstates his case, inasmuch as I can imagine a reader, perhaps an accomplished actor or orator, capable of manipulating syllable length and pause enough to achieve isochrony, or the perception of it anyway.[14] The single-word line in the passage could be interpreted dramatically. Since it introduces an elaboration of an idea, perhaps the reader is supposed to understand that the speaker of the poem is searching for the right words. Williams did argue that

> the language of the poem is made up of words and their configurations (the clause, the sentences, the poetic line—as well as the subtler, style); to these might be added the spaces between words (for measurement's sake) were these not properly to be considered themselves words—of a sort. (*Embodiment* 141)

If by "of a sort" Williams means pregnant pauses, chilly silences, and the like, then any two lines, no matter how visually unequal, can be made synchronous.

Further, one exception does not disprove the rule for variable feet any more than it does for metrical ones. Williams's letter to Eberhart explains that the perception of isochrony occurs "over the whole poem."[15] Still, Cushman's argument is potent because it points to the very crux of the variable foot: If a poet says his lines are measured, does that mean we must read them as such? It is as if a music aficionado felt obligated to find a new symphony beautiful simply because the composer insisted that it was. It brings to mind Stevens's complaint about feeling obligated to admire Modern art.

Comparison with traditional prosody underscores the theoretical problem of the variable foot. If a skeptic challenged Pope to enunciate his rhythmic principle, the Augustan poet could invite his adversary to count syllables, then open a dictionary and mark stresses. But Williams's foot involves so many factors—intonation, syllables, context, and so forth—that a full explication, such as Levertov's, leaves the reader with too many variables to check the assertion of isochrony. As Jespersen said of poetic rhythms, we must use our ears, and the truth of the world is that different readers hear differently.

With such difficulties in determining the aural organization of the variable foot, many have simply dismissed the poet's comments on the matter, and like Nathaniel Mackey, consider the variable foot merely a "trope" (204). Others have attended to aspects of the line clearly manifest. Hollander's assessment is echoed by many: the line is "of variable length, but graphically marked, and in general, syntactically bounded" (*Vision* 263). I shall take each aspect in turn.

The foot does vary in length, but rarely as extremely as the example that Cushman cites. Sometimes the lines are of similar lengths, such as this line from "The Sparrow":

> cannot surpass
>   the insistence
>   of his cheep! (II.292)

and this one from "Asphodel, That Greeny Flower":

The end
        will come
                in its time. (II.322)

Both lines have some claim to visual and accentual evenness. However, the poems rarely if ever approach the aural regularity of Pope or the visual uniformity of Williams's poems in the wheelbarrow stanza.

The "graphic marking" is usually called the "triadic line," a line that, like the first printing of Pound's "In the Station at the Metro," separates phrases into free-verse feet. Some are willing to make great claims for the visual aspect. Anne W. Fisher-Wirth considers the motion "fugal and incremental" (116). Marilyn Kallet gets more of a sinking feeling appropriate for the theme of "descent" is often prevalent in poems in the triadic line (59). She goes on to claim that the "typographic design" of these poems

> transmits a story in itself. The triadic lines stand out against the space of the white page to remind us of the space of the power of words to bring the void to account, emphasizing the dignity of speech against the blankness. (93)

Kallet seems to have in mind Mallarmé's explanation of the white space in *Un Coup de Dés.* However, *all* poems stand out against the page, though it is true that short-line poetry tends to give the reader a greater consciousness of white space because it provides more of it.

A more fundamental question is whether the triadic line is one line or three. Stephen Tapscott argues the triadic line is a "solution to the problem of reconciling the One and the Many" (116). It is unclear to me that blurring the distinction between the One and the Many really solves the "problem," but certainly the line may encourage some readers to ponder it.

In truth, most are fairly unimpressed with the typographical assertions of the triadic foot. Perloff complains that the visual form is "an extremely imposed geometric form, a kind of cookie cutter" ("To Give" 181). Perloff's major objection is that, as Hollander said, the lines are "syntactically bounded." Bollobás, following Berry and Perloff, calls the triadic line "a return to tradition"—the tradition, that is, of H.D. Set each lobe of the triadic line beginning "Asphodel" on the left margin, for example, and what's left might be out of *Sea Garden:*

Of asphodel, that greeny flower,
        like a buttercup
                upon its branching stem— (II.310)

For regulation H.D., though, the first word would have to be excised (characteristic for Williams, it "reaches" to the next line), as would the Keatsian "greeny." Still, for readers partial to heavily enjambed short lines, this line lacks forward propulsion. However, it isn't really a "return" inasmuch as Williams wrote syntactically bounded poetry throughout his career.

The lines in the variable foot do, however, evince a greater grammatical orderliness than do most of Williams's other poems, because when they break the decorum of ending lines (or lobes of the triadic line) with phrases, they usually do it in the same way. Thus:

> the fountain. His image (II.292)

and

> Stein—but (II.296)

and

> as this time); the reason for it (II.301)

That is, lines usually break the phrasal decorum in the middle of a lobe. Such expectability differs greatly from the unpredictability of strongly enjambed short lines. Far from the breakneck speed of the strongly enjambed verse, the poems in the triadic line tend to proceed, as Levertov puts it, at a "certain stateliness of pace" ("On Williams" 147).

Like Williams's other poems, the poems in the triadic line tend to go in and out of phase. Take these lines from "Asphodel":

> I am looking
>   into my father's
>   face! Some surface
>
> of some advertising sign
>   is acting
>   as a reflector. It is
>
> my own.
>   But at once
>   the car grinds to a halt.

Speak to him,
        I cried. He
                will know the secret

He was gone
        and I did nothing about it.
                With him

went all men
        and all women too
                were in his loins. (II.329)

These lines demonstrate the play of grammar across the line. Sometimes, phrase units act in consort with lobe endings, and triadic lines with larger phrases. The poem follows the traditional decorum that observation and narration receive stronger enjambment, while in the concluding statement the poem goes back in phase. When the car halts, so does the line with a full stop; when the speaker is most emotional (though emotion suffuses the whole passage), the line breaks are most unpredictable.

Thus, the triadic line affords two of what Wesling calls "scissoring points"—opportunities for enjambment: by the foot and by the line. However, it loses enjambment across the stanza, and in the triadic line there is nothing like the radical enjambment of "The Motor-Barge," where the word is split across a stanzaic break:

the broad river-
craft which
low in the water
moves grad-

ually, edging
between the smeared
bulkheads,
churning a mild (II.143–44)

As I have said, this sort of enjambment emphasizes the rigidity of the visual structure, and calls to the reader's attention the fracturing involved, whereas the variable foot seems comparatively more "natural," less subject to the demands of form.

These various organizing structures work together to form, theoretically, a very controlled verse. Though Hollander is right that any series of lines, of the same length and not unnaturally stressed, will evince a loosely accentual regularity that would not be of the poet's making—instead it would simply be an accident of a natural feature of language—it should be borne in mind that *all* prosodies control accidents of natural features of language. The point that traditional accentual-syllabic prosody controls a defining feature of English, rather than just a natural feature, begs the question of where the definition of English came from in the first place. Certainly English has traditionally been conceived of as an accentual language, and I have no reason to doubt it. Still, English speakers also use duration, pitch, and so forth just as "naturally" as they use stress. Further, part of Williams's system is based on syntax, which is surely as much a defining feature of English as accent.

I say that poets control "accidents" of language because poets generally seem to be intent on finding significance in coincidences in language. For example, when Hopkins found that "God" rhymed with "rod," he discovered what he considered a truth within the language that he was using. Whether you believe that God actually was revealing himself in the English language in that way depends upon your metaphysics; the point is that these are the sorts of concordances that poets find and use to add significance to their poetry. Alliteration, meter, assonance, and other prosodic features are all likewise manipulating natural features of language that, within the context of the poem, seem to imply meaning.

Hollander's point, of course, is that Williams doesn't manipulate sound in the way that Pope does, because the incidence of rhyme at the end of Pope's lines is much more frequent than could appear by chance. The strange thing is that Williams in a sense agreed with Hollander. He always claimed that he found his meter in speech. It is true that he wrote many times of creating a new measure, but equally true that he argued that the poet's task was to promote what was already in the language. Again, the salient feature is not that verse in some way reflects spoken English; such is the case for poets as disparate as Wyatt, Donne, Wordsworth, Frost, and a host of others. Using what he regarded as speech rhythms as the *only* factor for determining the line was "new."

In this regard, it is no use, as Perloff has done, to scan variable feet, even if you use, as Perloff did, a linguist's system of scansion. You will only find, like Perloff, that there is no consistent pattern.[16] In his "Statement on Measure" for Cid Corman, Williams states that traditional prosody used "mathematics" (202) but today "we have lost the ability to count" (204). No, Williams said, "I did not count the syllables that make it up but trusted entirely to my ear" (206). But if he is not counting stresses or syllables, what is he listening for? His rhythm is "purely intuitive" (204), he claims, "unconscious" (205). This may seem as if Williams is claiming a special pipeline to the muse, but given the fact that Williams said a poet must "discover a new metrical pattern among the speech characters of his day" (*Something* 166), his "intuitive" corresponds to what linguistics would call pragmatic knowledge of the language. And it is true that our knowledge of language is intuitive and unconscious. If you do not believe it, ask a hundred native speakers to give a full explanation of when to use "the" and when to use "a." Ninety-five, maybe ninety-eight, could not do it when put to the test; linguists today struggle with the task of specifying the rules.[17] Yet native speakers in English almost never make a mistake with their articles. They have intuited the rules, and experts in language acquisition believe the basic rules of language are imprinted on the mind at a very young age.

The theory of the variable foot is a good example of why we ought to attend to Williams's prose more carefully. Kenner claims that "Idiom was not the word he wanted" ("Rhythms" 37), and many accept his claim uncritically. In fact, though, "idiom"—"the syntactical, grammatical, or structural form peculiar to a language"—was precisely the word Williams wanted. As I mentioned earlier, Williams sometimes talked of his meter in terms of rhythm and sometimes in terms of meaning because he thought the two were related. If meaning and rhythm are related, then "idiom," the structure of language, should carry with it a rhythm. What Williams was after, and what he spent his entire career pursuing, was the sound not of *words* but of *meaning*. Recall that in his autobiography Williams said he sought to "recover underlying meaning" from the rhythm of everyday speech. Likewise, when Williams said the poet should listen to and copy impassioned speech, it was the passion he was after, or rather the "passionate welding" of thought and object. The problem was not that Williams chose a word that was wrong or vague; it is only that he was very vague on how to apply his term.

Though Williams did interrogate language, what and how humans meant their words was the focus of his investigation. All this comes together in the variable foot. Let's review what we know about it. First, it is graphically marked. Though length can vary widely, most of the lines are something like this long:

xxxxxxxxxxxx

By the unavoidable, accidental features of language—what we might call Hollander's Paradox—each line then should have a similar number of stressed syllables. In short, there is a loose accentualism present throughout.

Further, since lobes are often completed phrases, when "in phase" the variable foot will proceed from one unit of meaning to another within about the same period of time. We know further that hearers tend to organize sound into a kind of rough isochrony. Such a perceptual organizing should be greatly helped along if the phrases that the reader perceives are already organized into separate information units with a rough similarity of accent and duration.

Thus the pulse, or rhythm, or foot, or whatever you want to call it, is not very countable. Instead of Gates's "information/intonation" unit, I'd call it a perceptual unit, a unit of understanding. As the parsing meter isolates each detail on a line, giving the reader a momentary opportunity to take it in before moving to the next line, so the variable foot tries to provide the reader with an aural/visual/grammatical unit, and the intersection of the three loose prosodic systems may indeed be said to form the unit of meaning.

I am not saying that each line has the same number of beats while releasing the same amount of information. Instead, the true theory of the variable foot is that there is a rhythm of understanding, that we hear with our minds as much as with our tympana, so that the variable foot is a single unit of sounded meaning. It is a measure of "emphasis," to use the term Ruth Mary Weeks suggested in 1921. A phrase may have, say, three stresses, but only one main emphasis. In short, Williams seemed to grasp the linguistic fact that speech tends to be rhythmic along syntactic lines and tried to build it into the metric of his verse. Other poets, of course, had noticed and used the intersection of syntax and rhythm; Williams's theory is unusual in that it proposes to use syntactic rhythm instead of rather than along with other prosodies.

Further, Williams's variable foot is performance-based, which makes it radically different from traditional prosody, which sets up an abstraction, meter, that readers vary according to the way they emphasize different words and ideas. Williams's system attempts to use relatively consistent emphasis but variable stress. Williams felt traditional prosody was arbitrary, abstract, and unrelated to the living language, so he sought a system organized according to the non-abstract, non-arbitrary manner in which people speak.

I am arguing that this is the theory of the variable foot. This is not the same as saying this is actually how we, or most, or some, readers apprehend the line. It should be noted in closing that there is considerable resistance to Williams's theories, largely because they are, as I have shown, practically impossible to use as either a guide to writing or reading poetry. In "The Concept of Meter: An Exercise in Abstraction," Wimsatt and Monroe C. Beardsley take many of the assumptions of Williams's theory to task, arguing that since there are no rules, it follows that "you cannot make mistakes," nor can you be "right"—and in such an arena "you cannot create a public pattern" (155). In a like manner, Hollander argues that "Graphic form divorced from phonemic realities can easily . . . control inferred sound patterns" (*Vision* 239). That is to say, the fact that short lines can implicitly direct a reader to hear the lines in a certain way does not mean that the writer has uncovered some underlying truth in language. Indeed, Williams's "public pattern" may not at all represent the true rhythm of language; I have shown that many argue quite strenuously that he has not. However, theoretical vagueness in free-verse theory has been consistently troped as actual profundity, so these types of difficulties have often been seen as bolstering the case for free verse.

This being said, it should be borne in mind that many poets have believed in Williams's theory, or something very similar, and the corpus of, say, Denise Levertov helps demonstrate that whatever its theoretical difficulties, it has engendered good poetry. Since it really cannot be tested, a better way to characterize the variable foot is as an enabling myth that offers a quasi-scientific, seemingly rigorous justification for writing according to the "feel of the thing."

At the end of his statement to Corman, Williams comes close to acknowledging both the subjective nature of his foot and the need for an ideal reader. He writes that many may have difficulty hearing his rhythm, but adds that the reader must "follow" the poet. The poet's "concern for his reader is a generous concern, much like a father's love for his son," Williams wrote, but the poet does not relinquish "his privilege to outdistance the young man whenever the occasion should arise" (208). Hence, the writer writes, and readers look on and follow as best they can. The difference between this and traditional prosody is precisely that which I introduced in my discussion of the difference between "Fine Work" and "The Flatting Mill." Cowper makes a pill designed conforming to his audience's expectations, while Williams expects his audience to be instructed. The relationship Williams's prosody demands, then, is more Whitmanian than filial. As my first chapter argued, Whitman many times said that his poems needed a reader to "complete" them. But just as Williams's materialism often proceeds from transcendent ideals, so his non-abstract prosody amounts to the most abstract prosodic system ever invented. Whereas traditional prosody offers a metrical contract on a house already built, Williams's variable foot offers an agreement on a speculative venture. As I have shown, even granting its many assumptions about language, the variable foot's plethora of variables leaves you with one of two choices: take a leap of faith and try to fit the triadic line into the framework it is supposed to fit into, or simply reject it. The difficulty, again, is that apparently solid base of the variable foot, readerly performance, is actually quite vague and unstable. Like Whitman's catalogues, what you find in the variable foot depends on your confidence in the competence of the writer, and in the degree to which you are willing, at least provisionally, to share the writer's organic faith.

All the hoopla about a new measure and the American idiom sometimes distracts commentators from the fact that the poems using the variable foot have the distinction of being the most personal, idea-laden poetry Williams ever wrote. Often, a reader of *The Desert Music* and *A Journey to Love* meets a speaker talking about ideas in a voice that seems rather confessional. The personal nature of the poems does not concern me here, and anyway has been well documented by Mariani and others. However, the penchant for abstraction I noted in the short-line poems emerges to full-blown statement in the triadic line. "The Descent" informs its readers:

> No defeat is made up entirely of defeat—since
> the world it opens is always a place
>   formerly
>   unsuspected. (II.245)

Likewise, in "To a Dog Injured in the Street," Williams relates a lesson he says he learned from René Char:

> With invention and courage
>   we shall surpass
>   the pitiful dumb beasts,

let all men believe it,
            you have taught me also
                        to believe it. (II.257)

In "Asphodel," Williams permits himself a notion of love Dante would have approved of. The antecedent to "It" is love: Death

                        is not the end of it.
There is a hierarchy
                        which can be attained,

                                    I think,
in its service. (II.314)

Not all of the poems in the triadic foot contain such abstract truisms, but in this lineal form, Williams, for once, talks about, say, Memory ("The Descent") or Love ("Asphodel"), instead of his more usual approach of talking about a memory or a love. It seems that in this form, relatively relaxed compared to his rigidly visual stanzaic poems, Williams apparently felt he had a little more sanction to simply state his ideas without having to look around for things to stand for them.

Williams's contribution to twentieth-century prosody can be divided into practical and theoretical aspects. He brought some of the strongest enjambment in all of poetry in English to the parsing meter. By positioning function words (which have no meaning save to indicate relations within a sentence) at the area of greatest prominence, he emphasized the poem as a grammatical construction, as relationships among words. The grammatical relations within the sentence and across the line were allegorized as the movement of the mind. Thus, Williams's dynamic poems about still things: the flower isn't moving before the eye, the mind is moving over the flower.

Second, by bringing poems in and out of phase, Williams found he could not only use grammatical decorums for expressive purposes, but could isolate abstractions in a way suggesting that transcendent ideas are intrinsic parts of material wholes. He thus performed the significant service of showing how abstraction could be brought into the short line without the line losing its elemental feel.

Third, Williams created a visual prosody that endowed the poem with a sense of concision, yet did not demand any of what he considered archaic poeticisms. Partially because syntax is central for Williams's poetic, the preeminent sin as far as Williams's prosody was concerned was syntactic inversion. Pope used meter and syntactical inversion, oddly enough, to attain concision. Visual prosody, conversely, gives a poem a structure that announces the hand of the artist in the art without requiring syntactic reorganization.

Philosophically, Williams created a theoretical, perhaps mythic, framework to supplant traditional prosody. His claims for poetry remain the most prevalent justification for free verse, to the extent that even those who do not write in his line often echo his arguments. In chapter 1, I noted that proponents often assert without evidence that free verse is rigorously organized. Williams similarly asserted rigor, and his various explanations for his principles of organization always similarly left a crucial aspect unspecified. For example, the variable foot depends upon an accurate replication of the unspecified rhythms of American speech. Like Alice Corbin Henderson, Williams simply asserted that his poetry was guided by a "law" and left it at that. Further, Williams frequently gave reasons for readers to assume that free-verse form was particularly profound, whether it be because free-verse form represented the passionate welding of object and perception or that because it replicated the underlying principles of American speech. Concomitant with such profundity is the assumption that the form is not fully describable. Like many of the writers quoted in chapter 1, Williams put a greater burden on his readers, promising them a more natural and satisfying reading experience if they are willing to be led.

Finally, Williams promulgated a version of organic form that, while being every bit as all encompassing as that of Whitman or Coleridge, did not assume the existence of an extrahuman deity to regulate and compose the system. His organicism was such that the atheist, agnostic, and unconventionally religious could embrace it. I do not mean to argue that all of Williams's ideas are original to him. Certainly, he learned from his peers at least as much as he directed them. However, Williams has emerged as a central spokesman for free verse because, more than anybody else, he exemplified the Modern spirit of short-line free verse.

CONCLUSION

Avoiding Prosody?

Since free verse is a lineal form associated with a long quarrel with tradition, understanding its poetics in context is especially important. My conclusion furthers this aspect of my thesis; focusing on a few contemporary poems that claim to avoid traditional versification in significant ways, I show that the prosody of even these poems is revealing when their historical moment is considered. The fact that contemporary poets use the formal allegories common in the Modern period is further justification for my claim that most twentieth-century poets have considered verse form largely according to Modern paradigms. In the end of this chapter, I'll return to a more theoretical discussion of the need for historical analysis in prosody, an argument that has informed the method of this book.

As the cursory discussion in chapter 1 helps indicate, asserting that a poem avoids prosody brings up the question of whether any poem can truly do so. Such is the patterning of the language, and such is the human rage for order, that to truly write unpatterned poetry it would be necessary to go to extraordinary lengths to avoid some sort of repetition. However, as I have argued for other genres of free verse, the allegories poets make out of their poems' forms generally have little to do with empirical description. In chapter 1, I chose Masters and Lawrence to demonstrate the kind of free verse that avoids tradition because *Spoon River* had the reputation of being formless, and Lawrence's theoretical statements suggested a formless poetic. Can a clever and determined reader find some sort of patterning in their poems? Of course. Nonetheless, the notion that some poetry escapes prosody is an important myth about free verse that is as common today as it was eighty years ago. Consider "The Simple Truth," by Phil Levine, collected in *The Simple Truth* (1994). Typical of Levine's poems, "The Simple Truth" begins with a narrative and then moves to statement. Just as typical are the poem's colloquial diction and its emphasis on simplicity as an avenue for truth. The lines relevant for my discussion occur after the speaker describes buying potatoes from a roadside stand:

> Some things
> you know all your life. They are so simple and true
> they must be said without elegance, meter and rhyme,
> they must be laid on the table beside the salt shaker,
> the glass of water, the absence of light gathering
> in the shadows of picture frames, they must be
> naked and alone, they must stand for themselves. (Simple 44)

Linking "elegance" to "meter and rhyme," the speaker asserts that these qualities are not only unimportant to "truth," but also that "things," if they are "simple and true" enough, cannot be said in traditional lineal form.

Thus, in this poem Levine voices William Carlos Williams's critique of traditional versification. It should come as no surprise that Levine does so, since Levine has many times acknowledged Williams as a master. Levine told Jan Garrett that Williams gets Levine's vote for "greatest American poet of the twentieth century." Levine's Williams is the anti-rhetorical poet of the working class, the poet who created an "American style uncluttered by the silliness of English literary form" (*Don't* 132)—not the self-conscious maker of machines made out of words. When Calvin Bedient asked the poet if he were trying to create a new language, Levine replied,

> I don't know if I'm trying to create a language. I've never really thought about that. In a curious way, I'm not much interested in language. In my ideal poem no words are noticed. You look through them into a vision of . . . just see the people, the place. (*Don't* 101; orig. ellipses)

Molly Weigel points out that this means that Levine strives for a "transparent language" (228), in which the readers forget they are reading and treat the poem as reality, or at least as the reality of a person talking to them. Readers are thus not supposed to appreciate the poet's competence or cleverness, and the poems do not seek, as Williams's often do, to interrogate language. "My poems wouldn't be worth a damn if they were the surface of poems," Levine said to Arthur E. Smith (*Don't* 32); it is a poetry of the signified instead of the play of the signifiers.

This is the effect Levine's later poetry has had on many of his readers. For instance, Jonathan Holden quotes Levine's "Milkweed" to show "why good poetry depends upon something more than mere technique" (12); similarly, Ralph J. Mills, while acknowledging Levine's "command" of form, finds that Levine's style makes form "seem in a way secondary" (251): "A firm grip on existence takes a priority for Levine" (252).

It is a style that strikes many as style-less. Indeed, Louis L. Martz's comment, that "the endings and the beginnings of Levine's lines do not often have the firm significance and definition that one finds in Williams" ("Ammons" 70), holds true for "The Simple Truth." There is little occasion to find rhyme or pararhyme, and the poem uses the word, "edge," without putting it on the edge of a line. Everything about the surface of the poem seems intended to not call attention to itself. There is enjambment so that the poem does not have the progression of independent clauses characteristic of Pope, but not the strong enjambment evident in Williams. The poem goes in and out of phase rather gently. The lines vary widely in terms of syllables, and the visual standard is only loosely attended to. No words are split or articles put at the end of the line to maintain it. It is a poem that, as it says it does, eschews "elegance, meter and rhyme." In all, it is a prosody seeking invisibility. Levine's poems in this mode avoid "firm" gestures because they do not want you to know that they are gesturing at all. They want to appear prosodically innocent.

Like the irregular ode, what may be called "invisible prosody"[1] depends upon a history of visible prosody for its import. It is poetry whose prosodic virtues are the faults it has escaped. By denying itself the surface conventions of traditional prosody, it asks that the reader attend to its "truth." In such a sansculottist approach to poetry, traditional versification's function is to be the class wearing the culottes. It makes sense, then, that Levine should profess to be uninterested in language. In his fiction of composition, the poet hones his craft until he has something urgent to say, and then he says it without the elegance that might obfuscate or direct what he wishes to express. The narratives Levine so often incorporates into his poems can be traced to the Williams tradition Levine many times acknowledged being a part of: they are the things his ideas sprung from. Fidelity to fact keeps the writer from being seduced by highfalutin "poetic" language.

Although such a critique may well seem unfair to many traditional poets, it is the doctrine of the poem. It is not, however, truly the doctrine of Levine himself, or at least the whole doctrine of Levine, since he does write poems in other modes. Significantly, *The Simple Truth* does contain poems written in syllabics—though I doubt that too many of his readers have noticed that "Llanto" is written in a nine-syllable line or that "Winter Words, Manhattan" is written in a seven-syllable line. And about six years before "The Simple Truth" Levine articulated a comparable theory of prosody in a poem entitled, appropriately enough, "A Theory of Prosody." One thing that marks this as a twentieth-century poem is that fact that the poem's prosodic theory concerns itself entirely with the disposition of line breaks, and thus the poem does have the "firm significance and definition" of line that Martz find absent in much of Levine's verse. For instance, the opening lines,

> When Nellie, my old pussy
> cat, was still in her prime (Selected 276)

manipulate syntax in order to hint at the erotic implications of the traditionally female muse. It would seem that Nellie is a relative of Williams' jamcloset cat, because in the narrative of the poem she watches the poet compose and, "when the line / got too long," she paws him. Although the speaker seems to think that Nellie was spurred to action because she was paying strict attention to his words, the prosody of much of the poem suggests that she was merely counting to seven syllables before reaching her "sudden black foreleg down."

While the tone and the actual prosody of "A Theory" are quite different from "The Simple Truth," the theory is similar. The speaker says that the cat taught him that "it was poetic to end / a line anywhere" so long as it "drew blood"—that is to say, when the line touched something basic and vital to humans. The speaker does not say that Nellie was interested in creating lineal puns, forcing rhymes, controlling rhythm, or interrogating language. The end of the poem makes it clear that Levine does not believe his story literally and that he does not expect his reader to either. The speaker asks,

> Isn't that what it's about—
> pretending there's an alert cat
> who leaves nothing to chance.

He is telling us that he has presented a formal allegory, one that may be dubious factually, but is potent in its ability to help create poems.

Like Levine's "A Theory of Prosody," Robert Hass's "Measure" uses short-line poetics but argues for a prosody based on natural rhythms. Significantly, the poem was included in an article in *Forbes* (of all places) providing ideas for businessmen who might want to try writing poetry:

> Recurrences.
> Coppery light hesitates
> again in the small-leaved
>
> Japanese plum. Summer
> and sunset, the peace
> of the writing desk
>
> and the habitual peace
> of writing, these things
> form an order I only
>
> belong to in the idleness
> of attention. Last light
> rims the blue mountain
>
> and I almost glimpse
> what I was born to,
> not so much in the sunlight
>
> or the plum tree
> as in the pulse
> that forms these lines. (44)

The prosody is reminiscent of early H.D. Proceeding by short phrases with no radical enjambment, there is an orderly grammatical progression. In the context of the poem such a lineal decorum seems "natural," especially since the speaker locates the essence of poetic rhythm in natural recurrences (a word that recalls Lowell's idea of "return"). The notion that poetry is the result of "attention" is distinctly Williamsian. However, the poet is depicted as basically passive. He does not create order but rather, in moments of attention, "belongs to" it, so that the pulse forms the lines instead of being created by the lines. The poem, the speaker says, does not mirror nature so much as participate in the same rhythm that created nature. Again, it is important for such a poem to appear to be orderly in a way that does not correspond to traditional poetics. The speaker of the poem implies it is *ur*-poetic.

Since so many poems like this allegorize the fact that they are not traditional, an important part of the poems' formal allegory depends upon the reader noticing that their poetics are not traditional, though certainly such poems do not constantly refer to traditional meter as does haunted verse. These poems also demonstrate, of course, that traditional scansion is only used for the idea of the poem and does not tell us very much about the poems' rhythm.

Still, the assigned meanings are usefully considered as part of the prosody because they provide some clues to help an attuned reader. Pope's notion of form stems from (and helps create) his idea of the need for balance and order, and his notion that he was perfecting the ideals of previous generations of British poets. Whether Pope really created perfect order or just convinced himself that he did (and whether he perfected or degraded British poetics) depends on your point of view, but it seems likely Pope would have preferred that readers hear most of his lines as smooth. Similarly, for eighty years twentieth-century poets (particularly in America) have used free verse to push a kind of individualism that implies some sort of break with the past; again, different readers will have very different conclusions regarding their success. In poems like "Measure," while perhaps we are not to hear smoothness, the argument of the poem encourages us to find a kind of rhythm nonetheless.

Thus, the historical method of this book has tried to disclose the dynamic interaction between the form as it appears on the page and the way it is allegorized. Understanding both, as well as the historical moment in which the poem appeared, can be very telling. Consider, for example, this late-century free-verse sonnet by Rita Dove, "Flash Cards," which speaks to the traditional versification in a very complex manner:

> In math I was the whiz kid, keeper
> of oranges and apples. *What you don't understand,*
> *master,* my father said; the faster
> I answered, the faster they came.
>
> I could see one bud on the teacher's geranium,
> one clear bee sputtering at the wet pane.
> The tulip trees always dragged after heavy rain
> so I tucked my head as my boots slapped home.

My father put up his feet after work
and relaxed with a highball and *The Life of Lincoln.*
After supper we drilled and I climbed the dark

before sleep, before a thin voice hissed
numbers as I spun on a wheel. I had to guess.
Ten, I kept saying, *I'm only ten.* (*Grace Notes* 12)

If you read this and didn't notice that it was a sonnet (rhyming ABAB CDCD EFE GGF), I suspect you are not alone. When the poet read this poem on Garrison Keillor's *A Prairie Home Companion,* she read it according to its grammar, rushing over line breaks and in no way that I could hear emphasizing its formal structure. I doubt many listeners discerned she was reading a sonnet.

However, "Flash Cards" seems as eager to avoid tradition as participate in it. The first line can be read as being in fairly regular iambic pentameter, but no other line can claim such regularity. The lines vary in length from eight syllables to thirteen, with the average around eleven. Of course, scanning poetry that does not seem to have been composed in traditional metrical feet is problematic, but I reckon most lines with five stressed syllables, though line three seems to have three. Further, there are pararhymes instead of true rhymes. The poem, then, straddles the fence between traditional and free-verse poetics.

The prosody of the poem stems from the fact that Dove's notion of form is almost entirely ideational—she does not use the form to create the kind of predictable rhythms that Johnson thought so much a part of the pleasure of verse. Dove has explained that she uses poetic form to provoke ideas, not to create sound. The pressure of putting human experience into the form of poetic language, she has said, sparks her to greater creativity. "It's by language I enter the poem," she remarked in an interview, "and that leads me forward. That doesn't exclude perception and experiences and emotions or anything like that. But emotion is useless if there's no way to express it" (Kitchen et al. 237). She told William Walsh,

> For a writer to recognize that the language is both your tool and your clay—that you work with it and through it—is liberation, because there are a thousand different ways to get at the ineffable. To figure out what you're really writing about is extremely difficult to do by direct attack; you can end up destroying yourself in the process. But the language will help you by catching the subconscious off guard. (150)

Thus, she says, playing around with language can lead to a "discovery, a matter of seeing where words will lead me" (Taleb-Khyar 350); "often" she remarked in another interview, "a word or a phrase compels me" (Kitchen et al. 238). Sometimes this means looking up a word and tracing etymologies. Like Hass, Dove conceives of poetic language as an active force, and the pleasure of writing poetry, she has said, in part stems from "seeing words come alive" (Carroll 87). She believes that if a poet is willing to work with language, it will supply her with what she needs.

In order to surprise the subconscious, Dove is often willing to impose a rigid and rather arbitrary form. While in Germany, for instance, she tried to compose English poems using German syntax. Sometimes she tacks poems on the wall to look at them and revises them visually; at other times, she cuts a poem in half with scissors and works each half into a new poem without using any of the words from the first half. "It's too radical to yield actual poems" (Taleb-Khyar 350), she concedes, but such exercises help her see tendencies and find new combinations. Since manipulating language can lead to new revelations, denying an aspect of language, such as traditional versification, may deny the poet a path to truth. Still, Dove's aim is not to reproduce a preestablished standard, as she does not appear to regard the achievement of the perfection of received form as an end in itself.

Though it refuses to fall into traditional meter, the poem does avail itself of the resources and expectations of traditional versification. One of the poem's true rhymes occurs at the beginning and end of line three (schematically, the rhyme for "faster" is "keeper"). At the beginning of an enjambed line, "master" is thus adjacent to a rhymed position, and the effect that I hear is that "master" and "faster" chase each other around lines three and four. The repeating *aster* sound, linked with the fact that the lines are the shortest in the poem (only nine and eight syllables long), mimics the insistent speed the lines describe. Further increasing the speed is the fairly strong enjambment. Thus, the first quatrain bends the traditional rules of the sonnet to imitate the action described.

Noticeably different is the second quatrain, with longer lines (ten and twelve syllables), a true rhyme, and no internal rhymes to disrupt the pattern. The enjambment is relatively weak. The lines describe the natural rhythms of the rain and the speaker walking home, much different from the rushed rhythms of the lines describing the flash-card drills. It would seem that the versification is more "natural" than in the first quatrain, and that this milieu is much more fitting for the speaker, whose identification with nature is made literal when she drops her head in sympathy with the tulip trees.

In the sestet, the first three lines depicting the father's repose are lightly enjambed. The lines are comparatively long. When, in the final three lines, the speaker must respond to more flash cards, the enjambment becomes stronger, and the repetitions come striding—both "before" and "ten" repeat, and there is an internal rhyme with "sp*un*" and "*num*bers." Two of the final three lines are nine syllables long, so that, as in the opening quatrain, the lines simulate insistent speed with short lines and repetition. All together, the two stanzas describing agitated states are themselves agitated by the shortest lines in the poem, strong enjambment, and internal rhyme. The two stanzas describing more relaxed states use longer lines and light enjambment.

The sestet's alliteration, too, uses traditional decorum. The major stressed words of lines nine to eleven alliterate ("*f*ather / "*f*eet," "re*l*axed" / "*L*ife" / "*L*incoln," "*d*rilled" / "*d*ark"). Pope would have approved of the leisurely rolling *l*'s imitating the father's relaxation (and a relaxation of the demands on the speaker). And of course, the *s*'s hiss in "hi*ss*ed," prompting a "gue*ss*." However, the poem's complex interaction with traditional versification goes much deeper than using sound as an echo to the sense. As it helps itself to traditional versification for mimesis, so the poem uses its relationship to the sonnet form for allegory.

Reading the poem autobiographically helps bring out the formal allegory. In an interview with Grace Cavalieri, Dove implies that the poem is based on her own experience,[2] and many of the details in the poem agree with what Dove has told us about her life. Dove has described the household she grew up in as "stern" (Walsh 145); her father was an educated man, the first African-American to break the color barrier as a chemist at Goodyear, which certainly might lead him to value education and mental toughness. The speaker calls herself a "whiz kid," and Dove was a National Merit Scholar. The autobiographical reading is attractive because it adds undercurrents to her father's choice of recreation: he comes home from a grueling day at work where he has likely faced covert or overt racism, anesthetizes himself with a stiff drink, and then opens up a biography of the man who freed the slaves and supposedly made everything equal for everybody. After a few highballs, maybe he can believe that.

The book her father reads throws retroactive meaning onto "master," suggesting that her father is in some way acting out the oppression he has felt, and, in doing so, demanding that his daughter accept his view of society. Understanding is unimportant, he tells her; don't worry if it doesn't make sense, or, presumably like *The Life of Lincoln,* doesn't have much relation to everyday reality. The important thing is to be good at, to be one of the masters of, the existing system.

Even without insisting on autobiography, a sense of oppression comes through fairly clearly—especially in the end, where the speaker dreams she is Ixion spinning on the wheel (casting, by the way, her father as a powerful and arbitrary Zeus). More specifically, the poem addresses the oppression of numbers, which is why I suspect Dove cast the poem as a sonnet in the first place. The poem portrays a speaker sympathetic with natural forces who is forced to comply with an unnatural numerical system. Hence the poem's evasion of meter and perfect rhyme acts as evidence for the human attempt to find some breathing room in poetic numbers. Ironically, the speaker defends herself in the concluding line by offering a number of her own, one that she assumes (in contrast to the numbers on the flash cards) is significant. In the same way that her father reacts to oppression by visiting it on her daughter, so the daughter attempts to survive in a cruel system by participating, somewhat, in it. The number she gives, incidentally, is the number of syllables in an iambic pentameter line, the line of the conventional English sonnet.

With its implications regarding the legacy of slavery, "Flash Cards" has a political tinge to it. The poem avails itself of the free-verse critique of traditional verse—that conventional rhyme and meter are arbitrary, over-prescribed, and necessarily involves some falsification of the subject in order to find words to fit the pattern—so that, on the allegorical level, the speaker's voice is trying to make it through what Keats called the dull chains of the sonnet form. However, while using such an association for formal allegory, in practice Dove avoids the notion that traditional versification is intrinsically stultifying. Her remarks regarding her compositional processes make it seem that the poem's traditional form provided the avenue for its invention. Dove uses received form to facilitate the concentration and control she thinks a good poem needs, while evading the rules in significant ways.

Thus, "Flash Cards" presents a neat division in prosodic theory. On the one hand, there is the formal allegory of the poem itself, which protests against the controlling, perhaps "fascistic" (to borrow Williams's evaluation) aspect of a poet's numbers; on the other, there is the fact that such control enables poetry. Compare, in this regard, her book of free-verse sonnets, *Mother Love* (1995). In the introduction, she first toys with the idea that "any variation from the strictly Petrarchan or Shakespearean forms represents a world gone awry" (a Popean formulation of order), but then quickly counters that idea by suggesting the form can act as a "talisman against disintegration" (i). Received form staves off chaos; as a talisman, like Levine's acknowledgment of pretense, she concedes that such a view may be fictional, even superstitious, but that does not rob it of its power.

I conclude with a short critique of one other method that considers the kind of poetry that this study addresses. I do so in order to underscore the strengths of my approach, and, more important, to further specify what is the real concern of this book, the nature of free verse.

In the introduction, I pointed out that any historical views oversimplify if they rest on a single, coherent idea of how all the poets of a particular era understand poetic form. For "Flash Cards," of course, there are two obvious ideological readings that do so: either Dove is guilty of duplicity or bad faith by using a traditional form (associated by many of today's critics with white males, and Dove is black and female), or she subverts patriarchy by not following the rules exactly. My main objection is not the rather *ad* or *pro hominem* nature of the critiques, but the fact that such readings so little engage the text and are determined by *a priori* assumptions. The notion that such broad generalizations can be brought to bear on individual texts is belied by the dynamic situation in the contemporary world, indicated by Jorie Graham in the introduction to this book. My own *a priori* assumption is that people have always been complex.

In addition to attempting to bring such relationships to ideas into prosodic criticism, I have sought ways of understanding the rhythms of verse that obey decorums that are not well described by traditional versification. Like G. Burns Cooper, I have tried to do more than reiterate the "familiar bromides about poetry" and "impressionistic clichés" (190). While Cooper has dismissed these bromides and clichés as theoretically empty, I have tried to show that, historically contextualized, they can help readers hear and interpret free verse.

But Cooper can rightly claim that my own formulations have often been rather vague. In fact, it is only honest to admit that I critique their point of view from a position of considerable weakness, because the strength of the methods of Cooper, Richard Cureton, Donald Wesling, and others is that they embrace linguistic and other developments of the past eighty years in order to be precise about the types of features that I describe comparatively vaguely (I have not used their methods because they are ahistorical). Cooper and others like him offer a much fuller "hearing" of verse than has been ever attempted before, including such aspects as pitch, quantity, and so forth.

In trying to be more precise, Cooper and others like him follow in the rationalistic tradition of Poe and Sidney Lanier, who felt prosody should be, as Lanier titled his tome, *The Science of English Verse.* In the Modern period, William Patterson used (what was then) the most up-to-date recording equipment and "expert" readers.[3] More recent prosodists have tried to apply the theories of more recent linguists, because, Enikö Bollobás claims, "Linguistics has provided the possibility for 'scientific' exactness" in prosody (*Tradition* 33).[4] But just how much they have had to give up for such exactness is evident in Richard Cureton's *Rhythmic Phrasing in English Verse* (1992), which, at one point, spends forty-six pages—replete with charts, graphs, lists, and nomenclature old and new—analyzing twenty-one lines from William Carlos Williams's *Paterson.* Cureton explains in a defense of his book that his interest is to describe the "full range of our verse experience" ("A Response" 30). It certainly makes sense that poetry written under grammatical decorums may benefit from grammatical analysis, and finding a way to understand and measure the intonation poets put into their poems seems a very exciting new field. Furthermore, Bollobás, Wesling (especially in *Grammetrics*), Cureton, Cooper, and others grasp the idea that understanding poetic rhythm in part means examining human cognition, and thus are greatly interested in psychological and musicological studies of how people hear and order the world.

And yet, they still have not managed to negotiate a barrier I fear is insuperable. Christoph Küper, taking issue with Cureton's assumption of the first person plural pronoun ("our response"), points out that in *Rhythmic Phrasing,* the analyses are based on "Cureton's own readings of the cited texts" (2), and that different readers might hear differently. Similarly, Derek Attridge argues that "the history of prosodic theorizing is littered with assured claims about the existence of complex rhythmic features that have found no echo in the experience of other readers" ("Beyond Metrics" 19–20). Cureton's reply is revealing:

> *Rhythmic Phrasing in English Verse* is necessarily concerned with what the most skillful, alert, and considerate listeners experience and with what the most painstaking reflection on rhythmic experience might allow us to represent with full explicitness. Therefore, my representations cannot be dismissed because they are not readily accessible to some assortment of impatient, untrained, or inconsiderate listeners. ("A Response" 30)

Cureton's querulous tone suggests the manner of scholar who has worked very hard to create an extremely sophisticated mechanism only to have naysayers question his basic premises, as his reply better expresses his pique than it does the point at hand. Attridge and Küper were not arguing that impatient, untrained, and inconsiderate readers may not perceive a text in the way Cureton's "listener" does; they were saying that patient, trained, and considerate readers such as Attridge (whom even Cureton acknowledges as an expert) may disagree—and, in fact, Attridge *does* disagree with Cureton's scansion of Williams. In order to generate his impressive display of analysis, Cureton must assume the validity of his instrument, and that means assuming that everybody does—or should—"listen" to poetry in the same way.[5] Reading such works as Cureton's, I feel like a physicist reading a very complex new theory of quantum mechanics that either ignores or dismisses in a few sentences Heisenberg's Uncertainty Principle. In this age of theoretical pluralism, it does not seem very intellectually rigorous to accept any theory that requires us to swallow a good deal before we are allowed to ruminate.

Even if Cureton's theories are *true,* there is still another theoretical problem: who is this criticism for? Theories developed long after a poet has died cannot influence or direct that poet's work. I very seriously doubt that many future poets will sift through tomes on cognitive theory in order to learn how to write verse, so such theories fail (as traditional prosody does not) to provide a basis for future composition. The graphs and at times arcane vocabulary no doubt will confuse most poetry aficionados (and indeed most college professors), so Cureton and the rest are left talking to a very small group of like thinkers. It seems highly unlikely that many poets will attempt to write poetry for such an audience. The broader theoretical point as far as prosody is concerned is that, in order for linguistic and musicological analyses to gain wider acceptance, they will have to gain the kind of self-awareness that marks the better theories in other areas. Such critics will have to move away from trying to establish scientific verifiability and exactness and become flexible enough so that they will allow innovative poems to change the theory rather than simply squeezing poems into the shapes demanded by the theory.

Thus, if Cureton and Cooper may be said to reveal my Achilles heal, my approach exposes theirs. The varying ways that people read is an important reason why considering historical context is crucial. Using one approach to reading poetry of different eras, especially an approach that claims to be partly derived from studies in cognition, means assuming that people in different eras hear poetry in the same way. Yet this does not seem very tenable. In *An Essay on Criticism,* Pope remarks that the majority of his contemporary critics judged a poem by its "numbers," finding "smooth" to be "right" and "rough" to be "wrong." Very few read in this manner today. In fact, had Pope written in the past forty years, he may well have put it this way:

> Most by *lack* of *numbers* judge a Poet's song,
> And *roughly measured* to them is Right, and *smooth* is Wrong.

This book has largely examined Modern free verse, which occurred at a crucial juncture in this gradual paradigm shift. Simply put, free verse represents a dislocation of the "ideal reader," to the extent that today, many readers have only the vaguest notion of traditional meter and do not recognize a poet's numbers at all.

Further, for various reasons, twentieth-century poetry offers something not available in other centuries: a huge amount of undigested poetic theory. The Modern penchant for theorizing and pronouncing persisted throughout the century, resulting in innumerable articles, reviews, poems about poetry, introductions to volumes of verse, and dull tomes like this one. We have then, at hand, a large mass of documents that register this shift in the expectations of readers and the procedures of poets, and yet too often it is all dismissed simply because it is thought to be not "true." I have tried to show that searching for scientific verifiability tends to obscure the aesthetic myths these statements embody.

As I write, the current rage in criticism is a rather amorphous group of approaches that can be categorized as cultural studies. Surely the prosodic approach here can be applied to such studies fruitfully so long as the real dynamism of history is born in mind. This book appears in the very early twenty-first century, and as such has the advantage of taking a long look back over the previous century, particularly at the Modern period. In the United States presently, free verse is the institutional form, the form that is taught in colleges and expected by editors of most literary magazines. Critics throughout this century will surely look back on the previous one and not only be able to trace the shifting expectations of readers, but a good deal else about their concepts of form, of the nature and origins of verse, and, indeed, in the relation between a poetry that is difficult to measure and a world which is even more so.

Notes

INTRODUCTION

1. Wesling displays considerable learning on the historical debate on the form. Like Steele, however, he seeks to define and delimit free verse and proposes a new prosody constructed in part to help read free verse. Charles O. Hartman's *Free Verse* (1980) is directed by its attempt to determine the actual nature of free verse. Thus, it begins with a slew of definitions, all of which make what seem very sensible statements. Unfortunately, defining "free verse," like defining "art" or the novel only leads to definitions that leave a number of works some people consider a part of the definition out of the category the definition circumscribes. For example, Hartman begins by defining "verse" as "language in lines"—this, he says, is the "only" definition "that works absolutely" (11). The problem, however, is that it does not work "absolutely." A fuller discussion of the possibilities of unlineated poetry can be found in chapter 3 of this book.

2. See, in this regard, chapter 2.

3. Finch does quote Dickinson, but only to show that Dickinson refused to read Whitman because she thought he was "improper." This weakens, not strengthens, her argument.

4. It is noticeable that more recent anthologies of radical poetry from the nineteenth century—for example, Peter Scheckner's *An Anthology of Chartist Poetry* (1989) and Michael Scrivener's *Poetry and Reform* (1992)—tend to have more poems in ballad meter than sustained iambic pentameter. This is because ballads have traditionally been associated with the lower classes. However, both volumes have a fair number of poems in iambic pentameter. Furthermore, there was a very large amount of conservative, reactionary poetry in ballad meter during the century.

CHAPTER ONE: THE PROBLEM OF FREE VERSE

1. In the later essay, "The Music of Poetry," Eliot writes of the free-verse movement, "only a bad poet could welcome free verse as a liberation from

form. It was a revolt against dead form and a preparation for new form or for the renewal of the old; it was an insistence upon the inner unity which is unique to every poem, against the outer unity which is typical" (*On Poets* 31). He discounts what he considers the literal meaning of the term, and, significantly, speaks of the movement in the past tense.

2. See also Wood, p. 170, and Scott, p. 112. Stewart said that "what passes for free verse" is that which "1) does not preserve the set metrical and line structures of verse, and 2) is not like prose printed in continuous paragraphs" (201).

3. See pp. 34, 75, and 352, respectively.

4. Some won't even grant free verse the virtue of departing from traditional verse. Stephen Spender and Donald Hall's *Concise Encyclopedia of English and American Poets and Poetry* (1970) argues that free verse "pretends to adhere to no 'rule,' obey no 'law,' except that of rhythm. All one need really say about it is that it is the erecting into a principle of what has for centuries been the practice of poets" (223). The two seem to have in mind Graham Hough's earlier assertion, that free verse is "an extension of the liberties that have been normal in English verse over a great deal of history" (173).

5. Writing after Sutton, Rosemary Gates has offered something like a "systematic" analysis of Whitman's prosody. See "The Identity of American Free Verse: The Prosodic Study of Whitman's 'Lilacs'" in *Language and Style* 18.3 (1985): 248–76; "Forging an American Poetry from Speech Rhythms" in *Poetics Today* 8:3–4 (1987): 503–27; "T. S. Eliot's Prosody and the Free Verse Tradition: Restricting Whitman's 'Free Growth of Metrical Laws'" in *Poetics Today* 11.3 (1990): 547–78. Although I do not maintain that Gates has described Whitman's prosody with complete adequacy, they do call into question Sutton's claim that no such description is possible.

6. See chapter 2 for Curran's analysis of the ode.

7. Henderson may be referring to any of a number of studies made in the last part of the nineteenth century and into the twentieth using sound-recording devices to measure human speech. William Patterson, writing in 1916, provides an eight-page bibliography of studies of this nature, pp. 181–88.

8. Sally M. Gall has already addressed this passage, exploring the "Melic"—that is, musical—aspects of Pound's poetry. Her article scans "The Return" and other poems using musical notes in the place of the traditional marks of scansion. Though this is one way to understand Pound's rhythms, my interest is with what Jannaris has to say and how Pound adapted Jannaris's ideas for free-verse

theory. As Pound's discounting literal "fugal" organization helps indicate, it is likely he meant the connection to the Melic poets in a theoretical and figurative sense, not in the literal sense.

9. The first two appendices of Jannaris's *Grammar* outline the conclusions of his study of Melic poetry. Pound cites Jannaris because the classical scholar's approach to literature mirrored his own. Both writers' prose is precise and clear, and both insisted upon what Pound called in "The Tradition," "first-hand, untrammeled, unprejudiced examination" of primary texts (I.212); Jannaris's similar view is shown by the long title of his grammar of the Greek language: *An Historical Greek Grammar Chiefly of the Attic Dialect. As Written and Spoken from Classical Antiquity down to the Present Time. Founded upon the Ancient Texts, Inscriptions, Papyri and Present Popular Greek.* The two writers share a common critical temperament as well: both could be impatient, high-handed, and contemptuous toward those with whom they disagreed.

10. In the next appendix, Jannaris takes up the issue of quantity. He points out that in "the Homeric poems, as they have come down to us, the practice of quantitative versification appears as a fully developed system," but that this system is "by no means rigidly attended to" (522).

11. Jannaris claims that "there is not a word in the whole classical literature about quantity, as understood by us . . . nor is there a Greek word for 'quantity'"(526).

12. Campion's rules, set out in *Observations in the Art of English Poesie* (1602), adapt the rules of Latin to English without wholly neglecting the more native accentual tradition. Attridge's *Well-weigh'd Syllables,* pp. 219–27, outlines the way that Campion attempts to achieve "virtually complete coincidence of quantity and stress" (225). Anyway, there is no evidence Campion's example was followed by Modern poets—or really, by anyone.

13. Compare, in this regard, Pound's comment on Eliot's *Prufrock and Other Observations:* "Mr. Eliot is one of the few who have brought in a personal rhythm, an identifiable quality of sound as well as of style" (*Ezra* II.251). Pound seems to be referring to Eliot's signature style and not his personality.

14. It cannot be a typo, because he repeats the scansion later in the article.

15. Hollander's phrase adapts Coleridge's concept of a metrical *compact:* Coleridge speaks of a "*compact* between the poet and his reader, that the latter is entitled to expect, and the former is bound to supply" in order to afford the reader "pleasurable excitement" (*Collected* 7.I.65–66).

16. In Latin, *quaedam et definita lex est* and *Quare cum aures extremum semper*

exspectent in eoque acquiescant, ide vacare numero non oportet. The translations are by H. M. Hubbell from the Loeb Classical Library edition.

17. Holder states, "In the case of metrical verse . . . we would compare each line's pattern of stress distribution with the metrical paradigm's distribution norm, looking for significant deviations. The next step would be to consider how the phrases of a given line compare with each other in terms of their respective lengths and stress distributions, and how they compare on those same grounds with phrases in adjoining lines. Here, we would be looking for structural parallels and contrasts that might be related to expressive effects" (175).

18. Poe uses a 1 to 4 system to measure quantity. Jespersen admits that "in reality there are infinite gradations of stress" and that the difference between 2 ("half-stress") and 3 ("half-unstress") is "particularly hard to distinguish" (110). An exhaustive overview of prosodic systems is provided by Cureton, pp. 1–70.

19. This is not, by the way, the Mallarmèan line of "Un Coup de Dés" or Williams's "variable foot," because neither of those lines use space for obvious, emphatic, rhythm.

20. Carl Sandburg's "Muckers" (1915) uses ellipses to indicate a counter-pointed rhythm that is likewise imitative: "The muckers work on . . pausing . . to pull / Their boots out of suckholes where they slosh." (21) As in "London Nights," the pauses on the line with the ellipses are balanced against a line that runs smoothly.

21. In fact Robert Bridges's "Paper on Free Verse" takes issue with the sameness of free-verse lines. See my discussion in chapter 4 of this book.

22. The first two lines of Rodker's poem, quoted above, can be scanned / U U / U U / U U /. Other sections of the poem are more "free."

23. Küper lists four types: "the line as natural representation of rhythmic grouping" and its opposite, the line as creating "'tension'" between line breaks and grammar, "prose-like sentences," and a fourth type that "freely makes use of allusions to an assortment of metrical forms" (405). Küper does not go on from there. His first and second types seem to me to be most evident in what I call short-line verse. However, they are actually present in all lineated verse to some degree; the third type seems to correspond to what I call long-line verse, while the fourth, to the "haunted" verse of Eliot and Stevens.

24. Take, for example, Harry Hansen's comment in *Midwest Portraits*: "Carl poises a lance for the plain English idiom; his poems are filled with the expressive words that he had picked up in his tramps over the countryside: galoots,

mutts, slant-heads, jazzmen, knucks, fourflushers, longhorns, work plug, fade away, hank-pank, bootleg booze. He takes his phrases from the speech of the people and flings them at you, as in 'The Windy City,' where standing on the bastion of the bridge, he hears the 'black cataracts of people jazz the classics'" (19). Hansen goes on to voice the supposed complaints of effete academics.

25. Enjambed, that is, compared to the independent clauses typical of Pope.

26. The essay is an amalgamation of essays and reviews written in the eighties and nineties. The earliest part was first published in 1886.

27. Of course, a clever reader can find a rhythm in *anything*. Writing rhythmless poetry is as difficult as writing nonrepetitive music—John Cage, for instance, in *Fontana Mix* (1958) used computers to help him avoid repetition.

28. In "On Method," Coleridge posits a growing world in which an active God constantly takes exceptions, genially mutates, and harmonizes. He argues that everywhere in nature "particular laws" intervene "by which universal laws are suspended or tempered for the weal and sustenance of each particular class. Hence and thus we see that each species, and each individual of every species, becomes a system, a world, of its own" (*Collected* 7.II.517).

29. Though nowadays it is widely recognized that this passage owes a great deal to Schlegel, my interest in this paper is the received form of the ideas.

30. This inward naturalness, of course, differs markedly from the Augustan social, outward "natural."

31. Saintsbury's attitude can be summed up by his chapter subheadings: "Coleridge—The Christabel manifesto—Its looseness of statement—His prosodic opinions not clear—Supreme importance of his prosodic practice" (vii–viii).

32. Compare, in this regard, Wordsworth's preface to *Lyrical Ballads,* which describes meter as the "copresence of something regular"—copresent, that is, with the passions of the poet. Though meter may "divest language in a certain degree of its reality" (609), it is desirable because "the Reader has been accustomed to connect metre" to pleasure, and in especial the reader connects certain meters with certain feelings. Like Shelley, Wordsworth thought meter to be an inorganic, unnatural element that poetry absorbs in order to reach out to the reader.

Brennan O'Donnell's study of Wordsworth's poetics, *The Passion of Meter* (1995), describes this in terms of Wordsworth's familiar dictum that poetry is the spontaneous overflow of emotion recollected in tranquillity: "feeling overflows in expressive syntactic structures, figures, and imagery; metrical arrangement and all the patterns of rhythm and sound that go along with it may be regarded as a sign of the presence of the tranquilly purposeful mind directing and shaping the passion toward the proper end of poetry" (23). Thus, the poet's mind is the coadunating force that absorbs the inorganic strictures of meter for a greater organic whole.

33. Thus, in "A Backward Glance O'er Travel'd Roads," he quotes Taine approvingly that "All original art . . . is self-regulated, and no original art can be regulated from without; it carries its own counterpoise, and does not receive it from elsewhere—lives on its own blood" (443). In the 1855 preface, he says that although "The sailor and the traveler . . . the anatomist chemist astronomer geologist phrenologist spiritualist mathematician historian and lexicography are not poets," the poet uses "their construction" as the "structure of every perfect poem" (458).

34. Of course, the expressed desire for subtle readers to fully understand a work is by no means peculiar to free verse. Defenses or prefaces to difficult or arcane literature often make a similar point. For example, Marie de France prefaced her *Lais* (generally dated around the end of the twelfth century) by explaining that the custom of the "anciens" (she cites as her source Priscian) was to tell their tales obscurely so that later readers would have to gloss the text and put the finishing touches on the meaning (*"püessent gloser la letre / e de lur sen les surplus metre"* [1]). Like Whitman, Marie de France expects an alert reader will complete her meaning.

35. Eliot here does not dismiss (but greatly limits) eighteenth-century genre theory—on rare occasions, a poet may find himself with material appropriate for a sonnet. This, too, suggests a debt to Mallarmé, who remarks in "Crise de Vers," *"je demeure convaincu que dans les occasions amples on obéira toujours à la tradition solenelle"* (165). ("I remain convinced that on spacious occasions one always obeys the solemn tradition"—that is, the conventions of traditional versification.)

36. Eliot in this opinion seems also to have been influenced by Poe (though perhaps transmitted through the French Symbolists). In "The Philosophy of Composition," Poe writes, "What we term a long poem is, in fact, a succession of brief ones—that is to say, of brief poetical effects. It is needless to demonstrate that a poem is such, inasmuch as it intensely excites, by elevating, the soul; and all intense excitements are, through a psychical necessity, brief. For this reason, at least one half of *Paradise Lost* is essentially prose—a succession of excitements, interspersed, inevitably, with corresponding depressions" (orig. emphasis; 166).

37. This antipathy to personality is, in part, a reaction to the free-verse the-

ory that form is connected to the artist's "secret soul," as posited by Monroe and others.

38. Pound, "Mr. Hueffer and the Prose Tradition in Verse" ; Eliot, "The Borderline of Prose"; Ford, "Impressionism—Some Speculations": I; Lowell, "Vers Libre and Metrical Prose"; Fletcher, "A Rational Explanation of Vers Libre"; Aiken, "The Function of Rhythm"; Williams, "America, Whitman, and the Art of Poetry"; Flint, "Imagisme"; Ficke, "Metrical Freedom and the Contemporary Poet."

39. Thus, the glosses in *Rime of the Ancient Mariner* and the prose arguments preceding the chapters in *Paradise Lost* are clearly differentiated from the poetry and indeed are usually considered secondary. The prose sections in *The Canterbury Tales* are likewise set apart from the poetry and are introduced with explanations why they are in prose instead of verse. Devotional poetry such as Edward Taylor's also frequently quotes biblical prose, which is usually considered poetic anyway, and there is a clear separation between the Bible's words and the poet's own poetry. Blake's prophetic books and Ossian both proceed from a single mode of articulation and do not shift back and forth between the lyric and expository as, say, *Paterson* does. Prosimetric works, such as Boethius's *Consolation of Philosophy* and Dante's *La Vita Nuova* keep the prose and poetry visually separate and do not vary their mode of articulation. *Aucassin and Nicolette* also keeps the two visually separate. There is not the variety of tone, or the incorporation of other writer's prose, so characteristic of the twentieth-century montage poem like *The Waste Land* or *The Cantos.*

40. Hartman's distinction is, sensibly enough, based on lineation and all that follows from lineation. Again, he is more interested in statements for their truth-value than what theories of poetry they imply.

41. Thus Shelley, in his "Defence," argues that the prose of Bacon and the doctrines of Jesus Christ are really poetry. See also Walter Pater's essay, "Style."

42. At the time, Ford was using the surname Hueffer. In the article, Pound's citing French writers as models suggests a further debt to Ford.

43. Hugh Kenner, in fact, implies that Pound got the idea from Ford. See *The Pound Era,* on Ford's didactic roll, pp. 78–81.

CHAPTER TWO: THE LOOSE TRADITION IN VERSE FROM COWLEY TO ELIOT

1. See for example, "Out of the Cradle Endlessly Rocking," in the second section.

2. It's likely that one reason "Of Wit" has frequently been reprinted is that it is comparatively regular. The same thing can be said for the frequent reprinting of Whitman's "O Captain! My Captain!"

3. Here, and elsewhere, my schemes for longer poems begin each stanza with an A. I do this to avoid using superscripts or other typography—I am assuming, of course, that poetry of this nature does not interlock stanzas.

4. In chapter 3 of *Theory of Prosody in Eighteenth-Century England,* Paul Fussell points out that how a reader should pronounce elisions was a matter of debate throughout the century—even to the extent that some advocated pronouncing syllables marked for elision in the actual text of the poem, while others suggested eliding syllables not marked for elision.

5. Pegasus, the winged horse of Greek mythology, is associated with poetic flights. Hippocrene, a fountain on Mount Helicon whose waters inspire artists, was thought to have been made by a stamp from Pegasus's hoof.

6. That is, loHOW theYEARS toCOME aNUM 'rousAND wellFIT tedQUIRE. This presumes an unmarked elision plus a stressed "and." I suspect the line is deliberately irregular to emphasize that "well-fitted" does not equal "smooth." Still, most of the line is iambic.

7. The link to prose is Sprat's, not Cowley's, and not made in the sense that the Moderns tended to make the connection. It is based on the fact that the poems are not metrically uniform. The irregular ode's chief innovation was to subvert main elements of the metrical contract—stanza size, meter, rhyme—so as to disrupt, rather than establish, a predictable order. This is very different from the "prose virtues" of twentieth-century theory.

8. The distinction between inflectional and analytical languages I am referring to can be explained in this way: In English, a competent speaker knows the sentence, "John kisses Mary" means that John is kissing Mary (instead of being kissed by her) because "John" comes before the verb and "Mary" comes after the verb. The syntax of a more inflected language might be literally translated "Mary John kisses" in which the competent speaker knows John is doing the kissing because of inflectional endings on the words "John" and "Mary."

9. Usually the poems are not literally centered, but appear to be so because shorter lines are placed closer to the center of the page, so that tetrameter lines may be spaced five spaces in, trimeter lines ten, and so on.

10. Cowley seems to have had control over at least one edition of his poems, so I suspect his odes appear this way because he wanted them to. Most if not all of the poets whom I make this point about later also had some control over the

appearance of their poetry, and of course Herbert (and others) had been writing shaped poems before Cowley. Richard Bradford's study of visual poetics, *The Look of It,* starts its survey in the seventeenth century.

11. Or do not publish their scansions.

12. Langhorne characterized the poem as a "mixed kind of asclepiad and pherecratic verse" (139)—two loose classical measures that intermix lines such as—UU—UU—U- and—UU-U—. These are quantitative terms. This does not seem to me to describe the poem very well, since it is more clearly in iambics. Perhaps there is a quantitative overlay.

Milton's preface to *Paradise Lost,* which also mentions jingling, seems to have influenced Langhorne's low estimation of rhyme.

13. This gives the strophe and antistrophe thirteen couplets apiece—an appropriate number for an ode to fear.

14. Sayers was a minor poet and perhaps today mostly known as influencing the rhymeless metric of Robert Southey's *Thalaba the Destroyer* and *Curse of Kehama.* It is worth noting that the two epics Southey wrote while influenced by Sayers's theories are good examples of proto-free verse.

15. Lines ten and fifteen. If the decorum that rhymes only "count" when they match up with a rhyme in a stanza being used, there are several other unrhymed lines, notably line forty-five, which rhymes with line thirty-one in the previous stanza. That's very far and probably not hearable.

16. William E. Buckler, in his "Critical Reconstruction" of Arnold's poetry, lists the notion that Arnold's poetry was out of step with the aesthetic ideas of his prose as one of the prevailing "myths" of criticism about Arnold (3).

17. I focus my discussion here on "Dover Beach" because it is so familiar, but similar comments could be made for a poem such as "The Forsaken Merman."

18. Except perhaps descriptive poetry, though there's little description in the poem. Whether descriptive poetry ever describes, or intends to, is another matter.

19. Without including my entire scansion (but see below for some examples), for the most part irregularities are trisyllabic substitution and inverting the first foot. These are mainstream liberties.

20. That is, lines BAC are a grammatical unit, as is D. In Popean couplets, grammar coincides with rhyme, so that an AA rhyme would be one sentence or clause; neat quatrains generally have four-line clauses or sentences.

21. Did Arnold say "feth" (with a short *e*) or "brayth" (with a long *a*)? The concordance of his poems reveals that he almost always rhymes "breath" with

"death." Twice he rhymes it with "wreath," which suggests an eye rhyme. In one other poem, he rhymes "faith" and "breath"—"Euphrosyne," which also dramatizes a crisis in faith.

22. "Allegorizes" instead of "echoes" since it is an idea and not a natural sound described, and since the relation is an arbitrary one the poet thinks meaning into.

23. In "On Translating Homer."

24. Menken's *Infelicia* was greatly influenced by Whitman, and written in his style, although perhaps more histrionically—appropriately enough, since Menken gained fame portraying the scantily clad heroine in a stage adaptation of Byron's *Mazeppa*. Though she is most remembered today for her sensational public persona, she was a rather interesting and experimental poet. Today, her work appears in anthologies of nineteenth-century black women's poetry, and is worth a look at by critics of all sorts of persuasions. She was African American, a woman, outrageous, perhaps Jewish, and maybe a better poet that she is sometimes credited as being.

25. "Michael Field" was the pseudonym of Katherine Harris Bradley and her niece, Edith Emma Cooper.

26. Both Lambert and Fordham are black women, and their poems are available in the *Collected Black Women's Poetry* series edited by Joan Sherman.

27. Somewhat similarly, Adena Rosmarin argues the poem is a "mask lyric" along with poems such as "Andrea del Sarto," "To His Coy Mistress," and "Tintern Abbey."

28. John Paul Riquelme puts the poem with Victorian monologues, mainly Browning, which he views as a response to Romantic odes. His study mirrors mine in many respects, but his interest is not, as mine is, in lineal form.

29. Gardner does not use the term *iambic,* preferring to reserve that term for quantitative poetry. Her accentual-syllabic equivalent is "duple rising meter."

30. Transitionlessness and odd metaphors are, by the way, also characteristic of Cowley's "Pindarique" odes.

31. The slighting reference to Amy Lowell is more than just a parting blow in the Imagism wars: it helps indicate that one reason that Lowell was so readily accepted was that she was actually more traditional than she often portrayed herself as. Of course, she was also rich, related to James Russell Lowell, and so forth.

32. I scan this with just one line with trisyllabic substitution and two lines with an inverted foot at the beginning of a line. Such liberties are, of course, very conventional.

33. Except part IV of "The Dry Salvages," which quotes from Dante as, I suppose, some sort of compensation.

CHAPTER THREE: THE HAUNTING OF WALLACE STEVENS

1. Cook links Stevens and Eliot in her introduction to a special issue in the *Wallace Stevens Journal* 15.2 (1991); Taylor links the two similarly on p. 215 of the same issue. See also Gross, *Sound and Form,* p. 230.

2. A historical appreciation of lineal form is crucial to the interpretations of poems. Stein comes to the conclusion that the final section of "Peter Quince" *must* be satiric because it is traditional. Section 2 "exalts the creative act" (37), simply because it is nonmetrical, while the lines from section 4, "So gardens die, their meek breath scenting / The cowl of winter, done repenting" are "otiose rhyming" and "aberrant syntax," which combine to "disclaim credence in the sound and sense of poetry" (38). But such a prejudice against tradition is Stein's and not Stevens's, because, especially in *Harmonium,* Stevens could be quite traditional and in fact held such complete disregard for the past in great disdain. As is typical in Stevens, the idea expressed at the end of the poem, that beauty is or seems to be immortal, is not tested for its truth; Stevens is only interested if an idea satisfies. Thus, the ending of "Peter Quince" seems likely to be striving for the "finality" and "perfection" Stevens spoke of in "The Noble Rider."

It should also be noted here that Stevens was much too skeptical to assert that there is no such thing as truth. In "The Noble Rider," he says only that "we" shall never know it. He never asserts there is no truth, only that we cannot know if there is or not.

3. Unless otherwise noted, all quotations from poems in this chapter come from *Collected Poems.*

4. He makes these statements in *Letters,* pp. 294 and 351.

5. Note, too, the proximity of *c*'s close cousin, *g,* in these lines—the two sounds are very close in sound and in their place of articulation in the mouth.

6. As it is throughout the poem, *p* is often allied to *b.*

7. Brogan makes this point in *English Versification,* p. 71.

8. "Like that," not the same thing. Hopkins said he was following Welsh *Cyngnanedd* poetics.

9. If that indeed was his real name. "Latimer" used many pseudonyms and many of "his" letters were ghostwritten by others, usually politically minded

poets. Stevens knew Latimer was "an extraordinary person who lives in an extraordinary world" *(Letters* 391), but told Hi Simons, "I owe a great deal to him" (*Letters* 359)—including, most agree, such major poems as "Man with a Blue Guitar" and "Owl's Clover." The story of Latimer is recounted in greatest depth in Alan Filreis' *Modernism from Right to Left*.

10. Stevens claimed in 1954 that he "purposely held off reading highly-mannered people like Eliot and Pound, so that I would not absorb anything, even unconsciously. . . . As for W. Blake, I think that this means Wilhelm Blake" (*Letters* 813). However, in 1920, he remarked that he had just received an edition of Eliot's poems containing "nothing, I think, that I had not seen before" (*Letters* 217). A journal entry of 1904 demonstrates a familiarity with (William) Blake (see *Letters* 31).

11. The "article" goes on to say, "Some thirty representatives of the press were not there to greet him" (*Letters* 196).

12. Stevens here seems to be responding to sublime theory. Compare Longinus: "For all over-rhythmical passages at once become merely pretty and cheap, recurring monotonously without producing the slightest emotional effect" (293). As I noted in chapter 1, Longinus argued that this led to hearers paying attention to the rhythm and not the words. Stevens seems more probably making a comparable but different point—unhaunted free verse often has no rhythm.

13. Anca Rosu's identification of "Autumn Refrain" as a sonnet is perhaps more defendable, inasmuch as the poem is a discrete fourteen-line poem probably responding to Keats's ode, "To Autumn."

14. See *An Essay on Criticism*, ll. 350–51. Stevens's poem, by the way, might be called exhibit A in a trial of hackneyed rhymes. It pairs "white" with "light," "hue" and "blue," and "sleep" and "deep" (See *Letters* 157).

15. Hereafter, I will use consecutive letters for rhyme schemes and not start each stanza with the letter A.

16. It is generally recognized that Stevens's geography is consistent and significant. Thus, "New England Verses" quoted here is a collection of aphorisms that do not necessarily reflect Stevens' more complex view, while one of his most important statements of the transforming power of the imagination, "The Idea of Order at Key West," is set in one of the southernmost parts of the United States. "Farewell to Florida" provides a clear indication of Stevens's notion of place: the speaker bids *adieu* to the "ever-freshened keys" and to "oceanic nights calling / For music, for whisperings from the reefs." "My

North," he goes on, "is leafless and lies in wintry slime / Both of men and clouds, a slime of men in crowds."

17. It is, perhaps, a triple echo, since the poem also resembles Shakespeare's sonnet 73: "That time of year thou mayst in me behold / When yellow leaves, or none, or few, do hang" (1465).

18. Lines two and three combine for the "Mother Goose" rhythm, discussed below.

19. See the next two chapters for a fuller explanation of short-line free verse.

20. The important modifier here is "nothing more." Stevens sponsored Cummings for a Bollingen prize (See *Letters* 667) and praised Margaret Campion's attention to typography (*Opus* 215).

CHAPTER FOUR: STRAIGHT TALK, STRAIGHT AS THE GREEKS

1. Enikö Bollobàs, for example, calls "Prufrock" *vers libéré* in *Tradition and Innovation.*

2. Readers in the Modern period and since have always found something Greek about H.D.'s poetry. My Works Cited notes contemporary appraisals by Fletcher (1917), Bryher (1922), Untermeyer (1924), and Monroe (1925)—all address the Greekness of her poetry. More recent critics, such as Swann and Robinson (also in my Works Cited) also talk about H.D.'s classical sense, generally in the manner outlined by Guest. Eileen Gregory's *H.D. and Hellenism* is the most recent and best analysis of H.D.'s debt to Greek literature.

3. See *H.D. and Hellenism,* pp. 23, 24, and 26.

4. Murray's prose translations are scattered through his various critical works on Greek literature. When he published a translation of an entire work, he rendered the Greek into metrical, rhyming English verse.

5. See also Harmer, p. 142; Vanderwiden, p. 63; Swann, p. 4; and Coffman, p. 71.

6. Compare the opening of another of H.D.'s autobiographical novels, *Paint It Today:* "A portrait, a painting? . . . Do not paint it of yesterday's rapt and rigid formula nor of yesterday's day-after-tomorrow criss-cross jagged, geometric, prismatic . . . paint it today" (1).

7. Although it is sometimes asserted that English quantitative poetry is impossible to write, there is in fact a body of work in English written according to quantitative rules, generally those patterned on Latin prosody. Attridge's

Well-Weigh'd Syllables documents the quantitative verse of the Renaissance, and there is of course the work of Robert Bridges (for example "The Testament of Beauty") and Ezra Pound ("Apparuit") in the twentieth century.

In truth, the case against quantity rarely goes beyond the level of assertion, and is generally based on an unproven assumption regarding the "true" nature of the English language. The contention that quantitative rules oversimplify the language only says that quantitative prosody is like any other prosody. It is true there is no generally accepted system for quantity in English, and you cannot look up quantity in dictionaries. But then, neither could Homer, and from his poetry (and poetry like his) a quantitative system was devised.

8. In "On Translating Homer," Arnold is vague respecting quantity. Although he complained that English poets overly "rely on justification by accent," and thus "force the quantity," he quickly rules against following rules "which might easily be pushed too far." Thus, he seems to advocate accentual-syllabic prosody that does not ignore quantity, but is unwilling to submit to quantitative rules.

9. More precisely, the mechanism that allows the mind to conflate ancient islands and islands of personal history into a sense of irrecoverable pastness allows the mind to reexperience these places in the present—marked, of course, by the inescapable knowledge that the actual islands are not longer as the mind remembers them (hence "nostalgia").

10. Although *Beowulf* exists in one unique manuscript, analysis of handwriting and spelling has led most scholars to conclude that two scribes copied it.

11. Rosenmeyer goes on to explain some of the ways that the seemingly insurmountable textual cruxes have indeed been surmounted, and it is not my intention to argue that the received text of *Agamemnon* is extremely corrupt or unreliable. However, it is undeniably true that the editors who created the lineation of these choral passages did not speak the Greek of Aeschylus. It is thus not only plausible but indeed probable that the various editors' own notions of grammar—inculcated from birth and every day reinforced—interfered to some extent in the lineation of *Agamemnon*.

12. Note, too, the fact that this has an editorial reconstruction.

13. See Brinkley, pp. 607–8, and Hopkins's letter to Bridges, 21 Aug. 1877.

14. Hopkins's sprung rhythm actually attends to unstressed syllables as well, but only to register expressive effect. Only the number of stresses per line is regular. His approach differs from that taken by the *Beowulf* poet in that the Anglo-Saxon, purely accentual, poet rather assumes the reader does not hear unstressed syllables (insofar as rhythm), whereas Hopkins tries to control them for local effects.

15. He also finds similarity between *Samson* and "French and Welsh poetry," probably meaning by this French syllabicism and Welsh accentualism. However, his discussion seems to describe his own poetry better than it does Milton's.

16. The two books are Bridges's *Milton's Prosody* and Samuel Ernest Sprott's *Milton's Art of Prosody*. Watson Kirkconnell's *Awake the Courteous Echo* studies the prosody of *Comus*. Also worth serious consideration is John T. Shawcross's article, "The Prosody of Milton's Translation of Horace's Fifth Ode," in *Tennessee Studies in Literature* 13 (1968): 81–89. Brogan's authoritative bibliography of versification lists 113 entries for free verse, whereas Milton is the subject of about 171 entries.

17. Prince suggests that the "Italians" Milton alludes to are Tasso, Battista Gaurini, and especially Giovambattista Andreini, whose *Adamo* corresponds formally to the English irregular ode. *Adamo* is often cited as a source to *Paradise Lost*.

18. The terms mean, in order, "one strophe" (therefore there is no epode and perhaps no antistrophe), "non-stanzaic," and "a kind of progression where different speakers have speeches in succession" (instead of a chorus moving from strophe to antistrophe). These are not literal translations. John T. Shawcross tells me that Milton's amanuensis for this preface made at least one obvious error, and the whole thing is possibly suspect. He also tells me that (if the preface is at all reliable) it seems that by not "essential," Milton probably means not of the prosodic essence of the rest of the play (i.e., not iambic), and therefore not made of the same "material."

19. It is no use complaining that such does not accurately represent English pronunciation, since no prosodic system does.

20. See ll. 732 and 136.

21. His sanction for such hard enjambment again comes from Milton, who, the preface to *Prometheus Unbound* demonstrates, was very much on Shelley's mind.

22. Most of the rest are unrhyming quatrains in trochaic meter, usually tetrameter.

23. In other collections, Henley demonstrates that he is competent in traditional form—for example, the villanelle. It cannot thus be argued that Henley wrote free verse because metered verse was too difficult for him. In truth, the generic context for *In Hospital* is not the classical tragedy but the sonnet sequence. Its participation in this tradition resembles that of George Meredith's *Modern Love*—that is, it is a case of presenting a situation in which the neoplatonic values associated with the form are inadequate. Meredith's speaker finds

his notions of ideal love do not further his earthly love, while Henley's speaker finds he is in a situation in which ideals have nothing to do with the operation or recovery. Meredith, though, at least was concerned with love. Henley was original in applying the form to a hospital stay. Even the procedure Henley was in the hospital for was new and experimental—he was an early beneficiary of the growing acceptance that there was such a thing as a germ, and ways to fight infection that did not involve amputation.

24. An overview of contemporary reaction is available in Jerome Buckley, pp. 93–95.

25. Henley seemed to think so and wrote Wilde a letter thanking him for the notice. Later in life, Henley was not so gracious in his scathing review of *Ballad of Reading Gaol.*

26. Other poems in the volume follow the same pattern. Consider the first stanza of "Sea Poppies": "Amber husk, / fluted with gold, / fruit on the sand / marked with a rich grain" (21); or the first stanza of "Sea Lily": "Reed: / slashed and torn, / but doubly rich—/ such great heads as yours / drift upon temple-steps, / but you are shattered / in the wind"(14).

27. She could have shortened her poems, for example, by eliminating anaphora, and the elaboration attending anaphora.

28. Bridges differentiated between free verse, prose, accentual verse, and *verse libéré.* He hedges his assertion that a lack of lineal form is unique to free verse by adding, "I have made no examination of the practices of poets in this respect" (655).

29. That is, "thoughts," "seed-pods," "spent," "scattered," "shriveled," "poplar," and "seeds." I didn't "count" articles, prepositions, and "to be" verbs, which repeat as well.

CHAPTER FIVE: THE PARSING METER AND BEYOND

1. In chapter 1, I addressed the Modernist penchant for justifying prosodic innovation by asserting scientific verifiability. The relativity Einstein found and the variability in Williams's foot really are quite different. Mariani points out that Williams barely passed mathematics in college, so it is unlikely Williams could have understood Einstein's theories very deeply. The similarities between Einstein's and Williams's theories are based on verbal commonalties and not actual characteristics. For example, Einstein's Special Theory of Relativity does address "metrical simultaneity," but the physicist was not talking about poetic meter, thus the comparison does not extend our knowledge about the ideas of

Einstein or Williams. *The Encyclopedia of Philosophy* remarks that the theory of relativity is "utterly noncommittal concerning the theses of ethical relativism" (7–8.133). The same could be said regarding the implications of Einstein's theories for poetic meter.

2. Mayhew quotes from "This Florida: 1924" (I.364).

3. Coleridge says this in *Biographia Literaria,* chapter XIII.

4. See Doyle, pp. 54ff., and Hartman, pp. 91ff.

5. Wordsworth excoriates Cowper in the appendix to the preface of *Lyrical Ballads.* In a letter to John Thelwall, December 17, 1796, Coleridge describes Cowper's poems as "divine Chit chat" (*Collected Letters* I.279).

6. That is, *Biographia Literaria,* chapter XVII.

7. See, for example, Mariani, p. 695.

8. H.D. refers to the prologue to *Kora in Hell.*

9. That is to say, the "measureless oceans of space" (351) that Whitman's noiseless patient spider seeks to explore.

10. "Clipped," by the way, contains both a *c* and a *p.*

11. End-of-the-line prominence is discussed below.

12. This is different from Cummings because Williams does not usually consider the shapes of the letters of puns within words when he splits words. He uses the technique relatively infrequently.

13. Throughout the poem, the line is surely / U / U / U / U /. The poem has such lines as, "Which to follow, for to leave," and "When they come, they come in flocks," which do not make sense in Poe's scansion. Cranch wrote a number of poems in this line in *Poems* (1844), including "Beauty and Truth," "Gnosis," "Endymion," and "To the Aurora Borealis." Though Cranch wrote many conventionally formed poems in *Poems,* I have already noted "Correspondences" in chapter 1, and he also wrote irregular odes. Poe's choice of one of the more regular poems in the volume to make a point about prosodic variety seems almost willfully perverse.

14. I tried it, and succeeded at making the two lines equal in time—though admittedly it did not sound very natural.

15. That the very short line is juxtaposed against the long one suggests, perhaps, that Williams felt that the first was short and so used the second to compensate, the same way that sonneteers occasionally will follow a line of nine syllables with one of eleven. Compare also Fletcher's notion of a "suspended line" quoted in chapter 1.

16. Perloff used the Trager-Smith system, which differentiates among stresses

and length of pause. The system thus extends traditional scansion considerably. Attridge, in *Rhythms,* points out that it likewise magnifies the inaccuracies of traditional scansion.

17. See, for example, *The Semantics of Determiners,* ed. Johan van der Auwera (London: Croon Helm, 1980).

CONCLUSION: AVOIDING PROSODY?

1. I use the term in analogy to "invisible editing," a style of editing film which, like prosody, seeks *not* to call attention to itself. There are no jarring jump-cuts in invisible editing, for example.

2. Speaking of the poem, Dove said, "[T]he advice my father gave me . . . led me towards things that really mattered to me" (Cavaleiri 11). There seems little doubt that the speaker of the poem was Dove *in propia persona* and that the father character means to represent her actual father.

3. His phrase for this was "aggressively rhythmic."

4. It is worth noting that the man who invented the procedure Bollobás was referring to, Donald Wesling (for his "grammetrics"), backs away from such assertions in *Grammetrics*—because of the part of the reader in constructing poetic rhythms.

5. I quote Cureton on this issue because he is probably the most feisty of the new prosodists and thus serves as a kind of lightning rod for criticism. Cooper, in *Mysterious Music* (1998), tries to circumvent such problems by relying on poets' own readings of their texts (which introduces new problems with individual performance) or by assuming if he can hear it, it is at least potentially available to others. He does acknowledge that such procedures "still require subjective interpretation" (190).

Works Cited

Abrams, M. H. *The Mirror and the Lamp. Romantic Theory and the Critical Tradition.* New York: Oxford UP, 1953.

Adams, William. "The Poetry of Criticism: Mr. Matthew Arnold." *Gentleman's Magazine* n.s. 14 (April 1875): 467–80. Rpt. in Dawson, 266.

Aiken, Conrad. "The Function of Rhythm." *Dial* 65 (16 Nov. 1918): 417–18.

Alden, Raymond M. "The New Poetry." *Nation* 96 (17 April 1913): 386–87.

American Poetry: The Nineteenth Century. Ed. John Hollander. New York: Library of America, 1993. 2 vols.

Ammons, A. R. "Scribbles." *Worldly Hopes.* New York: Norton, 1982. 23–24.

Andrews, C. E. "The Rhythms of Prose and of Free Verse." *Sewanee Review* 26 (April 1918): 183–94.

——— and M. D. Percival. *Poetry of the Nineties.* Freeport, NY: Books for Libraries P, 1970 [1926].

Arnold, Matthew. *Essays in Criticism. Second Series. Contributions to 'The Pall Mall Gazette' and Discourses in America.* New York: AMS P, 1970. [1903–4].

———. *Matthew Arnold on the Classical Tradition.* Ed. R. H. Super. Ann Arbor: U of Michigan P, 1960.

———. *The Poems of Matthew Arnold.* Ed. Kenneth Allott. London: Longman, 1965.

———. *Poetry and Criticism of Matthew Arnold.* Ed. A. Dwight Culler. Boston: Houghton Mifflin, 1961.

Attridge, Derek. "Beyond Metrics: Richard Cureton's *Rhythmic Phrasing in English Verse.*" *Poetics Today* 17.1 (1996): 9–28.

———. "Poetry Unbound? Observations on Free Verse." *Proceedings of the British Academy* 73 (1987): 353–74.

———. *The Rhythms of English Poetry.* London: Longman, 1982.

———. *Well-Weigh'd Syllables: Elizabethan Verse in Classical Metres.* London: Cambridge UP, 1974.

Baker, Dorothy Z., ed. *Poetics in the Poem. Critical Essays on American Self-Reflexive Poetry.* New York: Peter Lang, 1997.

Barry, M. Martin. *An Analysis of the Prosodic Structure of Selected Poems of T. S. Eliot.* Washington, D.C.: Catholic UP, 1969. Rev. ed.

Baum, Paull F. *Ten Studies in the Poetry of Matthew Arnold.* Durham: Duke UP, 1958.

Bawer, Bruce. "The Poetic Legacy of William Carlos Williams." *New Criterion* 7.1 (1988): 14–26.

Bedetti, Gabriella. "Prosody and the 'Emperor of Ice Cream': The Elegiac Modern Lyric." *Wallace Stevens Journal* 8.2 (1984): 96–102.

Benet's Reader's Encyclopedia of American Literature. 3d ed. New York: Harper & Row, 1987.

———. 4th ed. New York: HarperCollins, 1991.

Berry, Eleanor. "Marine Technology and Technique in the Poetry of Marianne Moore and William Carlos Williams." *William Carlos Williams Review* 14.1 (1988): 50–68.

———. "Williams' Development of a New Prosodic Form: Not the 'Variable Foot' But the Sight Stanza." *William Carlos Williams Review* 7.2 (1981): 21–29.

Bollobás, Enikö. "Measures of Attention: On the Grammetrics of Lineation in William Carlos Williams' Poetry." *Poetry and Epistemology.* Ed. Roland Hagenbüchle and Laura Skandera. Regensburg, Germany: Friedrich Pustet Verlag, 1986.

———. *Tradition and Innovation in American Free Verse: Whitman to Duncan.* Budapest: Akadémiai Kiadó, 1986.

Borroff, Marie. *Language and the Poet: Verbal Artistry in Frost, Stevens, and Moore.* Chicago: U of Chicago P, 1979.

———. "Questions of Design in William Carlos Williams and Marianne Moore." *William Carlos Williams Review* 14.1 (1988): 104–15.

Bradford, Richard. *The Look of It: A Theory of Visual Form in English Poetry.* Cork: Cork UP, 1993.

Bridges, Robert. *Milton's Prosody.* New York: Oxford UP, 1901.

———. "A Paper on Free Verse." *North American Review* 216 (Nov. 1922): 647–58.

Brinkley, Roberta Florence. *Coleridge on the Seventeenth Century.* Durham: Duke UP, 1955.

Brogan, T. V. F. *English Versification, 1570–1980.* Baltimore: Johns Hopkins UP, 1981.

Brooker, Jewel Spears. *Mastery and Escape: T. S. Eliot and the Dialectics of Modernism.* Amherst: U of Massachusetts P, 1994.

Brooks, Cleanth, and Robert Penn Warren. *Understanding Poetry.* New York : Holt, Rinehart and Winston, 1976.

Browning, Robert. *Works.* New York: AMS P, 1966. 10 vols.

Bryant, William Cullen. *Prose Writings of William Cullen Bryant.* Ed. Parke Godwin. New York: Russell & Russell, 1964.

Bryher, Winifred [Ellerman]. "Spear-Shaft and Cyclamen Flowers." *Poetry* 19.6 (1922): 333–37.

Buckler, William E. *On the Poetry of Matthew Arnold.* New York: New York UP, 1982.

Buckley, Jerome Hamilton. *W. E. Henley: A Study of the 'Counter-Decadence' of the Nineties.* Princeton: Princeton UP, 1945.

Buckley, Theodore Alois. *The Tragedies of Aeschylus Literally Translated.* London: Henry G. Bohn, 1849.

Butterfield, R. W. (Herbie). *Modern American Poetry.* London: Vision P, 1984.

Calder, Angus. *T. S. Eliot.* Atlantic Highlands, NJ: Humanities P, 1987.

Cannell, Skipwith. "Poems in Prose and Verse." *Poetry* 2.5 (1913): 171–76.

Carroll, Rebecca, ed. *I Know What Red Clay Looks Like: The Voice and Vision of Black Women Writers.* New York: Carol Southern Books, 1994.

Cavalieri, Grace. "Rita Dove: An Interview with Grace Cavalieri." *American Poetry Review* 24.2 (1995): 11–15.

Cicero, Marcus Tullius. *Orator.* Trans. H[arry]. M[ortimer]. Hubbell. Loeb Classical Library. Cambridge: Harvard UP; London: Heinemann, 1952 [1939].

Coffman, Stanley. *Imagism: A Chapter for the History of Modern Poetry.* Norman: U of Oklahoma P, 1951.

Coleridge, Samuel Taylor. *The Collected Letters of Samuel Taylor Coleridge.* Ed. Earl Leslie Griggs. Corrected ed. Oxford: Clarendon P, 1966. 4 vols.

———. *The Collected Writings of Samuel Taylor Coleridge.* Gen. ed. Kathleen Coburn. London: Routledge & Kegan Paul, 1969.

———. *Shakespearean Criticism.* Ed. Thomas Middleton Rayson. 2d ed. Dent: London, 1960. 2 vols.

Collins, William. *The Poetical Works of William Collins.* Boston: Little, Brown, 1853.

Cone, Eddie Gay. "The Free-Verse Controversy in American Magazines, 1912–1922." Diss. Duke U, 1971.

Conte, Joseph M. *Unending Design: The Forms of Postmodern Poetry.* Ithaca: Cornell UP, 1991.

Cook, Eleanor. *Poetry, Wordplay, and Word War in Wallace Stevens.* Princeton: Princeton UP, 1988.

———. "Introduction." *Wallace Stevens Journal* 15.2 (1991): 115.25.

Cooper, G. Burns. *Mysterious Music. Rhythm and Free Verse.* Stanford: Stanford UP, 1998.

Cowley, Abraham. *Poems.* Ed. A. R. Waller. London: Cambridge UP, 1905.

Cowper, William. *The Poetical Works of William Cowper.* Ed. William Benham. London: Macmillan, 1927.

Cranch, Christopher Pearse. *The Collected Poems of Christopher Pearse Cranch.* Gainesville, FL: Scholars Facsimiles and Reprints, 1971.

Crane, Hart. *Complete Poems and Selected Letters and Prose.* New York: Liveright, 1966.

The Critic. Rev. of *Book of Verses.* 7 July 1888: 5.

Crombie, Winifred. *Free Verse and Prose Style.* London: Croon Helm, 1987.

Crowell's Handbook for Readers and Writers. Ed. Henrietta Gerwig. New York: Thomas Y. Crowell, 1925.

Cumberland, Richard. "Preliminary Observations on Samson Agonistes." Howe, 109–15.

Cummings, E. E. *Complete Poems, 1913–1962.* New York: Harcourt, Brace, 1963.

Cunliffe, John W. "Vers Libre." *Independent* 78 (16 Oct. 1916): 104.

Cunningham, J. V. *The Collected Essays of J. V. Cunningham.* Chicago: Swallow P, 1976.

Cureton, Richard. "A Response to Derek Attridge." *Poetics Today* 17.1 (1996): 29–50.

———. *The Rhythms of English Verse.* New York: Longman, 1995.

Curran, Stuart. *Poetic Form and British Romanticism.* New York: Oxford UP, 1986.

Current Literary Terms. Ed. A. F. Scott. New York: St. Martin's P, 1965.

Cushman, Stephen. *Fictions of Form in American Poetry.* Princeton: Princeton UP, 1993.

———. *William Carlos Williams and the Meanings of Measure.* New Haven: Yale UP, 1985.

Dawson, Carl, ed. *Matthew Arnold, the Poetry: The Critical Heritage.* London: Routledge & Kegan Paul, 1973.

de France, Marie. *Lais de Marie de France.* Ed. Karl Warnke. Paris: Libraire Générale Français, 1990.

De Quincey, Thomas. "Literature of Knowledge and Literature of Power." Perkins, 742–44.

Des Imagistes. New York: AMS P, 1982.

Deutsch, Babette. *Poetry Handbook.* 4th ed. New York: Funk & Wagnalls, 1974.

Dial. "The Muse in a Pet." *Dial* 55 (1 Oct. 1913): 245–47.

———. "New Lamps for Old." *Dial* 56 (16 March 1914): 231–33.

A Dictionary of Literary Terms. Ed. Harry Shaw. New York: McGraw-Hill, 1972.

Dodd, Wayne. "The Art of Poetry and the Temper of the Times." *Ohio Review* 37 (1986): 6–14.

———. "And the Look of the Bay Mare Shames Silliness Out of Me." *Ohio Review* 28 (1982): 36–44.

Doggett, Frank, and Robert Buttel, eds. *Wallace Stevens: A Celebration.* Princeton: Princeton UP, 1979.

Dolin, Sharon. "Enjambment as Modernist Metaphor in Williams' Poetry." *Sagetrieb* 9.3 (1990): 31–56.

D[oolittle], H[ilda]. *Bid Me to Live.* New York: Dial P, 1983.

———. *End to Torment.* Ed. Norman Holmes Pearson and Michael King. New York: New Directions, 1979.

———. *H.D. Collected Poems, 1912–1944.* Ed. Louis L. Martz. New York: New Directions, 1983.

———. "Letter to Norman Holmes Pearson." *Agenda* 25.3–4 (1987–88): 11–16.

———. *Paint It Today.* Ed. Casandra Laity. New York: New York UP, 1992.

Dondo, Mathurin. *Vers Libre: A Logical Development of French Verse.* Paris: E. Champion, 1922.

Douglas, Paul. "'Such the Life is, Such is the Form': Organicism Among the Moderns." *Approaches to Modernism.* Ed. Frederick Burwick. Dordrecht, Holland: D. Reidel, 1987. 254–66.

Dove, Rita. *Grace Notes.* New York: Norton, 1989.

———. *Mother Love.* New York: Norton, 1995.

Doyle, Charles. *William Carlos Williams and the American Poetry.* New York: St. Martin's P, 1982.

DuPlessis, Rachel Blau. "Objectivist Poetics and Political Vision: A Study of Oppen and His Poetry." *George Oppen: Man and Poet.* Ed. Burton Hatlen. Orono: National Poetry Foundation, 1981. 123–48.

Eastman, Max. "Lazy Verse." *New Republic* 8 (9 Sept. 1916): 138–40.

Eaton, Walter Prichard. "The Influence of Free Verse on Prose." *Atlantic Monthly* 124 (Oct. 1919): 491–96.

Ehrenpreis, Irving. "Strange Relation: Stevens' Nonsense." Doggett and Buttel, 219–34.

Eichner, Hans. "The Rise of Modern Science and the Genesis of Romanticism." *PMLA* 97.1 (1982): 8–30.

Eliot, T. S. "The Borderline of Prose." *New Statesman* 9 (19 May 1917): 157–59.

———. *The Complete Poems and Plays, 1909–1950*. New York: Harcourt, Brace, 1980.

———. *On Poets and Poetry*. London: Faber and Faber, 1957.

———. *The Sacred Wood: Essays on Poetry and Criticism*. New York: Knopf, 1930.

———. *To Criticize the Critic*. New York: Farrar, Strauss, & Giroux, 1965.

Emerson, Ralph Waldo. *Emerson's Essays*. New York: Dutton, 1971.

The Encyclopedia of Philosophy. Ed. Paul Edwards. New York: Macmillan, 1967. 8 vols.

Ficke, Arthur Davison. "Metrical Freedom and the Contemporary Poet." *Dial* 68 (1915): 11–13.

Filreis, Alan. *Modernism from Right to Left: Wallace Stevens, the Thirties, and Literary Radicalism*. London: Cambridge UP, 1994.

Finch, Annie. *The Ghost of Meter*. Ann Arbor: U of Michigan P, 1993.

Fisher-Wirth, Anne W. *William Carlos Williams and Autobiography*. University Park: Pennsylvania State UP, 1989.

Fletcher, John Gould. "H.D.'s Vision." *Poetry* 9.5 (1917): 266–69.

———. "A Rational Explanation of Vers Libre." *Dial* 66 (11 Jan. 1919): 11–13.

Flint, F. S. "Four Poems in Unrhymed Cadence." *Poetry* 2.2 (1913): 138–41.

———. "Imagisme." *Poetry* 1 (1913): 198–200.

Ford, Ford Madox. *Critical Writings of Ford Madox Ford*. Ed. Frank MacShane. Lincoln: U of Nebraska P, 1967.

———. "Impressionism—Some Speculations: I." *Poetry* 2.2 (1913): 177–87.

Fordham, Mary Weston. *Magnolia Leaves. Collected Black Women's Poetry*. Ed. Joan Sherman. New York: Oxford UP, 1988.

Foster, Finley Melville Kendall. *English Translations from the Greek*. New York: Columbia UP, 1918.

Fowler, Roger, ed. *A Dictionary of Modern Critical Terms*. London: Routledge & Kegan Paul, 1973.

Friedman, Susan Stanford. "Exile in the American Grain: H.D.'s Diaspora." *Agenda* 25.3–4 (1987–88): 27–47.

———. "Hilda Doolittle (H.D.)." *American Poets, 1880–1945. First Series. Dictionary of Literary Biography*. Ed. Peter Quartermain. Detroit: Gale Research, 1986. 115–49.

Fry, Paul H. *The Poet's Calling in the English Ode.* New Haven: Yale UP, 1980.
Frye, Northrup. "Introduction" to *The Tempest. Willliam Shakespeare: The Complete Works.* Gen. ed. Alfred Harbage. New York: Viking, 1977. [1969]. 1369–72.
Fuller, Henry B. "A New Field for Free Verse." *Dial* 61 (14 Dec. 1916): 515–17.
Fuller, Roy. "L'Oncle Tom: Some Notes and Queries." *Agenda* 23.1–2 (1985): 41–52.
Fussell, Paul. *Poetic Meter and Poetic Form.* Rev. ed. New York: Random House, 1979.
———. *Theory of Prosody in Eighteenth-Century England.* Handen, CT: Archon Books, 1966.
Gall, Sally M. "Pound and the Modern Melic Tradition: Towards a Demystification of 'Absolute Rhythm.'" *Paideuma* 8 (1979): 35–47.
Gardner, Helen. *The Art of T. S. Eliot.* London: The Cresset P, 1968.
Gaskill, Howard, ed. *The Poems of Ossian and Related Works.* Edinburg: Edinburg UP, 1996.
Gates, Rosemary L. "Forging an American Poetry from Speech Rhythms." *Poetics Today* 8.3–4 (1987): 503–27.
———. "The Identity of American Free Verse: The Prosodic Study of Whitman's 'Lilacs.'" *Language and Style* 18.3 (1985): 248–76.
———. "T. S. Eliot and the Free Verse Tradition: Restricting Whitman's 'Free Growth of Metrical Laws.'" *Poetics Today* 11.3 (1990): 547–78.
Gilman, Charlotte Perkins. "One Girl of Many." *The Later Poetry of Charlotte Perkins Gilman.* Ed. Denise D. Knight. Newark: U of Delaware P, 1996.
Ginsberg, Allen. *Collected Poems, 1947–1980.* New York: Harper & Row, 1984.
Golding, Alan. "Charles Olson's Metrical Thicket: Toward a Theory of Free-Verse Prosody." *Language and Style* 14.1 (1981): 64–87.
Graham, Jorie. "The Glorious Thing." Interview with Mark Wunderlich. *American Poet* Fall 1996. Rpt. The Academy of American Poets. www.poets.org/LIT/poet/jgrafst2.htm. 15 Dec. 1999.
Gregory, Eileen. *H.D. and Hellenism: Classic Lines.* Cambridge Studies in American Literature and Cultures, no. 111. London: Cambridge UP, 1997.
Gross, Harvey. *Sound and Form in Modern Poetry.* Ann Arbor: U of Michigan P, 1964.
———, ed. *The Structure of Verse.* Rev. ed. New York: Ecco P, 1979.
Guest, Barbara. *Herself Defined: The Poet H.D. and Her World.* New York: Doubleday, 1984.

Guichard, Léon. *Jules Laforgue et Ses Poesis.* Paris: Pes Universitaires de France, 1950.

The Guide to Modern World Literature. Ed. Martin Seymour-Smith. London: Wolfe, 1972.

Hall, Donald, ed. *Remembering Poets.* New York: Harper & Row, 1978.

Hansen, Harry. *Midwest Portraits.* New York: Harcourt, Brace, 1923.

Harmer, J. B. *Victory in Limbo: Imagism 1908–1917.* New York: St. Martin's P, 1975.

Hartman, Charles O. *Free Verse.* Princeton: Princeton UP, 1980.

Hass, Robert. *Field Guide.* New Haven: Yale UP, 1973.

Helms, Alan. "Intricate Song's Lost Measure." *Sewannee Review* 87.2 (1979): 249–66.

Henderson, Alice Corbin. "Humoresque." *Poetry* 3.1 (1915): 100.

———. "Poetic Prose and Vers Libre." *Poetry* 2.2 (1913): 70–74.

Henley, W. E. *Works of W. E. Henley.* London: D. Nutt, 1908. 7 vols.

Herbert, George. *Poems.* New York: Oxford UP, 1961.

Hirsch, Edward. "On the Line: A Lesson from Dr. Williams." *Ohio Review* (1987): 36–40.

Holder, Alan. *Rethinking Meter: A New Approach to the Verse Line.* Lewisburg, PA: Bucknell UP, 1995.

Holden, Jonathan. *Style and Authenticity in Postmodern Poetry.* Columbia: U of Missouri P, 1986.

Hollander, John. *Melodious* Guile. New Haven: Yale UP, 1988.

———. "The Sound of the Music and the Music of the Sound." Doggett and Buttel, 235–55.

———. *Vision and Resonance.* New York: Oxford UP, 1975.

Holley, Margaret. "The Model Stanza: The Organic Form of Moore's Syllabic Verse." *Twentieth-Century Literature* 30.2 (1984): 181–91.

Holman, C. Hugh, and William Harmon. *A Handbook to Literature.* 5th ed. New York: Macmillan, 1986.

Hopkins, Gerard Manley. *The Correspondence of Gerard ManleyHopkins to Richard Watson Dixon.* Ed. Claude Colleer Abbott. New York: Oxford UP, 1955. 2d ed.

———. *The Letters of Gerard Manley Hopkins to Robert Bridges.* Ed. Claude Colleer Abbott. New York: Oxford UP, 1955. Rev. ed.

Horrocks, Geoffrey. *Greek: A History of the Language and Its Speakers.* London: Longman, 1997. Longman Linguistics Library.

Hough, Graham. "Free Verse." *Proceedings of the British Academy* 43 (1957): 157–77.

Hovey, Richard. "Evening on the Potomac." *American Poetry Vol. 2.* 561–62.

Howe, Ralph E., ed. *John Milton's Samson Agonistes.* San Francisco: Chandler, 1966.

Howells, W. D. "Editor's Easy Chair." *Harper's Monthly Magazine* 131 (Sept. 1915): 634–37.

Huang, Guiyou. *Whitmanism, Imagism, and Modernisn in China and America.* London: Associated UP, 1997.

Hughes, Glenn. *Imagism and the Imagists.* New York: Humanities P, 1960.

Hughes, Langston. *Poetry Criticism.* Vol. 3. Ed. Robyn V. Young. Detroit: Gale Research, 1991.

Hulme, T. E. *Speculations.* New York: Harcourt, Brace, 1936.

Jannaris, Antonius N. *An Historical Greek Grammar Chiefly of the Attic Dialect. As Written and Spoken from Classical Antiquity down to the Present Time. Founded upon the Ancient Texts, Inscriptions, Papyri and Present Popular Greek.* Hildesheim: Georg Olms Verlagsbuchhandlung, 1968. [1897].

Janowitz, Anne. "Paterson: An American Contraption." *William Carlos Williams: Man and Poet.* Ed. Carroll F. Terrell. Orono : National Poetry Foundation, 1983. 301–32.

Jay, Gregory S. *T. S. Eliot and the Poetics of History.* Baton Rouge: Louisiana State UP, 1983.

Jesperson, Otto. "Notes on Metre." Gross, *Structure,* 107–28.

Jones, Llewellyn. "Free Verse and Its Propaganda." *Sewanee Review* 28 (July 1920): 384–95.

Johnson, Samuel. *Johnson, Prose and Poetry.* Oxford: Clarendon P, 1922.

Justice, Donald. "The Free-Verse Line in Stevens." *Antaeus* 53 (1984): 53–76.

Kallet, Marilyn. *Honest Simplicity in William Carlos Williams' "Asphodel, That Greeny Flower."* Baton Rouge: Louisiana State UP, 1985.

Keats, John. "Ode on a Grecian Urn." Perkins, 1182.

Kenner, Hugh. *A Homemade World.* New York: Knopf, 1975.

———. *The Invisible Poet: T. S. Eliot.* New York: Ivan Oblensky, 1959.

———. *The Pound Era.* Berkeley: U of California P, 1971.

———. "The Rhythms of Ideas." *Sagetreib* 3.2 (1984): 37–41.

Kermode, Frank. "Samson Agonistes and Hebrew Prosody." *Twentieth-Century Interpretations of Samson Agonistes.* Ed. Galbraith M. Crump. Englewood Ciffs, NJ: Prentice-Hall, 1968. 99–108.

Kilmer, Joyce. "How Does the New Poetry Differ from the Old?" *New York Times Magazine* (26 March 1916): 8.

[Kingsley, Charles]. "Recent Poetry and Recent Verse." *Fraser's Magazine* 39 (May 1849): 576–80. Rpt. in Dawson, 41–46.

Kirby-Smith, H. T. *The Origins of Free Verse.* Ann Arbor: U of Michigan P, 1996.

Kirkconnell, Watson. *Awake the Courteous Echo.* Toronto: U of Toronto P, 1973.

Kitchen, Judith, Stan Sanvel Rubin, and Earl G. Ingersoll. "A Conversation with Rita Dove." *Black American Literature Forum* 20.3 (1986): 227–40.

Kizer, Carolyn. "Amusing Our Daughters." *The Vintage Book of Contemporary Poetry.* Ed. J. D. McClatchy. New York: Random House, 1990. 205–6.

Kreymborg, Alfred. *Mushrooms.* New York: John Marshall, 1916.

Kugel, James L. *The Idea of Biblical Poetry.* New Haven: Yale UP, 1981.

Küper, Christoph. "Metrics Today I: An Introduction." *Poetics Today* 16.3 (95): 389–410.

Lambert, Mary Eliza (Perine) Tucker. *Loews Bridge, a Broadway Idyll. Collected Black Women's Poetry.* Vol. 1. Ed. Joan R. Sherman. New York: Oxford UP, 1988.

Langhorne, John. "Observations on the Oriental Eclogues and Odes." Collins 138–39.

Lanier, Sidney. "The Marshes of Glynn." *American Poetry.* Vol. 2, 412–16.

———. *The Science of English Verse.* New York: Charles Scribner's Sons, 1908.

Lawrence, D. H. "How Beastly the Bourgeois Is." *Norton,* 2127–28.

———. *Selected Literary Criticism.* Ed. Anthony Beal. London: Heinemann, 1955.

Lefevre, Andre. *Translating Literature: The German Tradition.* Amsterdam: Van Gorcum, 1977.

Leithauser, Brad. "The Confinement of Free Verse." *New Criterion* 5.9 (May 1987): 4–14.

Lensing, George. "Stevens' Prosody." *Teaching Wallace Stevens. Practical Essays.* Ed. John N. Serio and B. J. Leggett. Knoxville: U of Tennessee P, 1994.

———. *Wallace Stevens. A Poet's Growth.* Baton Rouge: Louisiana State UP, 1986.

Levertov, Diane. "The Ideas in the Things." Terrell, 141–51.

———. "On Williams' Triadic Line; Or, How to Dance on Variable Feet." McCorkle, 141–48.

Levine, Jessica. "Spatial Rhythm and Poetic Invention in William Carlos Williams' 'Sunday in the Park.'" *William Carlos Williams Review* 21.1 (1995): 23–32.

Levine, Philip. *Don't Ask.* Ann Arbor: U of Michigan P, 1981.

———. *New Selected Poems.* New York: Knopf, 1991.

———. "The Simple Truth." *New Yorker* 66.36 (1990): 48.

———. *The Simple Truth.* New York: Knopf, 1994.

Lindsay, Vachel. "The Firemen's Ball." *The Congo and Other Poems.* New York: Dover, 1992.

Literary Terms and Criticism. Eds. John Peck and Martin Coyle. London: Macmillan, 1985.

Longinus. *On the Sublime.* Trans. W. H. Fyfe. Rev. by Donald Russell. Cambridge: Harvard UP, 1995. Loeb Classical Library 119.

Lowell, Amy. "The Bombardment." *Poetry* 2.4 (1914): 60.

———. "Some Musical Analogies in Modern Poetry." *Musical Quarterly* 6 (Jan. 1920): 127–57.

———. "Vers Libre and Metrical Prose." *Poetry* 3 (March 1914): 213–20.

Lowes, John Livingston. *Convention and Revolt in Poetry.* Boston: Houghton Mifflin, 1922.

Mackey, Nathaniel. "Sound and Sentiment, Sound and Symbol." McCorkle, 194–218.

Maclean, Norman. "From Action to Imagery." *Critics and Criticism Ancient and Modern.* Ed. R. S. Crane. Chicago: U of Chicago P, 1952.

Mallarmé, Stephane. *Mallarmé.* Ed. Anthony Hartley. Baltimore: Penguin, 1965.

Mariani, Paul. *William Carlos Williams: A New World Naked.* New York: McGraw-Hill, 1981.

Martineau, Harriet. Rev. of *Poems* (1853). *Daily News* (Dec. 26, 1853). Rpt. in Dawson, 134–37.

Martz, Louis L. "Ammons, Warren, and the Tribe of Walt." *Yale Review* 72.1 (1982): 63–84.

———. "Introduction." *H.D. Collected Poems,* xi–xxxvi.

Masters, Edgar Lee. *Spoon River Anthology.* London: Collier, 1962.

Mayhew, Jonathan. "William Carlos Williams and the Free-Verse Line." Terrell, 287–300.

Mayo, Robert. "The Contemporaneity of Lyrical Ballads." *PMLA* 60 (1954): 486–522.

McCorkle, James, ed. *Conversant Essays.* Detroit: Wayne State UP, 1990.

Menken, Adah Isaacs. *Infelicia. Collected Black Women's Poetry.* Ed. Joan Sherman. New York: Oxford UP, 1988.

Meter in English. A Critical Engagement. Ed. David Baker. Fayetteville: U of Arkansas P, 1996.

Mill, John Stuart. "What Is Poetry?" *Norton,* 994–1000.

Miller, J. Hillis. "Williams: Poet of Reality." *William Carlos Williams: Modern Critical Views.* Ed. Harold Bloom. New York: Chelsea House, 1986.

Mills, Ralph J. *Cry of the Human: Essays on Contemporary American Poetry.* Urbana: U of Illinois P, 1975.

A Milton Handbook. Ed. James Holly Hanford and James G. Taafe. New York: Appleton Century Crofts, [1970].

Milton, John. *Paradise Lost.* Ed. Scott Elledge. 2d ed. New York: Norton, 1993.

———. *Samson Agonistes: A Dramatic Poem.* New York: Columbia UP, 1931.

Monroe, Harriet. "Carl Sandburg." *Poetry* 5.2 (1916): 90–93.

———. *Poets and Their Art.* Rev. ed. New York: Macmillan, 1932.

———. Rev. of *Collected Poetry of H.D. Poetry* 24.5 (1925): 268–75.

Moody, A. D. "'H.D., Imagiste': An Elemental Mind." *Agenda* 25.3–4 (1987–88): 77–96.

Moody, William Vaughn. *The Poems and Plays of William Vaughn Moody.* Ed. John M. Manley. Vol. 1. New York: AMS P, 1969. 2 vols.

Moore, Marianne. *Complete Poems of Marianne Moore.* New York: Viking, 1981.

Morris, Lewis. *The Poetical Works of Sir Lewis Morris.* London: Routledge, 1880.

Murray, Gilbert. *A History of Ancient Greek Literature.* London: Heinemann, 1897.

———. *Ten Greek Plays.* New York: Oxford UP, 1929.

Murry, John Middleton. *Pencillings.* New York: T. Seltzer, 1966.

The Nation. Review of *Book of Verses.* 26 Dec. 1889: 522.

The New Princeton Encyclopedia of Poetry and Poetics. Ed. Alex Preminger and T. V. F. Brogan. Princeton: Princeton UP, 1993.

Nicholson, Mervyn. "'The Slightest Sound Matters': Wallace Stevens' Sound Cosmology." *Wallace Stevens Journal* 18.1 (1994): 63–80.

The Norton Anthology of English Literature. Vol. 2. Gen. ed. M. H. Abrams. 6th ed. New York: Norton, 1993.

O'Donnell, Brennan. *The Passion of Meter: A Study of Wordsworth's Metrical Art.* Kent, OH: Kent State UP, 1995.

Ohio Review. Special issue: Free Verse. 28 (1982).

The Oxford Companion to French Literature. Ed. Paul Harvey and J. E. Heseltine. Oxford: Clarendon P, 1986.

Pater, Walter. *Appreciations, with an Essay on Style.* London: Macmillan, 1889.

Patterson, William Morrison. *The Rhythm of Prose.* New York: Columbia UP, 1916.

Peckham, H. Houston. "The Novelty Fallacy in Literature." *South Atlantic Quarterly* 16 (April 1917): 144–48.

Perkins, David, ed. *English Romantic Writers.* New York: Harcourt, Brace, 1967.
Perloff, Marjorie. "Return of the (Numerical) Repressed." *Radical Artifice.* Chicago: U of Chicago P, 1991. 134–70.
———. "To Give a Design: Williams and the Visualization of Poetry." Terrell, 159–86.
Pettersson, Thore. "Prose and Poetry." *Studia Linguistica* 36.1 (1982): 64–87.
Poe, Edgar Allan. *Edgar Allan Poe. Essays and Reviews.* Ed. E. M. Thompson. New York: Library of America, 1984.
———. *Poems and Essays.* London: Dent, 1977.
The Poet's Dictionary. William Packard. New York: Harper & Row, 1989.
Pondrom, Cyrena. "H.D. and the Origins of Imagism." *Sagetrieb* 4.1 (1985): 73–94.
Pope, Alexander. *Pastoral Poetry and* an Essay on Criticism. Ed. E. Audra and Aubrey Williams. London: Methuen, 1961. Vol. I of the Twickenham Edition. 10 vols.
———. The Rape of the Lock *and Other Poems.* Ed. Geoffrey Tillotson. London: Methuen, 1962. 3d ed. Vol. II of the Twickenham Edition. 10 vols.
Potter, R[obert]. *The Tragedies of Aeschylus.* London: J. Walker, 1809.
Pound, Ezra. *The Cantos of Ezra Pound.* New York: New Directions: 1986.
———. *Ezra Pound's Poetry and Prose: Contributions to Periodicals.* Ed. Lea Baechler, A. Walton Litz, and James Longenbach. New York: Garland, 1991. 11 vols.
———. "How to Read." *Literary Essays of Ezra Pound.* Ed. T. S. Eliot. New York: New Directions, 1935. 15–40.
———. "Mr. Hueffer and the Prose Tradition in Verse." *Poetry* 4 (1914): 111–20.
———. *Pound/Little Review.* Ed. Thomas L. Scott, Melvin J. Friedman, and Jackson R. Byre. New York: New Directions, 1988.
———. *The Spirit of Romance.* New York: New Directions, 1968.
Pratt, William, ed. *The Imagist Poem.* New York: Dutton, 1963.
Prince, P. T. *The Italian Element in Milton's Verse.* Oxford: Clarendon P, 1954.
Princeton Encyclopedia of Poetry and Poetics. Ed. Alex Preminger. Princeton: Princeton UP, 1974. Enlarged edition.
Prins, Yopie. "'Violence Bridling Speech': Browning's Translation of Aeschylus' Agamemnon." *Victorian Poetry* 27.3–4 (1989): 151–70.
Ramsey, Paul. "Free Verse: Some Steps toward Definition." *Studies in Philology* 65.1 (1968): 98–108.

Rapp, Carl. *William Carlos Williams and Romantic Idealism.* Hanover: UP of New England, 1984.

The Reader's Companion to World Literature. New York: Holt, Rinehart & Winston, 1956.

The Reader's Encyclopedia of American Literature. Ed. Max J. Herzberg. New York: Thomas J. Crowell, 1962.

A Reader's Guide to Literary Terms. Ed. Karl Beckson and Arthur Ganz. New York: Farrar, Strauss, & Giroux, 1960.

Reed, John. Letter. *Poetry* 2.3 (1913): 111–12.

Rice, Wallace. "Mr. Ezra Pound and 'Poetry.'" *Dial* 54 (1 May 1913): 370–71.

Richards, I. A. *Practical Criticism.* New York: Harcourt, Brace, 1929.

Richardson, Joan. *Wallace Stevens: The Early Years, 1879–1923.* New York: William Morrow, 1986.

Riley, James Whitcomb. *Complete Poetical Works of James Whitcomb Riley.* New York: Garden City Publishers, 1942.

Riquelme, John Paul. *Harmony of Dissonances: T. S. Eliot, Romanticism, and Imagination.* Baltimore: Johns Hopkins UP, 1991.

Robinson, Janice S. *H.D. The Life and Work of an American Poet.* Boston: Houghton Mifflin, 1982.

Rodker, John. "London Nights." *Poetry* 2.3 (1914): 121–23.

Rosmarin, Adena. *The Power of Genre.* Minneapolis: U of Minnesota P, 1985.

Rosenmeyer, Thomas G. *The Art of Aeschylus.* Berkeley: U of California P, 1982.

[Rossetti, William Michael]. "The Strayed Reveler and Other Poems." *Germ* 2 (Feb. 1850): 84–96. Rpt. in Dawson, 56–66.

Rosu, Anca. "Images of Sound in the Poetry of Wallace Stevens." *Wallace Stevens Journal* 15.2 (1991): 178–90.

Ryan, Lawrence V. "The Classical Verse of R. D. Blackmore." *Victorian Poetry* 22.3 (1985): 229–47.

Saintsbury, George. *A History of English Prosody.* London: Macmillan, 1906–10. 3 vols.

Sanborn, Robert Alden. "Lento." *Part of the Climate.* Ed. Jaqueline Vaught Brogan. Berkeley: U of California P, 1991.

Sandburg, Carl. *Chicago Poems.* Ed. John Halwas. Urbana: U of Illinois P, 1992.

Saner, Reg. "Noble Numbers: Two in One." *Ohio Review* 28 (1982): 6–15.

Sato, Hiroaki. "Lineation of Tanka in English Translation." *Monumenta Nipponica* 42.3 (1987): 347–56.

Sayers, Frank. *Disquisitions, Metaphysical and Literary.* New York: Garland, 1977.

Sayre, Henry. *The Visual Text of William Carlos Williams.* Urbana: U of Illinois P, 1983.

Scheckner, Peter, ed. *An Anthology of Chartist Poetry: Poetry of the British Working Class, 1830s–1850s.* Madison, NJ: Fairleigh Dickinson UP, 1989.

Scott, A. F. *Current Literary Terms.* New York: Macmillan, 1965.

Schwab, Ulrike. *The Poetry of the Chartist Movement : A Literary and Historical Study.* Studies in Social History (International Institute for Social History) 13. Dordrecht; Boston : Kluwer Academic, 1993.

Scott, A. F. *Current Literary Terms.* New York: Macmillan, 1965.

Scrivener, Michael, ed. *Poetry and Reform: Periodical Verse from the English Democratic Press, 1792–1824.* Detroit: Wayne State UP, 1992.

Selver, Paul. *The Art of Translating Poetry.* Boston: The Writer, 1966.

Shavit, Uzi. "David Fogel and Hebrew Free Verse: Is There a Fogelian Nusah in Hebrew Poetry?" *Prooftexts* 13.1 (1993): 65–86.

Shelley, Percy Bysshe. *The Complete Works of Shelley.* Ed. Roger Ingpen and Walter E. Peck. New York: Gordian P, 1965. 10 vols.

Simms, William Gilmore. "The Lost Pleiad." *American Poetry.* Vol. 1. 363–64.

Simpson, Louis. "Irregular Impulse: Some Remarks on Free Verse." *Ohio Review* 28 (1982): 54–57.

Sitwell, Edith. *Poetry and Criticism.* London: Hogarth, 1925.

Skinner, Constance Lindsay. "Songs of the Coast-Dwellers." *Poetry* 2.1 (1914): 8–15.

Smith, Barbara Herrnstein. *Poetic Closure.* Chicago: U of Chicago P, 1968.

Snodgrass, W. D. "Whitman's Selfsong." *Southern Review* 32.3 (1996): 572–602.

Some Imagist Poets. Boston: Houghton Mifflin, 1915.

Spender, Stephen, and Donald Hall, eds. *The Concise Encyclopedia of English and American Poets and Poetry.* London: Hutchinson, 1970.

Sprat, Thomas. "Introduction." *Abraham Cowley: Poetry and Prose.* Oxford: Clarendon P, 1959.

Springer, Mary Doyle. "Repetition and 'Going Round' with Wallace Stevens." *Wallace Stevens Journal* 15.2 (1991): 191–208.

Sprott, Samuel Ernest. *Milton's Art of Prosody.* Oxford: Basil Blackwell, 1953.

Spurr, David. "Eliot, Modern Poetry, and Romanticism." *Approaches to Teaching the Poetry and Plays of T. S. Eliot.* New York: Modern Language Association, 1988.

Stalker, James C. "Reader Expectation and the Poetic Line." *Language and Style* 15.4 (1982): 241–52.

Steele, Timothy. *Missing Measures.* Fayetteville: U of Arkansas P, 1990.

Stein, William B. "Tinkling Symbols and Green Roaring Horses." *Wallace Stevens Journal* 3.1–2 (1979): 35–41.

Stevens, Wallace. *The Collected Poems of Wallace Stevens.* New York: Vintage, 1982.

———. *Letters of Wallace Stevens.* Ed. Holly Stevens. New York: Knopf, 1966.

———. "Letters to Ferdinand Reyher." *Hudson Review* 44.3 (1991): 381–409.

———. *The Necessary Angel.* New York: Knopf, 1954.

———. *Opus Posthumous.* Ed. Milton Bates. New York: Knopf, 1989.

———. *Souvenirs and Prophecies.* Ed. Holly Stevens. New York: Knopf, 1977.

Stewart, George R. *The Technique of English Verse.* New York: Kennikat P, 1966.

Storer, Edward. "Form in Free Verse." *New Republic* 6 (11 March 1916): 154–56.

Sutton, Walter. *American Free Verse.* New York: New Directions, 1973.

Swann, Thomas Burnett. *The Classical World of H.D.* Lincoln: U of Nebraska P, 1962.

Taafe, James G. *Abraham Cowley.* New York: Twayne, 1977.

Taleb-Khyar, Mohammed. "An Interview with Rita Dove." *Criticism* 14.2 (1991): 346–66.

Tapscott, Stephen. *American Beauty: William Carlos Williams and the Modernist Whitman.* New York: Columbia UP, 1984.

Tarlinskaja, Marina. "Beyond 'Loose Iamb': The Form and Themes of the English 'Dolnik.'"

Poetics Today 16.3 (1995): 493–522.

Taylor, Dennis. "The Apparitional Meters of Wallace Stevens." *Wallace Stevens Journal* 15.2 (1991): 209–28.

The Teacher's and Writer's Handbook of Poetic Forms. Ed. Ron Padgett. New York: T & W Collaborative, 1987.

Terrell, Carroll, ed. "Introduction." *William Carlos Williams. Man and Poet.* Orono: National Poetry Foundation, 1983.

Thompson, Francis. *A Renegade Poet and Other Essays.* Boston: Ball, 1910.

Timrod, Henry. "The Cotton Boll." *American Poetry.* Vol. 2. 206–10.

Tucker, Mary Eliza Perine. *Loew's Bridge: A Broadway Idyl. Collected Black Women's Poetry.* Ed. Joan Sherman. New York: Oxford UP, 1988.

Untermeyer, Louis. *The Forms of Poetry.* New York: Harcourt, Brace, 1926.

———. "The Perfect Imagist." *Saturday Review of Literature* 1.15 (1924): 260.

Vanderwiden, Betty. "'No Before nor After': Translating the Greek Tradition.'" *Classical and Modern Literature* 13.1 (1992): 63–74.

Vendler, Helen. *On Extended Wings.* Cambridge: Harvard UP, 1969.

Walsh, William. "Isn't Reality Magic? An Interview with Rita Dove." *Kenyon Review* 16.3 (1994): 142–54.

Warfel, Harry. "A Rationale of Free Verse." *Jahrbuch für Amerikanstudien* 13 (1968): 228–35.

Warner, H. E. "Verse—Free or Confined?" *Dial* 61 (28 Dec. 1916): 572.

Warr, George C. W., trans. *The Oresteia of Aeschylus.* New York: Longman, 1900.

Weeks, Ruth Mary. "Phrasal Prosody." *English Journal* 10 (1921): 11–19.

Weigel, Molly. *The Leonard L. Milberg Collection of American Poetry.* Ed. J. Howard Woolmer. Princeton: Princeton UP, 1994.

Weinstein, Mark. *William Edmondstoune Aytoun and the Spasmodic Controversy.* New Haven: Yale UP, 1968.

Wendorf, Richard. *William Collins and Eighteenth-Century English Poetry.* Minneapolis: U of Minnesota P, 1981.

Wesling, Donald. *The Scissors of Meter : Grammetrics and Reading.* Ann Arbor: U of Michigan P, 1996.

———. *The New Poetries.* Lewisburg, PA: Bucknell UP, 1985.

———, and Enikö Bollobás. "Verse Form: Recent Studies." *Modern Philology* 81.1 (1983): 530–60.

West, Martin L., ed. *Aeschyli Agamemnon.* Stuttgart: B. G. Teubner, 1991.

Whitman, Walt. *Leaves of Grass and Selected Prose.* Ed. Lawrence Buell. New York: McGraw-Hill, 1981.

Wilde, Oscar. *The Artist as Critic: Critical Writing of Oscar Wilde.* Ed. Richard Ellman. New York: Random House, 1969.

Williams, William Carlos. "America, Whitman, and the Art of Poetry." *Poetry Journal* 8 (Nov. 1917): 27–36.

———. *The Autobiography of William Carlos Williams.* New York: Random House, 1951.

———. *The Collected Poems of William Carlos Williams.* 3d ed. Ed. Walton A. Litz and Christopher MacGowan. New York: New Directions, 1991. 2 vols.

———. *The Embodiment of Knowledge.* Ed. Ron Loewinsohn. New York: New Directions, 1974.

———. "Letter to Frances Sterloff." *Antaeus* 30/31 (1978): 24–25.

———. *Interviews with William Carlos Williams.* Ed. Linda Welshimer Wagner. New York: New Directions, 1976.

———. *I Wanted to Write a Poem.* Ed. Edith Heal. Boston: Beacon P, 1967.

———. *Paterson.* New York: New Directions, 1963.

———. *Selected Essays of William Carlos Williams.* New York: Random House, 1951.

———. *The Selected Letters of William Carlos Williams.* Ed. John Thirwall. New York: McDowell, Obolensky, 1957.

———. *Something to Say: William Carlos Williams on Younger Poets.* Ed. James E. B. Breslin. New York: New Directions, 1985.

———. *William Carlos Williams and James Laughlin. Selected Letters.* Ed. Hugh Witemeyer. New York: Norton, 1989.

———. *The Williams-Siegel Documentary.* Ed. Martha Baird and Ellen Reis. New York: Definition P, 1970.

Williamson, George. *T. S. Eliot: A Reader's Guide.* New York: Farrar, Strauss & Cudahy, 1953.

Wimsatt, W. K. *The Verbal Icon.* Lexington: U of Kentucky P, 1954.

———, and Monroe C. Beardsley. "The Concept of Meter: An Exercise in Abstraction." Gross, *Structure,* 147–72.

Wood, Clement. *Poet's Handbook.* Garden City, NY: Garden City Publishing, 1942.

Wordsworth, William. *William Wordsworth.* Ed. Stephen Gill. New York: Oxford UP, 1984.

The Writer's Encyclopedia. Ed. Kirk Polking et al. Cincinnati: Writer's Digest Books, 1983.

Xie, Ming. "Pound, Waley, Lowell, and the 'Chinese Example' of Vers Libre." *Paideuma* 22.3 (1993): 39–68.

Yeats, W. B. "Modern Poetry: A Broadcast." *The Collected Writings of W. B. Yeats. Later Essays.* Ed. William H. O'Donnell. New York: Charles Scribner's Sons, 1994.

Zukofsky, Louis. *All.* New York: Norton, 1965.

———. *Prepositions.* Expanded ed. Berkeley: U of California P, 1981.

Index

MAJOR REFERENCES IN BOLD

Abrams, M. H., 48, 87
accent, 20, 149
accentualism, accentual poetry, 14, 16, 21, 34, 63, 123, 207, 209, 215, 217, 239n. 12, 246n. 29, 250n. 8, 250n. 14, 251n. 13, 252n. 28
Adams, Percy G., 82
Adams, William, 82
Aeschylus, 149, 157, 250n. 11
WORKS:
Agamemnon, 250n. 11 (trans. Browning, 147–51, 157; trans. Buckley, 144; trans. Murray, 138; trans. Potter, 141–42; trans. Warr, 142); *Prometheus Bound,* 138
Aiken, Conrad, 55, 243n. 38
Alden, Raymond, 16
Aldington, Richard, 56, 137; "The River," 171
allegory, 5–6, 9, 60, 68–70, 71, 75, 103, 105, 107, 116, 118, 180, 186, 201, 205, 220, 223, 226, 228, 231, 232, 246n. 22
alliteration, 94, 95, 144, 174, 215. *See also* Dove, Rita; Pope, Alexander; Stevens, Wallace
Ammons, A. R., 30; "Scribbles," 201
Andreini, Giovambattista: *Adamo,* 251n. 17
Andrews, C. E., 1, 83
Arensberg, Walter, 102
Aristotle: *Poetics,* 63
Arnold, Matthew, 28, 63, 91, 143, 166, 245–46n. 21
WORKS:
"Dover Beach," **78–82**, 87, 88, 90, 94, 245n. 17; *Empedocles on Etna,* 159–60; "Euphrosyne," 246n. 21; "The Forgotten Merman," 245n. 17; preface to *Merope,* 80; "On Translating Homer," 78, 246n. 23, 250n. 8; "Philomela," 160–61; "The Study of Poetry," 80
Attridge, Derek, 22, 210, 234, 235, 239n. 12, 249–50n. 7, 254n. 16
Aucassin and Nicolette, 243n. 39
Auden, W. H., 7, 181
Auwera, Johan van der, 254n. 17
Aytoun, William, 82

Bacon, Francis, 243n. 41
Bailey, Philip James: *Festus,* 82
Baker, Dorothy Z., 5
Barry, M. Martin, 87–88, 94
Barthes, Roland, 7
Baum, Paull F., 79
Bawer, Bruce, 179
Beardsley, Monroe C., 218
Bedetti, Gabriella, 109
Bedient, Calvin, 224
Benet, William Rose, 109
Benet's Reader's Encyclopedia, 24
Benet's Reader's Encylopedia of American Literature, 15
Beowulf, 35, 105, 149, 154, 170, 250n. 10, 250n. 14
Berry, Eleanor, 181, 199–200, 201, 203, 209, 212
Bible, 39, 57, 59, 98, 243n. 39; Exodus, 183; Genesis, 156; Job, 39; Psalms, 39
Binyon, Lawrence: "Red Night," 83

Blackmore, R. D., 143
Blair, Hugh, 144–45, 146
Blake, William, 39, 243n. 39, 248n. 10
Bloom, Harold, 87
Bly, Robert, 26
Boethius: *Consolation of Philosophy,* 243n. 39
Bollobás, Enikö, 2, 61, 187, 201, 212, 234, 249n. 1, 254n. 4
Borroff, Marie, 102, 197, 201
Bowra, C. M., 137
Bradford, Richard, 152, 245n. 10
Bradley, Katherine Harris, 246n. 25
Bridges, Robert, 56, 151, 250n. 13, 252n. 28
WORKS:
Milton's Prosody, 172, 251n. 16; "A Paper on Free Verse," 172, 240n. 21; "Testament of Beauty," 250n. 7
Brinkley, Roberta Florence, 250n. 13
Brogan, T. V. F., 13, 247n. 7, 251n. 16
Brooker, Jewel Spears, 87
Brooks, Cleanth, and Robert Penn Warren: *Understanding Poetry,* 28
Browning, Elizabeth Barrett: *Aurora Leigh,* 82
Browning, Robert, 62, 83, 246n. 28
WORKS:
Agamemnon (trans.), **147–51**, 157; "Andrea Del Sarto," 246n. 27
Bryant, William Cullen, 76
Bryher (Winnifred Ellerman), 249n. 2
Buckler, William E., 245n. 24
Buckley, Jerome, 252n. 16
Buckley, Theodore Alois, 144, 145
Bunyan, John: *Pilgrim's Progress,* 5
Butterfield, R. W., 188
Byron, George Gordan, Lord: *Childe Harold,* 8; *Manfred,* 83; *Mazeppa,* 246n. 24

cadence, 19–26, 27, 30, 31, 33, 34, 36, 56, 103, 140, 145, 153
Cage, John, 241n. 27
Calder, Angus, 87, 88
Campion, Margaret, 249n. 20
Campion, Thomas, 14, 207
WORKS:
Observations in the Art of English Poesie, 239n. 12; "Rose Cheeked Laura," 37
Cannell, Skipwith: "Poems in Prose and Verse," 33–34
capitalization, 103, 113
Carpenter, Edward: *Towards Democracy,* 39
catalogue, 40, 50–51, 159, 170, 219
Cavalieri, Grace, 231
Char, Rene, 219
Chaucer, Geoffrey, 16, 61, 69, 80, 165; *Canterbury Tales,* 243n. 39
Chomsky, Noam, 198
Cicero: *Orator,* 28
Coffman, Stanley, 249n. 5
Coleridge, Samuel Taylor, 14, 31, 76, 80, 86, 88, 108, 143, 151, 189, 221, 241n. 31; metrical contract, 27, 28, 239n. 15; organicism, 3, 47–49, 50, 51, 52, 53, 54, 62–63, 182, 183, 184, 185
WORKS:
Biographia Literaria, 48, 263n. 3, 253n. 6; "Christabel," 123, 152, 241n. 31; "Dejection: an Ode," 62, 77–78; "Ode to the Departing Year," 62, 77; "On Method," 241n. 28; *Rime of the Ancient Mariner,* 243n. 39
Collins, William, 63, 73–75, 76, 79, 80, 82
WORKS:
"Ode on the Poetical Character," 74; "Ode to Evening," 73; "Ode to Fear," 74; "Ode to Liberty," 74; "The Passions," 74
Cone, Eddie Gay, 2
Conte, Joseph M., 3
contextual prosody, 63, 67–70, 76–78, 81–82, 90, 153, 154
Cook, Eleanor, 102, 247n. 1
Cooper, Edith Emma, 246n. 25
Cooper, G. Burns, 233–34, 235, 254n. 5
Corman, Cid, 216, 218
Cornhill, The, 166

Cowley, Abraham, 28, 61, **63–73**, 75, 79, 80, 82, 151, 153, 175, 205, 244n. 7, 245n. 10, 246n. 30; disruption of normal patterns, 63–67; organicism, 63, 64, 67, 70; rhyme, 71–73, 74, 89–90, 114; sublime, 67–70; theory of imitation, 64
WORKS:
"First Olimpique Ode," 64–65; "The Muse," 72; "Ode. Upon Liberty," 72; "Of Wit," 64, 72, 244n. 2; *Pindarique Odes,* 63, 64; preface to *Poems,* 66; "The Praise of Pindar," 67, 69–70; "To Dr. Scarborough," 89; "To Mr. Hobs," 65–66; "The Resurrection," 66–68
Cowper, William, 185, 253n. 5; "The Flatting Mill," 185–86, 218
Crabbe, George, 165
Cranch, Christopher Pearse, 39, 83, 208, 253n. 13
WORKS:
"Beauty and Truth," 253n. 13; "Correspondences," 39, 253n. 13; Endymion," 253n. 13; "Gnosis," 253n. 13; "My Thoughts," 207; *Poems,* 253n. 13; "To the Aurora Borealis," 253n. 13
Crane, Hart, 53
Creeley, Robert, 38, 180
Critic, The, 164, 166
Crombie, Winifred, 55
Crowell's Handbook for Readers and Writers, 24
Cumberland, Richard, 151
Cummings, E. E., 32–33, 37, 103, 113, 249n. 20, 253n. 12
WORKS:
"Chansons Innocents," 32; "[1(a]" 176–77; *Tulips and Chimneys,* 32
Cummington Press, 123
Cunliffe, John, 25
Cunningham, J. V., 172, 173
Cureton, Richard, 10, 233, 234–35, 239n. 18, 240n. 18, 254n. 5
Curran, Stuart, 17, 62–63, 75, 238n. 6
Current Literary Terms, 15
Cushman, Stephen, 5, 6, 180, 183, 198, 199, 201, 207, 210–11

Dante Alighieri, 113, 220, 247n. 33; *La Vita Nuova,* 177, 243n. 39, 247n. 33
de France, Marie: *Lais,* 242n. 34
Demuth, Charles, 194
De Quincey, Thomas, 57, 59
Deutsch, Babette, 25
Dial, 1, 19
Dickinson, Emily, 6–7, 62, 237n. 3
Dictionary of Literary Terms, A, 24–25
dochmiac, 157–58
Dodd, Wayne, 18, 26
Dolin, Sharon, 197–98
Dondo, Mathurin D., 53
Donne, John, 215
D[oolittle], H[ilda], 11, 42, **135–40, 151, 168–75, 177–78**, 179, 180, 190, 195, 199,202–3, 212–13, 227; decorums of *Sea Garden,* 168–75; and Gilbert Murray, 138–40;grammar and enjambment, 170–71, 175, 192, 193, 199, 200; and Greek poetry, 137–38, 249n. 2; model Imagist, 135–36; theory of translation, 142–43, 146–47
WORKS:
Bid Me to Live, 142; "Cliff Temple," 169; *Collected Poems,* 137; *End to Torment,* 136; "The Helmsmen," 170; "Hermes of the Ways," 136, 139; "Mid-Day," 173–74; "Oread," 31, 135; *Paint It Today,* 249n. 6; "Pursuit," 168–69; "Saturn," 175; *Sea Garden,* 137, 168, 169, 191, 212; "Sea Iris," 169; "Sea Lilly," 252n. 26; "Sea Poppies," 251n. 26; "Sea Rose," 169; *Trilogy,* 177
Dorn, Alfred. 4
Dos Passos, John: *USA,* 55
Douglas, Paul, 46, 51–52
Dove, Rita, 11, **228–33**, 254n. 2; alliteration, 231; enjambment, 230, 231;

meter, 229, 232; repetition, 231; rhyme, 229, 230
WORKS:
"Flash Cards," 228–33; *Mother Love,* 232
Doyle, Charles, 184, 253n. 4
Drayton, Michael: *Idea,* 177
Dunbar, William, 108; "Ane Ballat of Our Lady," 108
DuPlessis, Rachel Blau, 173

Eastman, Max, 16, 71
Eaton, Walter Prichard, 27, 28, 56
Eberhart, Richard, 207, 210, 211
Ehrenpreis, Irving, 102
Eichner, Hans, 47
Einstein, Albert, 19, 180, 252–53n. 1
Eliot, T. S., 6, 10–11, 14, 15, 16, 18, 37, 46, 51–53, 54, 55, 56, 58, 61, 63, **87–99**, 101–2, 108, 110, 113, 134, 181, 239n. 13, 240n. 23, 242n. 35, 242n. 36, 242n. 38, 247n. 1, 248n. 10; enjambment, 97; genre, 87–89, 101, 133; ghost of meter, 42–44; and Laforgue, 90–91; meter, 91, 93–96; organic theory, 91; repetition, 90, 98–99, 131, 134; rhyme, 89–90, 91, 96, 97; and Sanskrit, 93, 96; visual poetics, 92, 97
WORKS:
"The Borderline of Prose," 56; "Ezra Pound: His Metric and Poetry," 51–52; *The Four Quartets,* **96–99**, 247n. 33; "Hamlet and His Problems," 43; "The Love Song of J. Alfred Prufrock," 10, 34, 52–53, 63, **87–90**, 101, 131, 133, 162, 189–90, 249n. 1; "The Music of Poetry," 237–38n. 1; "Portrait of a Lady," 102; *Prufrock and Other Observations,* 91, 239n. 13; "Reflections on *Vers Libre,*" 43, 52, 63, 96; "Rhapsody on a Windy Night," 114; "Tradition and the Individual Talent," 19, 25, 53; *The Waste Land,* 39, 51, 53, **91–96**, 97, 98, 99, 136, 147, 243n. 39
Emerson, Ralph Waldo, 3, 83, 120, 140–41; "The Poet." 3, 58
Encyclopedia of Philosophy, 253n. 1
enjambment, 40, 42, 159, 162, 163, 177, 225, 227, 241n. 25. *See also* D[oolittle], H[ilda]; Dove, Rita; Eliot, T. S.; Pope, Alexander; Williams, William Carlos
Euripides, 20

Fenollosa, Ernest, 137
Feo, Jose Rodriguez, 125
Ficke, Arthur Davison, 55, 243n. 38
"Field, Michael," 246n. 25; "Across a Gaudy Room," 83
Filreis, Alan, 248n. 9
Finch, Annie, 6–7, 28, 237n. 3
Fisher-Wirth, Anne W., 212
Fletcher, John Gould, 23–24, 31, 55, 56, 243n. 38, 249n. 2, 253n. 15; "Blue Symphony," 171
Flint, F. S., 55, 59, 243n. 38
WORKS:
"Four Poems in Unrhymed Cadence," 34; "I," 171
Ford, Ford Madox, 55, 58–59, 119, 187, 243n. 38, 243n. 42, 243n. 43
Fordham, Mary Weston, 246n. 26; *Uranne,* 83
Foster, Finley, 143–44
Fowler, Roger, 15
Frazer, Sir James, 51
Frazer, Katherine, 123
free verse, "free-verse fanatics," 44, 46, 54–55, 108, 109, 111; historical approach, 6–9, 11; indescribable form, 16–18; "negative" definition, 15–16, 18, 25; problem of definition, 1, 4, 10, 13–15; and propaganda, 1–2, 13, 180, 221; and prosody, 9–10, 28–31; and rhythm, 18–27, 31–37, 44, 46, 53–54; and truth, 2–4;
GENRES, 10–11, 13, 37–46; avoids tradition, 10, 11, 44–46 (*see also* Hass, Robert; Levine, Philip);

"haunted," 10–11, 42–44, 45, 52, 135, 240n. 23 (*see also* Eliot, T. S.; Stevens, Wallace); long-line, 10, 39–42, 45, 57, 240n. 23; short-line, 10, 11, 42, 133 (*see also* "D[oolittle], H[ilda]; Williams, William Carlos). *See also* cadence; meter; rhythm; *chapters on individual poets*
Friedman, Susan Stanford, 135–36, 146
Frost, Robert, 165, 215
Fry, Paul H., 75
Frye, Northrup, 92
Fuller, Henry B., 23
Fuller, Roy, 44, 53
Fussell, Paul, 38, 40, 47, 244n. 4

Gall, Sally, 238–39n. 8
Garden, Mary, 112
Gardner, Helen, 87, 94, 246n. 29
Garrett, Jan, 224
Gaskell, Howard, 144
Gates, Rosemary, 201, 209–10, 217, 238n. 5
Gerber, John W., 182, 187
Gilbert, Sandra, 7
Gilman, Charlotte Perkins, 7
WORKS:
"One Girl of Many," 7; "The Yellow Wallpaper," 7
Ginsberg, Allen, 39, 42, 180; *Howl*, 40, 42
Goethe, Johann Wolfgang Von, 48, 53, 80, 145, 146, 148
Golding, Alan, 25, 66
Goldsmith, Oliver: *She Stoops to Conquer*, 95
Graham, Jorie, 9, 233
Gray, Thomas, 73, 74, 75
WORKS:
"The Bard," 73; "Sonnet on the Death of Mr. Richard West," 59
Gregory, Eileen, 137–38, 146, 168, 169, 249n. 2, 249n. 3
Gross, Harvey, 61–62, 102–3, 123, 247n. 1
Guarini, Battista, 251n. 17
Gubar, Susan, 7
Guest, Barbara, 137, 249n. 2
Guichard, Léon, 91
Guide to Modern World Literature, 15

Hall, Donald, 91; *Concise Encyclopedia of American Poets and Poetry*, 238n. 4
Handbook to Literature, A, 25
Hansen, Harry, 53–54, 240–41n. 24
Hardy, Thomas, 10
Harmer, J. B., 249n. 5
Hartman, Charles O., 2, 4, 9, 26, 27, 30, 38, 56, 61, 74, 184, 201, 210, 237n. 1, 243n. 40, 253n. 4
Hass, Robert, 11; "Measure," **226–28**
Helms, Alan, 30
Henderson, Alice Corbin, 18, 19, 21, 22, 31, 56, 221, 238n. 7; "Humoresque," 31
Henley, William Ernest, **161–66**, 173, 251–52n. 23, 251n. 25
WORKS:
In Hospital, 161, 164, 165, 166, 251n. 23; "Ave, Caesar," 163; Clinical," 162, 164; "Discharged," 161–62, 164–65; "Pastoral," 161, 165; *Poems*, 161; "Vigil," 162–63
Herbert, George, 10, 204–5, 206, 245n. 10
WORKS:
"The Altar," 205; "Easter Wings," 205
Hirsch, Edward, 201
Holden, Jonathan, 225
Holder, Alan, 10, 28, 240n. 17
Hollander, John, 5, 7, 28, 40, 102, 180, 198, 199, 202, 204, 205–6, 207, 211, 212, 215, 217, 218, 239n. 15
Holley, Margaret, 78
Holman, C. Hugh, and William Harmon, 25, 46
Homer, 13, 20, 22, 143, 170, 250n. 7
Honig, Edward, 117
Hopkins, Gerard Manley, 14, 31, 62, 71, 151–52, 215, 247n. 8, 250n. 13, 250n. 14; "Wreck of the Deutschland," 107–8
Horace, 108

Horrocks, Geoffrey, 20
Hovey, Richard: "Evening on the Potomac," 84–85
Howe, Susan, 9
Howells, William Dean, 56
Hough, Graham, 15, 16, 44, 238n. 4
Huang, Guiyou, 172
Hubbell, H. M., 239–40n. 16
Hughes, Glenn, 56, 137, 140
Hughes, Langston, 41
Hulme, T. E., 136; "Mana Aboda," 136

iambic pentameter, 6–7, 8, 18, 21, 27, 40, 53, 68, 73, 85, 87, 88, 90, 94, 96, 117, 119, 123, 124, 133, 147, 152, 175, 178, 179, 187, 202, 229, 232, 237n. 4
Imagism, 56, 135, 136–37, 142, 171, 172, 175, 177. *See also* D[oolittle], H[ilda]; Pound, Ezra)
Imagistes, Des, 171

Jannaris, Antonius N., 19–22, 27, 187, 238–39n. 8, 239n. 9, 239n. 10, 239n. 11; *An Historical Greek Grammar,* 20–22, 239n. 9
Janowitz, Anne, 181
Jay, Gregory, 87
Jespersen, Otto, 29–30, 211, 240n. 18
Johnson, Samuel, 28, 64, 65, 70–71, 80, 151, 229
Jones, David: *In Parenthesis,* 56
Jones, Llewelyan, 2
Joyce, James, 55
WORKS:
Finnegan's Wake, 55; *Portrait of the Artist as a Young Man,* 55; *Ulysses,* 55
Justice, Donald, 102, 103, 123, 172

Kallet, Marilyn, 212
Keats, John, 20, 76, 80, 232
WORKS:
"Epistle to John Hamilton Reynolds," 113; "Ode to Psyche," 76; To Autumn," 248n. 13; "To One Who Has Been Long in City Pent," 118
Keillor, Garrison, 229
Kenner, Hugh, 102, 142–43, 180, 185, 187, 188, 201, 216, 243n. 43
Kermode, Frank, 153
Kilmer, Joyce, 21, 57
Kingsley, Charles, 82
Kirby-Smith, H. T., 3, 144
Kirkconnell, Watson, 251n. 16
Kizer, Carolyn: "Amusing Our Daughters," 38
Klaeber, Franz, 154
Kreymborg, Alfred, 34, 54, 55, 102
WORKS:
"Children," 34–35; *Mushrooms,* 34; "Vista," 34
Kugel, James, 57
Küper, Christoph, 38, 234, 235, 240n. 23

Laforgue, Jules, 43, 87, 91, 166
Lambert, Mary Eliza Tucker, 246n. 26; *Loews Bridge,* 83
Langhorne, John, 73, 245n. 12
Langland, John: *Piers Plowman,* 37, 108
Language poetry, 2, 7
Lanier, Sidney, 10, 161, 207, 234
WORKS:
"The Marshes of Glynn," 85–86; *The Science of English Verse,* 85, 234
Latimer, Ronald Lane, 108, 109, 247–48n. 9
Laughlin, James, 204, 205
Lawrence, D. H., 45–46, 54–55, 56, 109, 110, 223; "How Beastly the Bourgeios Is," 45
Leithauser, Brad, 26, 195
Lensing, George, 110, 123
Levertov, Denise, 181, 190, 195, 209, 211, 213, 218
Levine, Jessica, 192
Levine, Philip, 11, 223–26, 233; "invisible

prosody," 225; rhythm, 226–27
WORKS:
"Llanto," 226; "Milkweed," 225; "The Simple Truth," **223–25**; *The Simple Truth,* 223, 226; "A Theory of Prosody," 226; "Winter Words, Manhattan," 226
Lindsay, Vachel, 31, 37
WORKS:
The Congo, 36; "The Firemen's Ball," 31, 35–36
Literary Terms and Criticism, 15
Longfellow, Henry Wadsworth, 25, 62, 82; "The Building of a Ship," 83
Longinus, 28, 67, 80, 248n. 12
Lowell, Amy, 18, 19, 21, 22, 25, 31, 55, 56, 57, 135, 167, 227, 243n. 38, 246n. 31
WORKS:
"The Bombardment," 36; "Venus Transiens," 171–72
Lowell, James Russell, 246n. 31
Lowes, John Livingston, 57, 59
Loy, Mina, 102

Mackey, Nathaniel, 211
Maclean, Norman, 67, 70, 71
Macpherson, James, 144, 145
Mahabharata, 93
Mallarmé, Stephane, 43, 52, 240n. 19
WORKS:
Un Coup de Des, 212; *"Crise de Vers,"* 43, 242n. 35
Mariani, Paul, 188, 190, 201, 219, 252n. 1, 253n. 7
Marston, John Westland: *Gerald,* 82
Martineau, Harriet, 28, 82
Martz, Louis L., 168, 225, 226
Marvell, Andrew: "To His Coy Mistress," 246n. 27
Masters, Edgar Lee, 44, 52, 56, 223
WORKS:
"Lydia Puckett," 44–45; *Spoon River Anthology,* 44, 56, 223
Maupassant, Guy De, 58
Mayhew, Jonathan, 182, 188, 199, 210, 253n. 2
Maynard, Theodore, 53
Mayo, Robert, 62
McGreevey, Thomas, 111
Melic poets, 19–22, 187, 238–39n. 8, 239n. 9
Menken, Adah Isaacs, 83; *Infelicia,* 246n. 24
Meredith, George: *Modern Love,* 4, 251–52n. 13
meter, **27–31**, 37, 41, 45, 47, 48–50, 58–59, 70, 81–82, 83, 140, 143, 145, 147, 148, 152, **153–55**, 157, 161, 165, 241n. 32, 244n. 7. *See also* Dove, Rita; Eliot, T. S.; prosody; Stevens, Wallace; Williams, William Carlos
Meter in English, 10
Mill, John Stuart, 58
Miller, J. Hillis, 197, 201
Milton, John, 31, 73, 151, 159, 203, 251n. 16, 251n. 17, 251n. 18, 251n. 21
WORKS:
Paradise Lost, 118, 152, 199, 203, 242n. 36, 243n. 39; preface to *Paradise Lost,* 13–14, 113, 245n. 12; *Samson Agonistes,* **151–58**, 160, 163, 251n. 15
Milton Handbook, A, 152
Mills, Ralph J., 225
Monroe, Harriet, 2, 21, 31, 53–55, 110, 136, 243n. 37, 249n. 2
Moody, A. D., 168, 170–71
Moody, William Vaughan, 84
WORKS:
"Daguerrotype," 84, "Ode in a Time of Hesitation," 84; "A Prairie Ride," 84
Moore, Marianne, 6, 108, 180, 181, 206; "Marriage," 92
Moore, Merrill, 184, 191
Morris, Sir Lewis, 91; "Ode on a Fair Spring Morning," 88–89
Morse, Samuel French, 117
Murray, Gilbert, 137, 138–40, 170, 249n. 4

Murry, John Middleton, 145, 147
Nation, 164
New Formalism, 2
New Princeton Encyclopedia of Poetry and Poetics, The, 38, 107
New Princeton Review, 164
Nicholson, Mervyn, 114
Norton Anthology, The, 56

ode, 17, 39, 148, 161, 175, 225, 238n. 6., 244n. 7, 245n. 13, 246n. 28, 251n. 17, 253n. 13; Collins, 74–75; late nineteenth-century irregular odes, 83–87; Romantic, 76–78. *See also* Arnold, Matthew; Cowley, Abraham; Eliot, T. S.
O'Donnell, Brendan, 241–42n. 32
Ohio Review, 25
Olds, Sharon, 9
Olson, Charles, 3, 180
Oppen, George, 173, 180
organic form, 3, 6, 10, 17, **46–55**, 60; Modern, 51–55; Romantic, 47–49; Whitman, 49–51. *See also* Coleridge, Samuel Taylor; Cowley, Abraham; Eliot, T. S.; Pope, Alexander; Stevens, Wallace; Williams, William Carlos
Ossian, 39, 144–45, 243n. 39
Others, 31
Oxford Companion to French Literature, 166

Panini, 93
Pater, Walter, "Style," 243n. 41
Patterson, William, 38, 135, 234, 238n. 7
Pearson, Norman Holmes, 146
Peckham, H. Houston, 1
Percival, M. D., 83
Perloff, Marjorie, 8, 188, 195, 201, 210, 212, 215–16, 253–54n. 16
Petrarch, Francesco, 177, 232
Pettersson, Thore, 201
Pindar, 63–64, 67, 80, 151
Poe, Edgar Allan, 27, 114, 207, 208, 234, 240n. 18, 253n. 13
WORKS:
"The Philosophy of Composition," 242n. 36; "The Rationale of Verse," 29, 207
Poetry, 1, 18, 19, 58, 136
Poetry Handbook, 25
poetry/prose debate, 55–60
Poet's Dictionary, The, 15
Pondom, Cyrena, 135
Pope, Alexander, 16, 18, 47, 64, 69, 80, 103, 109, 121, 173, 211, 221, 228, 231; alliteration, 231; enjambment, 150–51, 198, 225, 241n. 25; metrical contract, 28–29, 90, 235–36; organicism, 47; rhyme, 71–72, 75, 79, 107, 212, 215
WORKS:
Essay on Criticism, 29, 47, 71, 113, 150, 153, 154, 235–36, 248n. 14; *The Rape of the Lock,* 37, 103, 150–51
Potter, Robert: *Aeschylus,* (trans.), 141–42, 143
Pound, Ezra, 41, 43, 44, 45, 46, 51, 54, 55, 56, 58–59, 135, 137, 138, 140, 147, 164, 180, 187, 190, 201, 208, 239n. 9, 243n. 42, 248n. 10; contextual prosody, 153, 154; free-verse propaganda, 1–2, 164, 166; Imagism, 135, 136; poetry vs. prose, 59, 243n. 38; rhythm, 19–22, 23, 140, 238–39n. 8, 239n. 13; translation theory, 142, 143, 145–46, 148, 172
WORKS:
"Apparuit," 250n. 7; *The Cantos,* 60, 243n. 39; *A Draft of XXX Cantos,* 54; "How to Read," 143; "In the Station at the Metro," 31, 212; "Mr. Hueffer and the Prose Tradition in Verse," 58, 243n. 38; *The Spirit of Romance,* 18–19; "The Tradition," 19–21, 239n. 9
Pratt, William, 15, 140
Prince, P. T., 152, 251n. 17
Princeton Encyclopedia of Poetry and Poetics, The, 14, 38, 151, 181

Prins, Yopie, 147, 148
Priscian, 242n. 34
prosody, 10, 11, 20–21, **26–31**, 153–54, **233–36**

quantitative prosody, 14, 16, 20–21, 143, 152, 207, 239n. 10, 239n. 11, 239n. 12, 245n. 12, 246n. 29, 249–50n. 7, 250n. 8

Ramayana, 93
Ramsey, Paul, 16, 38
Rapp, Carl, 188, 189
Reader's Companion to World Literature, The, 24
Reader's Encyclopedia of American Literature, The, 16
Reader's Guide to Literary Terms, A, 25
Reed, John, 1
repetition. *See* Dove, Rita; Eliot, T. S.; Stevens, Wallace
Reyher, Ferdinand, 2, 110, 112
rhyme, **71**, 75, 78–81, 145, 147, 161, 165, 225, 244n. 7, 245n. 20, 245–26n. 22, 248n. 14. *See also* Cowley, Abraham; Dove, Rita; Eliot, T. S.; Pope, Alexander; Stevens, Wallace
rhythm, **27–37,** 145, 151, 226, 239n. 13, 248n. 12. *See also* cadence; Levine, Philip; Pound, Ezra; prosody; Stevens, Wallace
Rice, Wallace, 1
Richards, I. A., 27–28, 30, 47, 108
Richardson, Joan, 102
Riley, James Whitcomb: "Little Orphant Annie," 32–33
Riquelme, John Paul, 246n. 28
Robinson, Janice S., 249n. 2
Rodker, John, 37, 240n. 22; "London Nights," 34, 240n. 20
Roethke, Theodore, 180
Rosenmeyer, Thomas G., 149–50, 157–58, 168, 250n. 11
Rosmarin, Adena, 246n. 27
Rossetti, Christina, 82
Rossetti, Dante Gabriel, 82, 168
Rossetti, William Michael, 82, 83
Rosu, Anca, 132, 248n. 13

Sainte-Beuve, Charles-Augustin, 50
Saintsbury, George, 48, 123, 152, 154, 155, 241n. 31
Sanborn, Pitts, 112
Sanborn, Robert Alden, "Lento," 31
Sandburg, Carl, 39, 42, 44, 53–54, 167, 240–41n. 24
WORKS:
Chicago Poems, 167; "Fog," 89; "Muckers," 240n. 20; "Who Am I," 42
Saner, Reg, 38
Sappho, 140
Sato, Hirosake, 172–73
Sayers, Frank, 76, 245n. 14
Sayre, Henry, 203
Scheckner, Peter, 237n. 3
Schlegel, Friedrich, 241n. 29
Schwartz, Delmore, 111
Scott, A. F., 15, 238n. 2
Scrivener, Michael, 237n. 3
Shakespeare, William, 8, 43, 47, 61, 73, 177, 232
WORKS:
Hamlet, 43–44; sonnet, 73 249n. 17; *The Tempest,* 92
Sharp, William: "The White Peacock," 83
Shavitt, Uzi, 44
Shawcross, John T., 251n. 16, 251n. 18
Shelley, Percy Bysshe, 76, 241n. 32
WORKS:
"A Defence of Poetry," 48–49, 243n. 41; "Mont Blanc," 87; *Prometheus Unbound,* 158–59, 251n. 21
Sherman, Joan R., 83, 246n. 26
Sidney, Sir Philip: *Astrophil and Stella,* 4, 177
Simms, William Gilmore: "The Lost Pleiad," 84

Simons, Hi, 248n. 9
Simpson, Louis, 25, 26
Sitwell, Edith, 53
Skinner, Constance Lindsay: "Songs of the Coast-Dwellers," 35
Smart, Christopher: *Jubilate Agno,* 39
Smith, Arthur E., 224
Smith, Barbara Herrnstein, 25, 37–38
Snodgras, W. D., 41
Some Imagist Poets, 171
sonnet, 4, 5–6, 39, 51–52, 73, 96, 101, 102, 112, 118, 161, 177–78, 183–84, 188, 228–29, 232–33, 248n. 13, 249n. 17, 253n. 15
Southey, Robert: *The Curse of Kehama,* 245n. 14; *Thalaba the Destroyer,* 245n. 14
spasmodic verse, 82–83
Spender, Stephen: *Concise Encyclopedia of English and American Poets and Poetry*, 238n. 4
Spenser, Edmund, 8
WORKS:
Amoretti, 177; *Faerie Queene,* 8
spenserian stanza, 8, 73, 78–79, 112, 143
Spire, André, 53
Sprat, Thomas, 70, 71, 244n. 7
Springer, Mary Doyle, 130–32
Sprott, Samuel Ernest, 251n. 16
Spurr, David, 87
Stalker, James C., 201–2
Steele, Timothy, 2–3, 19, 48, 56, 58–59, 207, 237n. 1
Stein, Gertrude, 55, 125, 130–31
WORKS:
Tender Buttons, 55; *Useful Knowledge,* 55
Stein, William Bysshe, 103, 247n. 2
Stendhal (Marie Henri Beyle), 58
Sterloff, Frances, 59, 186
Stevens, Wallace, 2, 6, 11, 36, **101–34**, 167, 171, 173, 174, 180, 211, 240n. 23, 248n. 9, 248n. 10, 248n. 12, 248n. 16, 248n. 20; alliteration, 103–8, 109, 115, 134; compared to Eliot, 101–2; ghost of meter, 102–3, 111–12; grammar, 109; and irregular ode, 101; meter, 103, 114, 117–23, 125, 127–28, 130; organicism, 108–112; repetition, 130–34, 174; rhyme, 103, 113–17, 118, 125–26, 128–130, 248n. 14; rhythm, 109, 110, 114, 122; sonnet, 112, 248n. 13; terza rima, 112–13; visual prosody, 123–24
WORKS:
"Anything Is Beautiful If You Say It Is," 121; "The Bird with the Coppery, Keen Claws," 117–18; *The Collected Poems,* 133, 247n. 3; "The Comedian as the Letter C," **105–7**, 198; "Continual Conversation with a Silent Man," 122, 129; "Death of a Soldier," 106; "Domination of Black," 132; "Earthy Anecdote," 106, 120, 131; "The Emperor of Ice Cream," 109, 117; "Farewell to Florida," 248–49n. 16; "Floral Decorations for Bananas," 106; "From the Journal of Crispin," 112; *Harmonium,* 105, 115, 117, 121, 130, 172, 247n. 2; "The High-Toned Old Christian Woman," 105, 106; "Idea of Order at Key West," 248n. 16; "Indian River," 104, 106; "Infanta Marina," 103–4; "In the Carolinas," 120; "Invective Against Swans," 115; "The Irrational Element in Poetry," 115; "The Jack Rabbit," 106, 120; "Life is Motion," 120; "Like Decorations in a Nigger Cemetery," 121–22; "A Load of Sugar-Cane," 104–5; "Le Monocle de Mon Oncle," 102, 106, 115–116, 190; "On the Manner of Addressing the Clouds," 106; "The Man on the Dump," 112; "The Man Whose Pharynx Was Bad," 118–19; "The Man with the Blue Guitar," 111, **124–30**, 132, 248n. 9;

"Martial Cadenza," 132–33; "New England Verses," 120, 248n. 16; "The News and the Weather," 121; "The Noble Rider and the Sound of Words," 113–14, 247n. 2; "Notes Toward a Supreme Fiction," 102; "Not Ideas About the Thing But the Thing Itself," 133; "Ode," 101, 133; "The Ordinary Women," 105; "Owl's Clover," 248n. 9; "Peter Quince at the Clavier," 103, 120, 247n. 2; "Ploughing on a Sunday," 36; "Sunday Morning," 102, 105; "Theory," 130; "Thirteen Ways of Looking at a Blackbird," 120; "A Thought Revolved," 120–21; "To the Roaring Wind," 104; "The Weeping Burgher," 116–17
Stewart, George, 15, 16, 238n. 2
Storer, Edward, 23, 26, 53
Stravinsky, Igor: "Grotesques," 36
sublime, 10, 63, 67–70, 80, 86, 87, 111, 114, 145, 248n. 12
Sutton, Walter, 14, 16–17, 18, 208, 238n. 5
Swann, Thomas Burnett, 137, 178, 249n. 2, 249n. 5
Swift, Jonathan: "Description of a City Shower," 89
Swinburne, Charles Algernon: "Nephilidia," 108
syllabic prosody, 16, 226

Taafe, James, 69
Taine, Hippolyte, 242n. 33
Tapscott, Stephen, 212
Tarlinskaja, Marina, 8
Tasso, Torquato, 251n. 17
Taylor, Dennis, 61, 102, 112, 247n. 1
Taylor, Edward, 243n. 39
Teacher's and Writer's Handbook of Poetic Forms, 17, 18
Tennyson, Alfred Lord, 16, 20, 62, 82, 83; *Maud,* 82
Terrell, Carroll, 179–80
terza rima, 102, 112–13
Thelwall, John, 253n. 5
Thirwall, John, 188
Thompson, Francis, 164, 165; "The Hound of Heaven," 83
Tietjens, Eunice, 167
Timrod, Henry, 89; "The Cotton Boll," 84, 86
Toomer, Jean: *Cane,* 55
Tourneur, Cyril: *Revenger's Trajedy,* 53
translation theory, **140–48;** Browning, 147–48; and meter, 143–46; nineteenth- and twentieth-century, 141–42; Ossian, 144–45. *See also* D[oolittle], H[ilda]; Pound, Ezra; Whitman, Walt
transcendental, 140–41; translatable *logos,* 145; verse translation, 143
Tupper, Martin: *Proverbial Philosophy,* 39

Untermeyer, Louis, 11, 135, 249n. 2; *Forms of Poetry,* 24

Vanderwiden, Betty, 146, 249n. 5
Vendler, Helen, 102
Virgil, 68; *Georgics,* 143
visual poetics, 32–33, 37, 72–73, 79–80, 87, 152, 176–77, 244n. 9, 244–45n. 10. *See also* Eliot, T. S.; Stevens, Wallace; Williams, William Carlos

Wallace Stevens Journal, 247n. 1
Walsh, William, 229
Warfel, Harry, 15–16
Warner, H. E., 26
Warr, George C.: *Agamemnon* (trans.), 142, 143
Weeks, Ruth Mary, 172, 217
Weigel, Molly, 224
Weinstein, Mark, 82
Wendorf, Richard, 74
Wesling, Donald, 2, 4, 9, 10, 22, 26, 38, 48, 61, 62, 195, 201, 214, 233, 234, 237n. 1, 254n. 4
West, Martin L., 149

Weston, Jesse, 51
Whitman, Walt, 14, 16–17, **39–42**, 57, 58, 59, 62, 76, 82, 83, 91, 144, 160, 164, 183, 191, 201, 219, 221, 237n. 3, 238n. 5, 242n. 34, 246n. 24, 253n. 9; organicism, 49–51, 54–55, 64; poet as translator, 64, 141
WORKS:
"A Backward Glance o'er Traveled Roads," 242n. 33; "Democratic Vistas," 49, 50; 1855 preface to *Leaves of Grass,* 41, 49, 141, 242n. 33; *Leaves of Grass,* 39, 141; "A Noiseless Patient Spider," 253n. 9; "O Captain! My Captain!" 243n. 2; "Out of the Cradle Endlessly Rocking," 243n. 1; "Poets to Come," 50; "Poetry To-Day," 50; *Song of Myself,* 40, 41, 50, 141; "Starting from Paumanok," 40
Wilde, Oscar, 164–65; *Ballad of Reading Gaol,* 252n. 25
Williams, William Carlos, 11, 14, 16, 19, 38, 42, 46, 55, 59, 102, 110, 135, 151, 166–67, 168, 173, 175–76, 177, **179–221**, 224, 225, 227, 232, 243n. 38, 252–53n. 1, 253n. 12, 253n. 15; concision, 190–91; enjambment and grammar, 192–202, 213–15, 220, 225; "idiom," 216; importance to twentieth-century poetics, 179–81, 220–21; isochronous theory, 208–11; meter, 184, 187, 204, 215, 217; organicism, 179, 181–90, 221; relationship to reader, 218–19, 221; rhythm, 179, 186–87, 210, 216; variable foot, 11, 19, 179, 180, 181, **207–220**, 240n. 19, 252–53n. 1; visual prosody, 202–7, 211–13, 221
WORKS:
"Apres le Bain," 204; "Asphodel, that Greeny Flower," 211–12, 212–13, 213–14, 220; *Autobiography*, 182–83; "Calypsos," 199; "Christmas, 1950," 175–76; "The Crimson Cyclamen," 194–95; "Descent," 193"The Descent," 210, 219, 220; *The Desert Music,* 183, 219; "The Fight," 204; "Fine Work with Pitch and Copper," 181–82, 185–86, 218–19; "It Is a Small Plant," 196–97; *I Wanted To Write a Poem,* 187; *A Journey to Love,* 219; *Kora in Hell,* 55, 253n. 8; "Metric Figure," 192–93; "The Motor-Barge," 214; "The Nightingales," 203; "Passer Domesticus," 206; "Pastoral," 166–67, 193; *Paterson,* 60, 188, 192, 195, 234, 243n. 39; "Poem," 184–85; "The Poem," 198; "Portrait of a Woman in Bed," 188, 189; "[so much depends]," 167, 177, 188, 202; "The Sparrow," 211; *Spring and All,* 55, 187, 191–92, 196, 197–98; "Statement on Measure," 216; "Stillness," 192; "Summer Song," 195–96; "10/14," 200; "The Term," 197, 199; "This Florida," 253n. 2; "Three Sonnets," 200; "To a Dog Injured in the Street," 219; "To a Poor Old Woman," 198–99; "To Be Written on a Small Piece of Paper which Folded into a Tight Lozenge Will Fit in Any Girl's Locket," 167; "The Unfrocked Priest," 204; *The Williams-Siegel Documentary,* 183; "War, the Destroyer," 200; "The Winds," 196
Williamson, George, 88
Wimsatt, W. K., 71, 113, 218
Wood, Clement, 15, 16, 238n. 2
Woolf, Virginia, 61
Wordsworth, William, 10, 27, 48, 58, 86, 116, 124, 133, 163, 189, 202, 215
WORKS:
preface to *Lyrical Ballads,* 59, 109, 241n. 32, 253n. 5; "Ode: Intimations of Immortality from Recollections of Early Childhood,"

17, 76–77; "Tintern Abbey," 246n. 27
Wright, James, 26
Writer's Encyclopedia, The, 15
Wunderlich, Mark, 9
Wyatt, Thomas, 215

Xie, Ming, 172

Yeats, William Butler, 55

Zukofsky, Louis, 176, 180
WORKS:
'A,' 177; *Fifty Flowers,* 177; *Prepositions,* 19; "THE," 176, 177